best
sports
stories
1975

best sports stories 1975

A PANORAMA OF THE 1974 SPORTS WORLD INCLUDING THE 1974 CHAMPIONS OF ALL SPORTS WITH THE YEAR'S TOP PHOTOGRAPHS

Edited by Irving T. Marsh and Edward Ehre

PZ
1
B57
1975

E. P. DUTTON & CO., INC. / NEW YORK / 1975

Published simultaneously in Canada by Clarke, Irwin & Company
Limited, Toronto and Vancouver

ISBN: 0-525-06621-7
Library of Congress Catalog Number: 45-35124

Contents

Illustrations

best
sports
stories
1975

Preface

Entering the fourth decade of the *Best Sports Stories* annuals, the editors welcome three first-time winners of the awards and a new judge to the anthology that started back in 1944 and has continued without a break since.

The new judge who joins John Chamberlain and John Hutchens as a member of the selection panel is Jerry Nason, retired sports editor of the *Boston Globe*, who replaces Red Smith, resigned because of the pressure of other duties. Nason has been a member of the *Best Sports Stories* family for many years. Not only has he been a contributor to the series about a dozen times but he has won three awards in the news-coverage and news-feature divisions, the last in 1973.

But all of the 1975 award winners, as noted above, gained prizes for the first time. More, John S. Radosta of *The New York Times*, who took the title and the $250 in the magazine division for his article on stock-car racing in his paper's Sunday magazine, and Dr. Ross Thomas Runfola, the professor-writer who won the news-feature story competition with his off-beat hockey piece that also appeared in *The New York Times* (sports section), were contributing to the series for the first time.

Thus they captured the diadem in their maiden effort, as the patois of the racetrack would have it.

The third winner, Dwain Esper of the *Pasadena Star-News*, who took the news-coverage award for his dramatic story on the USC–Notre Dame football game, has appeared in *Best Sports Stories* many times before.

The only victor who scored a sweep (unanimous No. 1 choice of all three judges) was Dr. Runfola. Radosta took two of the three magazine story first places, while the third No. 1 ballot in this category went to Ms. Catherine Bell for her article on Rosie Casals which ran in *Tennis* magazine. Ms. Bell is one of the few women writers whose efforts have appeared in this series, although two ladies were prize winners in the past.

The closest competition came in the news-coverage division,

where two second-place ballots for a total of four points nosed out four other pieces with a three-point total. Seven stories received mention in this division. Of the 50 stories in the book, 20 were selected for a spot in the balloting. Altogether, considerably more than 1,000 separate entries—the high-water mark in the series thus far—were read by the editors.

It is interesting to note that three of the four accounts on the 1974 World Series were chosen by the judges for a first place, indicating that our Series coverage this year is the best it has ever been, if first-place votes are an adequate yardstick.

As in the past, the stories that were sent to the judges went to them "blind." That is, they were identified only by a word or two (known in newspaperese as a "slug") with no indication as to the writer or his publication. You may note that's how the stories are identified by the judges in the box score and in their comments which follow.

THE BOX SCORE

News-Coverage Stories	Chamberlain	Hutchens	Nason	Total Points*
USC [*Davis Triggers the Explosion* by Dwain Esper]	2	2	—	4
1st Series [*A Rare Display of Camaraderie* by Phil Pepe]	—	3	—	3
2d Series [*The Dodgers Even It Up* by Jim Hawkins]	3	—	—	3
5th Series [*The Spoiled Brats Take It All* by Maury Allen]	—	—	3	3
Tennis [*Connors Buries Rosewall at Forest Hills* by Dave Hirshey]	—	1	2	3
Wimbledon [*Connors Buries Rosewall at Wimbledon* by Bud Collins]	1	—	—	1
Superbowl [*The Dolphins Win a Game of Inches* by Dave Casstevens]	—	—	1	1
News-Feature Stories				
Hockey [*A Model of Legalized Violence* by Dr. Ross Thomas Runfola]	3	3	3	9
No-Hitter [*Don't Jinx the No-Hitter* by Hal Lebovitz]	2	—	—	2
K-State [*Was the Ticket Worth the Money?* by Hank Inman]	—	2	—	2
Aaron [*Henry Aaron Was Able* by Bob Hunter]	—	—	2	2
Ebbets [*Ebbets Field Revisited* by Jeff Prugh]	1	—	1	2
Form [*The Most Expensive Daily* by Frederick C. Klein]	—	1	—	1
Magazine Stories				
Stockcar [*Stock-Car Streaking* by John S. Radosta]	3	3	—	6

*Based on 3 points for a first-place vote, 2 for a second, 1 for a third.

Rosie [*Rosie Casals: Why Hasn't She Lived Up to Her Potential?* by Catherine Bell]	—	—	3	3
Fight [*Ali—You Gotta Believe!* by Peter Bonventre and Pete Axthelm]	1	2	—	3
Toad [*Death Stalked the River* by Walt Walbert]	2	—	—	2
2d Base [*How to Play Second Base* by Laurence Sheehan]	—	—	2	2
Winning [*Where Winning Is God* by Eddie Donnally]	—	—	1	1
Reggie [*Reggie Jackson: Blood & Guts of the Fighting A's* by Murray Olderman]	—	1	—	1

JUDGES' COMMENTS

John Chamberlain
News-Coverage Stories

1. 2d Series [*The Dodgers Even It Up* by Jim Hawkins]
2. USC [*Davis Triggers the Explosion* by Dwain Esper]
3. Wimbledon [*Connors Buries Rosewall at Wimbledon* by Bud Collins]

1. I like the 2d Series particularly for the way it combines personal stories with on-the-spot reporting of the Dodgers' lone victory over Oakland. All the other Series game stories are good, making a lot of the high points. But the writer of 2d Series brought some knowledge of the players to bear on what he saw happening. There is psychological depth to this account of Don Sutton's revenge for Charlie Finley's slight.

2. USC reads like the story of two separate games, which means that it is entirely true. The writer makes the most of a situation in which ten men came to block after being out of it for almost an entire half. Anthony Davis, who scored after that, was hero enough, but not the only hero. The other ten men also must be given an accolade.

3. Wimbledon, the story of 21-year-old Jimmy Connors' demolition of 39-year-old Ken Rosewall, combines the spot news with intelligent interview stuff. Connors comes through as something inhuman on the court, but perfectly human in his understanding of his own position as the disliked killer. It's all in a sentence tossed

off by Connors: "Those problems are for them—I have to play for me."

News-Feature Stories

1. Hockey [*A Model of Legalized Violence* by Dr. Ross Thomas Runfola]
2. No-Hitter [*Don't Jinx the No-Hitter* by Hal Lebovitz]
3. Ebbets [*Ebbets Field Revisited* by Jeff Prugh]

1. Hockey is a searing experience to read. It is offered as a "tragic footnote" to the larger history of sports violence, but this is to belittle it. The truth is that this low-keyed narrative of what happened in Canada when a young white hockey player taunted a young black player beyond endurance is a tragic footnote to something much bigger than sports. It is the story of the beast that is in everybody, but it is also the story of the good that gives one hope that men, someday, will be civilized in their necessary competitiveness.
2. No-Hitter builds to a terrific tension. A first-rate mood piece.
3. Ebbets takes one back. It's the *Boys of Summer* theme, but, as an old hatitué of Ebbets Field, I thrill personally to every repetition. Worth third place by a hair over four other stories.

Magazine Stories

1. Stockcar [*Stock-Car Streaking* by John S. Radosta]
2. Toad [*Death Stalked the River* by Walt Walbert]
3. Fight [*Ali—You Gotta Believe!* by Peter Bonventre and Pete Axthelm]

1. I am not a fan for anything in sports that involves machinery. But I found Stockcar profoundly interesting. It is sport, it is sociology, it is Americana, all put together with a deftness that keeps its encyclopedic details from becoming boring. Deserves No. 1 rating by a big margin.
2. Toad is more of an adventure story than a sport story, but it is very good narrative. And man against nature is always a contest. The writing makes it No. 2.
3. Fight sets a good tropical scene, but, more important, it makes you see what happened in the ring and also what went on between Ali and the press. The detail about the prostitute eating the butterfly is an inspired bit.

JOHN HUTCHENS
News-Coverage Stories

1. 1st Series [*A Rare Display of Camaraderie* by Phil Pepe]
2. USC [*Davis Triggers the Explosion* by Dwain Esper]
3. Tennis [*Connors Buries Rosewall at Forest Hills* by Dave Hirshey]

1. A lively, good-humored piece about an event—the opening game of a World Series—that is too often treated with the solemnity reserved for the reconstruction of the Battle of Gettysburg. And, not at all incidentally, it's full of solid information as well.

2. It would take a long memory to recall a comeback victory like USC's over Notre Dame, perhaps the greatest of its kind within most gridiron addicts' experience. The writing, terse and spare, does justice to it.

3. Jimmy Connors' defeat of Ken Rosewall at Forest Hills could have lent itself to cruel jesting or funereal analysis. Instead, an obviously good reporter gives us a description both decently objective and humanely compassionate.

News-Feature Stories

1. Hockey [*A Model of Legalized Violence* by Dr. Ross Thomas Runfola]
2. K-State [*Was the Ticket Worth the Money?* by Hank Inman]
3. Form [*The Most Expensive Daily* by Frederick C. Klein]

1. A story that needed to be written about the increasing and mindless brutality that is infecting a great sport, seen here in the tragedy that befell two teen-age Canadian high school players— death for one, a manslaughter conviction for the other, with the real villain a bloodthirsty, racially bigoted crowd. I found it a profoundly moving chronicle.

2. A lively little off-beat piece about all that you don't get for your time and money at a college football game. The first of its kind that I, at least, have ever encountered.

3. An in-depth account of a totally unique American daily newspaper that must fascinate not only all full-time horseplayers but also those who put down only an occasional quid or two at the off-track betting studios and the parimutuel windows.

Magazine Stories

1. Stockcar [*Stock-Car Streaking* by John S. Radosta]
2. Fight [*Ali—You Gotta Believe!* by Peter Bonventre and Pete Axthelm]
3. Reggie [*Reggie Jackson: Bloot & Guts of the Fighting A's* by Murray Olderman]

1. A fine, thorough, frequently hair-raising picture of a world unknown to most of us except perhaps on TV—its ethics, if any, its skills and rewards and bravado.

2. To those (and I must confess I am one of them) who have been a bit reluctant to join the ranks of Muhammad Ali's admirers, this may come as a pleasant surprise. It is pegged on the self-professed Greatest One's destruction of George Foreman in the small hours of the morning in far-off Africa, and it is a splendid eyewitness picture of it. But it is chiefly memorable as a profile of a heavyweight champion like no other who comes to mind, a superb natural showman, arrogant and charming, and, on this occasion, exceedingly smart.

3. Another striking portrait of a major athlete of his time, the unpredictable and mighty right fielder of the Oakland A's, who stands for no nonsense from a manager, an owner, or his own fellow players—and who has a way of winning important games.

JERRY NASON
News-Coverage Stories

1. 5th Series [*The Spoiled Brats Take It All* by Maury Allen]
2. Tennis [*Connors Buries Rosewall at Forest Hills* by Dave Hirshey]
3. Super Bowl [*The Dolphins Win a Game of Inches* by Dave Casstevens]

1. The Oakland Athletics are more than a championship baseball team. The talent and temperaments, and the tantrums of this assembly of outspoken athletes in the employ of a flamboyant and controversial owner make them a unique "public property," unique for any sport in that respect. What I relished about this report of the winning of the World Series by them in the fifth game was that the writer, while maintaining complete fidelity to the facts of the game itself, as a good reporter should, also wove into the fabric of his story a genuine picture of what the A's are like and what makes them tick . . . as a good writer should.

2. The story of killer Connors humiliating old Ken Rosewall at Forest Hills pushed hard on my judgment, too. Perhaps seldom has a one-sided contest in sports been written on-scene with greater understanding or more tasteful compassion for the routed contestant of the second part than this one. The writer, whoever he is, made it clear to my mind that he not only was conversant with the game, but unusually sensitive to the agonies and ecstacies of those who play it professionally. This piece, too, served to illustrate vividly the facts of life—that the best sports writing today is not necessarily found only among the topical Big Three of baseball, football, and boxing.

3. The Super Bowl report was a classroom model for tight, bright writing, a story convincingly told without a superfluous display of verbiage, yet not without a lilt to its composition. Note the lead-in paragraph—a gem, burnished in post-game haste.

News-Feature Stories

1. Hockey [*A Model of Legalized Violence* by Dr. Ross Thomas Runfola]
2. Aaron [*Henry Aaron Was Able* by Bob Hunter]
3. Ebbets [*Ebbets Field Revisited* by Jeff Prugh]

1. So well documented was the entry labeled "Hockey" that it could almost have qualified as a contestant in the coverage category. This story deals with hockey's violence generally and the tragic hockey happening at Mississauga specifically. The manslaughter charges resulting from this teen-age quarrel, spawned on a Midget League hockey rink, were unknown to me. This story is a shocker, but does not depend upon its shock effect for attention to declare itself an excellent example of reporting. It is written with candor and yet with restraint, but the message is clear: a boy was victim not only of another's violence, but of Canadian hockey's almost casual acceptance of such violence while not actually condoning it. A blue-ribbon writing job in my estimation.

2. Right behind it I rated "Aaron." If, 30 years from now, you were to research the historic feat of Henry Aaron's 715th and record home run this is the piece you'd seek out as a source. It tells it all —the scene, the cast of characters, what they did, what they thought while they were doing it. Most of all, in simple but somehow profound paragraphs, it gives you a portrait of Henry as he stepped past Babe Ruth into baseball immortality.

3. Third comes "Ebbets," a piece that surely must tug at the heartstrings of those baseball fans who remember the present-day Los Angeles Dodgers as "Dem Bums" of Brooklyn, and who remember, too, the field at which their addicts once congregated in loud and often profane worship of their idols. The field, victim of high-rise, is no more.

Magazine Stories

1. Rosie [*Rosie Casals: Why Hasn't She Lived Up to Her Potential?* by Catherine Bell]
2. 2d Base [*How to Play Second Base* by Laurence Sheehan]
3. Winning [*Where Winning Is God* by Eddie Donnally]

1. There was a tremendous amount of good reading submitted for judgment in this category, a more leisurely type of writing in which the deadline is measured more by days, or weeks, than by hours or minutes. Not everybody is for tennis—but what reader of sporting instinct could resist "Rosie"? I couldn't, and thus tapped it No. 1—a simply superb typewriter portrait of complex, electrifying, classic-stroking, yet somehow failure-prone Rosemary Casals. A real pro had to be responsible for this piece. He [she—Ed.] left the reader not only knowing a lot more than he'd ever known before about tennis, but more importantly he was left with an intimate acquaintance with Rosie. To personalize, this was a considerable feat, because this judge is not particularly fond of tennis.

2. "Second Base" is a reading delight for any adult male who can recall his own days and deeds, or misdeeds, upon attaining that dizzy pinnacle of juvenile success—a regular position on the ol' Horace Mann grammar school baseball nine. So much is written about baseball at another pinnacle—stardom in the major leagues —that, frankly, it was refreshing to encounter a little gem like "Second Base" tucked innocently among all the "biggies."

3. Why is it that such a paucity of top-drawer writing is devoted to the durable and daring race rider of the so-called Sport of Kings? This thought will occur to you after reading "Winning" by a writer who will put you astride a thoroughbred race horse in the midst of the hazards, the dirty tricks and traps, the desperation and the elation that is the daily diet of these mighty little men. This writer does it so well that he leaves his reader with saddle sores. Well-done and different.

As for the photos, seldom, if ever, have we selected a shot that had more action than the winner of the $100 award in this division—"Sit Down Strike" by Jim Vincent of the *Portland Oregonian,* a veteran contributor whose picture is the seventh of his we have run in this series.

And the feature-photo award to "Undesignated Pinch Runner Continues Streak" by James Roark of the *Los Angeles Herald-Examiner,* a first-time contributor, is entirely in keeping with the latest (now almost extinct) collegiate vogue of streaking. Strictly in keeping, too, with our uninhibited society.

So, for your edification and enjoyment, here is *Best Sports Stories* —*1975.* May you get as much fun out of it as readers have (they have told us) from the previous 30.

IRVING T. MARSH
EDWARD EHRE

THE PRIZE-WINNING STORIES

Best News-Coverage Story

DAVIS TRIGGERS THE EXPLOSION

By Dwain Esper

From the Pasadena Star-News

Copyright, ©, 1974, Pasadena Star-News

In a series loaded with lore, USC may have etched the most dramatic chapter Saturday afternoon.

The Trojans rallied from a 24–0 first-half deficit to roll up an astonishing 55–24 victory over Notre Dame while an on-hand throng of 83,552, to say nothing of a national television audience, watched in stunned disbelief.

To a man, the Trojans agreed that A. D. Davis provided the trigger to the explosion that buried the Fighting Irish under an avalanche of points.

Trailing 24–6 as the third quarter began, Davis accepted the kickoff 2 yards deep in the end zone, sped upfield behind two superb blocks by Ricky Bell and Mosi Tatupu, and romped all the way to a touchdown.

"A.D.'s run was the spark," chortled Charlie Phillips, the great roverback who picked off three Notre Dame passes, the last for a 58-yard trip to the end zone.

"It was like a fireworks," said Phillips. "After that, there was no way Notre Dame was going to win."

The Trojans outscored the Irish 49–0 in the second half, 35–0 in the third quarter.

In all the history of Notre Dame football, only three other opponents bettered USC's second-half point total over a full game—Wisconsin 54–0 in 1900 and 58–0 in 1904, and Army 59–0 in 1944.

USC's previous high against the Irish was 45–23 in 1972.

How did this all happen?

How could there be a 79-point swing in one game—perhaps the greatest turnabout in college football history?

USC coach John McKay refused to divulge his half-time chat. One can surmise it had a few expletives pretty explosive in themselves.

"We needed a catalyst and it came in the kickoff return," McKay said. "We discussed with our players that there was no NCAA rule against blocking on kickoffs. The other ten men have to want him to score, and on the long run, he got some excellent blocks."

Once Davis posted his miraculous touchdown, the entire momentum of the game swung to the Trojan side.

Davis scored three other touchdowns, giving him 11 in a glorious career against the nation's most respected opponent.

Quarterback Pat Haden passed to four touchdowns, equaling a Trojan school record. During the incredible third quarter, Haden completed 5 for 5, for 123 yards and two scores.

And the defense which had stumbled all over the field in the first half finally came to life.

Time after time the big plays were made as the Irish were forced into six turnovers—three interceptions and three fumbles.

Said linebacker Kevin Bruce, who recovered two fumbles: "We knew we could win if we just kept hitting and taking it to them."

The final statistics make the Trojans look respectable. But a glance at the first half depicts an entirely different ball game.

The Irish had an 18–7 edge in first downs, 257–145 lead in total yardage in the first two quarters. At the end it was Notre Dame 24–20 in first downs, USC 400–367 in total yards.

Of course, the most revealing statistic lies in return yards—187 for USC to three for Notre Dame. Davis contributed his 102-yard kickoff return, Phillips his 58-yard pass interception return, and Marvin Cobb added a 56-yard punt return to set up another touchdown.

"Well, obviously there were two different games out there today," admitted a downcast Ara Parseghian, Notre Dame coach. "We just made too many mistakes in the second half."

Parseghian is concerned over the startling change in climate from 20–30 degrees in South Bend, Ind., to the summerlike 75 degrees in Los Angeles.

"I don't want to sound like I'm making an excuse," said Parseghian. "But I'm going to discuss playing this game on a comparable day in October every year with our administration."

USC made the move to October for the South Bend game back in 1961. Previously every renewal was held late in the year.

Parseghian blamed the Notre Dame collapse on other factors too.

"Their kicking game provided them with good field position," he reasoned. "They didn't have to travel very far to score."

But in the first half Notre Dame showed why it was ranked No. 4 on both wire service polls. USC was third on the UPI and fifth on the AP.

The Irish quickly capitalized on a Trojan miscue when linebacker Drew Mahalic picked off a Haden pass, which tight end Jim Obradovich bobbled at the USC 39.

Quickly Tom Clements rifled a 21-yard pass to flanker Al Samuel. In five plays the Irish had their touchdown, a two-yard bolt off tackle by fullback Wayne Bullock.

On the next series, USC faced a fourth-down-and-inches situation at the 30-yard line.

McKay elected to go for it, always looking at the positive side of things.

"You have to have confidence that your offense can gain less than a yard."

Haden tried to get it off tackle, but Mahalic piled him up short at the 29.

Immediately Clements rolled right and speared Pete Demmerle on a cross-over pattern for a touchdown.

"We thought it was a good time to hit them with a pass right there," said Parseghian. "They might not have expected it."

Phillips, the former Blair all-star, took full blame.

"Demmerle was my responsibility," he declared. "I didn't read my key right and took my eyes off of him."

So after Dave Reeve's second conversion, the Trojans were down 14–0 midway through the first quarter.

Then the Irish embarked on a 16-play drive, mostly on the ground, to set up Reeves for a field goal from the 10 less than 2 minutes into the second quarter.

Said Trojan defensive tackle Art Riley: "I couldn't believe they were gaining like that on the ground. We just weren't hitting."

The Trojans made a neat foray into Irish territory on a 23-yard swing pass from Haden to Davis. But Mahalic ruined that effort with a fourth-down sack of Haden, costing 11 yards.

As the half was coming to a close, the irrepressible Clements (or so it seemed at the time) rallied his forces for a 9-play, 79-yard drive to another touchdown, a 9-yard tailback delay by Mark McLane.

So there it was all lit up on the scoreboard: Notre Dame 24, USC 0! And only 53 seconds left to intermission.

Parseghian was upset that place-kicker Pat McLaughlin was too cautious on the first kickoff, sending it out of bounds.

"We ordered a squib from the 35, and they were able to bring it back to good field position."

Ricky Bell was the man who returned 13 yards to the 41.

Making judicious use of the time-out and sideline passes, Haden gave a hint of what was to come with a nifty 6-play, 59-yard drive to a touchdown in the span of 40 seconds.

The payoff was a swing pass to Davis, who churned seven yards into the end zone.

After Kevin Nosbusch blocked Chris Limahelu's conversion try, the Trojans were down 24–6.

"We reminded them of the 1964 game," said McKay. "It was 17–0 then and 24–6 today; so there wasn't that much difference."

The Trojans came back to win it 20–17 and knock Notre Dame out of No. 1 and an unbeaten season.

Despite the seeming hopeless adversity, the USC players felt to a man they could come back.

"You never give up against anybody," said Davis.

And he proceeded to deliver the bomb that literally shot the Trojans into orbit.

McLaughlin's kickoff was high and deep. Davis fielded it in the east end zone. He wasted no time, this fellow. Davis shot up field, got the blocks from Bell and Tatupu around the 20, and soon was clear.

"I want to point out one thing," said A.D. "It wasn't my kickoff return, it was USC's. Everyone had to do the job, else I couldn't have gone all the way."

It was the sixth kickoff return to a touchdown for Davis, an all-time NCAA record. Three have come against Notre Dame.

The aroused Trojans streamed on the field to congratulate this dynamic young man who may very well have secured the Heisman Trophy with Saturday's performance.

Special team star David Lewis then leveled McLane at the Notre Dame 8 on the ensuing kickoff, wiping out a failure on the two-point conversion.

The defense slammed the door in Notre Dame's face, bringing on a punt which Phillips brought back eight yards to the Irish 38.

On second down Haden unloaded a 31-yard strike to split end John McKay, followed by Davis' 6-yard bolt off right end for the touchdown.

Again the USC defense asserted itself. Desperately trying to get out of a hole, Clements hit Demmerle for what appeared to be first down.

But Danny Reece made a tremendous hit, forcing a fumble which Bruce gobbled up at the Irish 36.

Said the fiery Bruce from St. Francis High School: "I go on the theory that every loose ball is mine."

In five plays, highlighted by a 17-yard scramble pass from Haden to McKay, the Trojans got their go-ahead touchdown—a pitchout to Davis, who squirted into the end zone from the 4. He added the 2-point conversion on another pitchout around end.

Cobb's 56-yard punt return set up an 18-yard Haden to McKay touchdown pass, and a Phillips interception led to a 45-yard scoring effort by the same pair.

Said McKay: "Notre Dame was so conscious about shutting off our running game and taking away the short outs that they were giving the long pass. And we take what we can get."

That capped the 35–0 third quarter, but there was more to come.

Eric Pennick, who stunned USC with an 85-yard touchdown run in a 23–14 Irish win last year, couldn't find the handle on a Clements handoff. His fumble again was snapped up by the alert Bruce at the Notre Dame 15.

Haden rolled left and speared flanker Sheldon Diggs with another touchdown shot, bringing his career total to 31, bettering the USC record of 30, set by Jimmy Jones.

So it remained for Phillips to cap the amazing afternoon with his third interception at the Trojan 42 and subsequent 58-yard romp to the touchdown.

Phillips tantalized Notre Dame's Terry Eurick by holding the ball at arm's length as he dashed along the sidelines.

"Naw, I wasn't trying to embarrass anybody," said the 6-foot-3, 208-pounder who will be making a third visit to his home town New Year's Day when USC takes on Ohio State.

"It's just that I felt so happy."

Back on the Notre Dame bench, the television cameras picked up the glowering Parseghian, going through one of the worst experiences of his coaching career.

One doesn't have to wonder if he'll remember the final day of November, 1974.

An incredible day of football, to say the least.

Best News-Feature Story

A MODEL OF LEGALIZED VIOLENCE

By Dr. Ross Thomas Runfola

From The New York Times

Copyright, ©, 1974, The New York Times Company

Reprinted by permission

As a mirror reflection of American life, the most popular sport in America is professional football: brutal, precise, competitive, and highly standardized. In football, as in much of American society, the competitor is The Enemy, and the all-consuming passion is to win, often at any cost.

In Canada, sport is also a reflection of the culture; significantly, then, the most popular sport in Canada is professional hockey. Like the American brand of football, hockey also serves as a model of legalized violence—only on a simpler and grander scale befitting a society that still contains a frontier.

Hockey, of course, allows for the most aggressive type of behavior with a formalized rule structure. In hockey, one is free to use whatever personal resources one might have to defeat the opposition as efficiently as possible, including public humiliation through verbal baiting as well as pure physical power. No other team sport in recorded history accepts fighting as such a crucial aspect of the game.

No one has yet been able to chart acceptable parameters for hockey violence. The inability of the hockey establishment to give definition as to what constitutes "civilized violence" was personified recently when the Ontario Hockey Association suspended Gerry Henderson, president of the Bramalea Junior B hockey team, for two years when he withdrew Bramalea from the playoffs after such a violent and brawl-filled first game with the Hamilton Red Wings that he feared for the lives of his players.

A tragic footnote to the suspension of the Bramalea official is the manslaughter conviction of Paul Smithers for the death of Barrie Cobby on February 18, 1973, in a post-game brawl following a midget league hockey game.

Henderson, a concerned official, is considered a threat to the good order of organized hockey; Smithers, a young hockey player, is considered a threat to Canadian society. Both stand guilty of an inability to distinguish the hazy ethical line that separates acceptable and unacceptable levels of hockey violence.

The case of Paul Smithers is the greater tragedy because he stands broken and disillusioned at 17 years old. It is all the more tragic because in some ways—with one notable exception—he is a typical young Canadian. The exception is that he is black. A product of a developing middle-class suburb of Toronto, he lived quietly in a modest townhouse with his parents and 8-year-old brother. There was nothing very important to clutter his young life. Who to ask to the next dance? What record album to buy? And, of course, the next hockey game.

Hockey was a large part of his life. The numerous medals and trophies that filled the bookshelves in his bedroom bore visual proof both of his hockey proficiency and his youthful priorities.

By most standards, then, Paul Smithers was like many youngsters growing up in Canada who skate at 5 and dream of playing in the NHL. If he was somehow different from his peers, it was because he was an extraordinary hockey player, the best player in the Mississauga Midget League. Paul Smithers was also the only black player in the league.

Black hockey players are virtually nonexistent for numerous reasons, including the very small number of blacks living in Canada. Few blacks live in Mississauga—only a couple of hundred out of a population of more than 200,000. Despite this, the Smithers family experienced few problems. Paul's mother, Joyce, who is white, explains why: "We never bother other people and they don't bother us. We are a quiet family that sticks close together."

The quiet, everyday life of the Smithers family ended forever the night of February 18. Paul Smithers had a game that night against Applewood, but his parents did not attend because they were celebrating their wedding anniversary.

Unknown to them, a few miles away at Cawthra Park Arena, a

nightmare was unfolding. *The Toronto Sun* coldly captured the tragedy for them in bold print: MURDER AFTER HOCKEY: BOY CHARGED. As Don and Joyce Smithers stared tearfully at the banner headline the next day, it appeared to them that *The Sun* had already convicted their son.

When their son played for Cooksville in the Toronto Metro Hockey League, he was keyed up for every game. After his parents moved from Toronto and he was forced to play in the Mississauga Hockey League, the poor quality of the coaching and officiating caused him to quit playing for part of the previous season.

A member of the opposing Applewood team, Barrie Ross Cobby, also would have been happier playing in another league. After he was dropped from the Dixie Beehives, Cobby had no choice but to play in the Mississauga Midget League. In the lesser league, he was as much a star for his team as Smithers was for Cooksville.

Only a few weeks before the game of February 18, Cobby wrote an essay in school on the lesson he learned from reading *The Adventures of Huckleberry Finn*. The book showed young Cobby that "Negroes are human. I often wondered if they were any different, although I don't think I was prejudiced. . . . But most important of all I learned about friendship between two races and I hope that some day we'll be able to get along together."

The essay by young Cobby arguing racial harmony obviously did not include Paul Smithers. A member of the Cooksville Midgets recalls that Cobby always directed racial barbs at Smithers whenever the teams met. While tough talk and baiting are as much a part of hockey as fighting, Smithers remains convinced that his blackness and not his ability made him the target for verbal abuse.

And so young Smithers laced up for the Applewood game with mounting anxiety. The game met Smithers' worst fears. It was not hockey they were playing at Cawthra Arena on February 18; they were waging war, a war orchestrated by a crowd that at times appeared to be emotionally deranged.

Never before had Smithers been conscious of the crowd. But against Applewood, his ears rang whenever play stopped or he skated into the corner to dig out the puck. As the game progressed, the crowd reaction assumed an increasingly ugly character almost in perfect cadence to the illicit violence and racist baiting on the ice.

At the trial, several witnesses, including John Barme, coach of the Applewood Midgets, testified that his team subjected Smithers to numerous racial slurs. Early in the game, Barrie Cobby told Smithers, "I'm going to get you, you black bastard." As the verbal assault escalated, Cobby called Smithers a "stupid nigger" and a "coon" and his mother a "nigger lover" and a "white pig."

At one point, the game threatened to get completely out of hand when the entire Applewood team and parents in the arena started to taunt Smithers and yell, "Get the nigger." As Smithers describes it, the referees ignored his plea to take action to halt the tripping, slashing, and verbal abuse. Soon afterward, Cobby speared Smithers. Just before he entered the penalty box, Cobby challenged Smithers, "Let's fight, you stupid nigger." Smithers scored a goal while Cobby was serving the penalty. The goal only served to further incense Cobby and the crowd. Eventually, Cobby and Smithers were ejected from the game for their continuing battle.

Just four months past his 16th birthday, Smithers reacted to Cobby's challenge to fight by waiting for him outside the Applewood dressing room. Almost a year and a half later, Smithers' father attempts to capture his son's mental state after the Applewood game:

"Paul was just a young boy. Who can say he should have controlled his emotions when players and fans were calling him 'nigger' every game? He was bound to explode."

The inevitable explosion came when young Smithers followed Cobby outside the arena to the parking lot, determined to get an apology or a fight. Smithers punched Cobby once and was then grabbed by four Applewood players. With his arms and neck pinned, he kicked out instinctively as Cobby lunged toward him. Cobby crumpled to the ground, clutching his groin. Minutes later he was dead, choked on his own vomit.

A tragic accident by any standard. At the trial, not one doctor could say with any medical certainty that there was a direct connection between the kick to the groin and the death of Cobby. A pathologist attributed Cobby's death to the inhaling of his own vomit, but found no evidence of bodily harm. Dr. William Butt, the Mississauga coroner, testified that even extreme tension could have caused the vomiting.

If Smithers' attack on Cobby had occurred during the game, Smithers would have been liable for a five-minute major penalty. Off the ice, he was liable for a term in prison.

In view of the extenuating circumstances, Judge B. B. Shapiro of Peel County Court informed the all-white jury that it could find Smithers guilty of common assault rather than manslaughter under the same criminal code section. In a surprising move, the jury found Smithers guilty of the harsher manslaughter conviction. Judge Shapiro had little choice but to sentence Smithers on June 4 to six months in the Brampton Adult Training Center. Outside the court-room, Len Cobby, father of the dead boy, was visibly upset by the sentence. "I think it's a pretty poor effort," he told a crowd of reporters, "when Smithers gets six months for taking 50 years from my boy."

Early the next afternoon, Smithers was released on bail pending appeal. Minutes after his release, I haltingly asked him why Cobby's mother sent him a Christmas card in which she refers to her son as being in "profound sleep." As tears well in his eyes, I quickly shifted the subject to why he thought he was convicted of manslaughter. Without pause, he blurted out, "Because I'm black." But then he quickly offered an opinion designed to be more acceptable to his father, who is standing nearby.

"No. The fact that I'm black is not the point. Any 12 decent people would have found me not guilty. I think I got a bad deal from the jury, especially in view of the medical testimony."

As Paul Smithers waits for his appearance, expected sometime in the fall, Don and Joyce Smithers are attempting to prepare their family for an uncertain future. They recently purchased a 25-acre farm in Orangeville, Ontario, to rebuild their shattered lives.

It will not be easy. Although their son Paul had never been in trouble before the hockey incident, the week after he was found guilty the Mississauga police went to the Smithers home to question him about the robbery of a corner gas station.

"Luckily, I was in the hospital for typhoid fever, so they couldn't get me for that," said Smithers.

Who, then, is to blame for a tragedy that has taken one young life and threatens to destroy another? Barrie Cobby, who grew up with a Manichean "Good vs. Evil" view that is so much a part of the contemporary sports scene? Paul Smithers, who finally resorted to physical violence after a season of particularly cruel verbal violence? Or societies that increasingly tend both to glorify violence and desensitize young people to the growing spectacle of human brutal-ity by teaching them techniques of controlled violence to crush opposition on rival teams?

Perhaps the most important question is also the one that is the most difficult for Canadians to contemplate. The popular heroes in Canada are men who express themselves in the most aggressive and assertive ways. Dare anyone confront the thought that perhaps fans at Cawthra Arena were screaming insults at a black, 16-year-old youngster because he symbolized the assertiveness and unbridled aggression that they themselves demand in "the future custodians of the Republic"?

It is, after all, the widespread belief of fans that outcomes in the sporting arena are inextricably intertwined with outcomes in the real world that gives the Paul Smithers case a social significance that transcends the sports world. In a word, how far removed is Mississauga from Mississippi?

Best Magazine Story

STOCK-CAR STREAKING

By John S. Radosta

From The New York Times Magazine

Copyright, ©, 1974, The New York Times Company

Reprinted by permission

When 40 of the noisiest automobiles in America line up for the 16th annual Firecracker 400 on July 4 at Daytona Beach, Florida, the race will differ in one respect from the 15 previous Firecrackers. It will retain the "400" in its name, but in a deferential (and public-relations) nod to the fuel situation, its length will be cut 10 percent to 360 miles, just as the Daytona 500 of last February and other important stock-car races have been curtailed this season. Apart from that one change, which is bound to be temporary, other characteristics of the Firecracker and similar races remain immutable:

(1) Most of the racing teams, with techniques that are artful and arcane, will have found ways of cheating on the rules, which are as complex as the income-tax laws.

(2) Most of the teams will be jealously protecting some newly discovered competitive secret known as "the tip"—whether it's some way of coaxing one more horsepower out of a 450-h.p. engine or some ruse like polishing the sidewalls of the tires with silicone.

(3) If Richard Petty, the Babe Ruth–Jack Nicklaus–Gordie Howe–O. J. Simpson of stock-car racing, doesn't win, then his old enemy, Bobby Allison, will. Or David Pearson, hottest of this season's hot dogs. And if none of these good ol' boys makes it, they will force whoever does to sweat hard for his purse.

(4) Most important, the race will be one hell of a show, up to three hours of hard-chargin', fender-bangin' competition over the two-

and-a-half mile oval track at 175 miles an hour (that's nearly three miles a minute), giving the 60,000 to 65,000 spectators more than their money's worth before sending them home at some sensible time, like 1 P.M.

Auto racing is as old as the automobile itself, and over the years it has evolved into many specialized formats, notably stock-car racing, road racing (on courses that simulate country roads), drag racing, and Indianapolis. An estimated 40-million paying spectators attend all motor racing in the United States, and stock-car racing accounts for more than half of them. This is all the more unusual in view of the fact that the stockers' appeal is virtually concentrated in the southeastern part of the country; it is popular in varying degrees elsewhere (it has even spread to Canada and West Germany), but Dixie is its main turf, and Daytona Beach its Mecca.

As a whole, auto racing in the U.S. generates about $1 billion a year in expenditures, from big-buck sponsorships and television contracts to cotton candy purchased at concession stands. Stock-car racing, combining elements of sport, industry, and show business, is one of the more conspicuous financial successes in the realm of motor sports. Beneath the Dixie trappings of fried chicken, corn pone, busty beauty queens, patriotic display and politicians, beer, Coke, and earnest invocations by local Protestant ministers, there is a hardnosed, tightly organized business establishment that brings together talented race drivers, the most ingenious auto mechanics to be found anywhere, and a band of sophisticated race promoters and car owners.

The very words "stock car" are an astute bit of merchandising con, a deadpan form of mislabeling. They are intended to imply that the race car on the track is the same as the Plymouth, Chevrolet, or Ford sedan you drive to work. No so. "Stock-appearing" is a closer description. The brand names and body contours are the only things the race car and the ordinary passenger car have in common. For the racing stock car is a highly specialized piece of hand-built machinery that costs about $20,000, including a $4,000 engine (more if you're counting on winning often). It is created to do what a conventional passenger car cannot do—run long races without falling apart and killing its driver. The racing stock car also happens to be at least ten times safer, mechanically and structurally, than the car you buy from your friendly neighborhood dealer. Collisions and flipovers seldom injure, let alone kill, the drivers of racing stock cars.

One of the big reasons why stock-car racing is more prosperous than road racing or Indianapolis racing is that it offers the fan vivid identification factors. Fans are interested in the cars because the trade names are the same as those of their own cars parked outside the stadium. Fans are interested in the drivers because they are folk heroes who also happen to be first-name neighbors, or seeming neighbors. When the fans say "Richard" or "Bobby" or "David," they can mean only Richard Petty, Bobby Allison, and David Pearson, the sport's three million-dollar winners.

The drivers' names evoke partisanship as violent as the races themselves. As recently as last April, in Wilkes County, North Carolina, a man was shot to death and two others beaten ("stomped") in a barroom brawl that was touched off by the appearance of three of Bobby Allison's pit crewmen. Allison is about as popular as a revenue agent in Wilkes County, which, a sheriff's spokesman emphasized, "is Cale Yarborough and Richard Petty country."

It's quite the opposite at Hueytown, Alabama, where Bobby and his younger brother Donnie are based. People come from miles around just to drop in on the Allison shop and say hello. "Everybody's real friendly," says Donnie, "even the coloreds."

The Yankee may consider stock-car drivers a picturesque crowd of men, but that's not the way Southerners regard them. The drivers are just as plain as can be, and most of them come from farm areas and small towns. Few have made it through high school. Most started poor or close to poor, with motel rooms an unattainable luxury. These men are not glamorous world travelers like the Grand Prix jet-set, nor are they womanizers, heavy drinkers, carousers, or pot smokers. As a rule they prefer "heck" and "goldang" to (expletive deleted). They are family men in their 30's and late 20's; when school and family circumstances permit, they take the kids to the races around the circuit. Most of them attend Protestant churches regularly, and some are active in church or community work. They support a tiny mobile chapel that travels from one race to the next. Its minister, a sort of evangelist known as Brother Bill, also leads the quiet prayer that concludes the private drivers' meeting just before a race.

The leader of the lot is Richard Petty, who apprenticed (and sometimes competed) with his father, Lee Petty, a magnificent driver of a generation ago. Richard Petty has won the national championship four times. He has won 158 stock-car races, more than twice as many as anyone else. He is the only driver ever to win more than once the Daytona 500, the best of all stock-car races; in fact, he's won it four times.

Petty could be a Joe Namath if he wanted to, but he remains the serious country boy who sticks to his business enterprises. He has a smile that dazzles like an Ultrabrite ad; he has no "side" or poses, and he often uses the old-fashioned word "cat" in referring to people. He lives with his wife and four children on a 22-acre property at Level Cross, the North Carolina hamlet where he was born July 2, 1937, and where the only bright lights are in the traffic signals. "There is something clean and pure and fresh as a pine forest about him," a Georgia admirer once said of Petty. He may be modest, but not all that modest. When a writer asked Richard how far he wanted to go in racing, he answered, "I'm there."

Petty's closest personal rival is Bobby Allison, 36 years old, one of the few Catholics in the sport. Petty and Allison used to be authentic enemies, and they banged up each other's cars. They've toned down some, though this is not to say they're bosom buddies yet.

This is a world in which fans like the unlikely diminutives: Tiny Lund and Buddy Baker are giants. Bobby Isaac is 39 years old, and Donnie Allison is 34. There are other catchy names like Coo Coo Marlin, Hoss Ellington, Soapy Castles, Banjo Matthews, Cotton Owens, Turkey Minton, Junior Johnson.

And it is a world in which drivers are enshrined in the memories of the fans. For instance, there was Tim Flock, who raced with his monkey mascot, Jocko Flocko; the monkey rode in a special seat and wore a helmet and fire-retardant racing suit. Then there was Curtis Turner, a hard drinker and brilliant racer who once went straight from an all-night party to a race, driving in his white linen suit. Turner liked to land his airplane on highways and race tracks and to park rented cars in motel swimming pools. He was suspended between 1961 and 1964 for trying to organize a drivers' labor union.

The origins of stock-car racing go back, in part, to moonshining, a lucrative business that thrived on evasion of alcohol taxes. The delivery of corn whiskey from mountain stills to city customers provided a sort of training ground for future race drivers. They learned car preparation, speed, evasion, high-speed U-turns at the *po*lice barriers and secret compartments for booze (still useful on the track for hidden fuel, if not discovered at tech inspection). The necessary elements of car preparation were road-holding, stability, endurance, acceleration and—the crucial consideration if the driver wanted to stay out of jail—finishing first and vanishing into the darkness. "You have to run good, otherwise you get caught," said Curtis Turner, who learned his trade this way.

As each hill and valley produced its own master mechanic and its own hero "leadfoot" driver, parochial bragging led to informal races among the good ol' boys who created the cars and drove them with consummate skill and audacity. Men who could scarcely read and write suddenly became the most affluent in the neighborhood.

Moonshining, of course, is not the only source of stock-car racing. In the socioeconomic ethos of the South, a car is the most prized possession of many a family. And if in the nineteen thirties and forties a young man didn't have a ball game to go to, or the money to attend one, he could at least tinker with his car or hang around watching others doing it. So stock-car racing developed in the rural areas, on rough country roads and in meadows. No prizes at first, maybe only a small bet. In time, there were slightly more formal races at county-fair horse tracks, with paid attendance and purses —if the promoter was honest. There were no garages or pits. Mechanics simply hung block and tackle on the limb of a sturdy oak to lift engines. They were called shade-tree mechanics.

It was a raffish sport in the forties. Promoters cheated drivers by running off with gate receipts. They lied to fans about what drivers would appear. Cheating was rampant, rules were chaotic, and nobody had the clout to enforce rules anyway.

In 1948 a race driver and promoter named William Henry Getty (Big Bill) France introduced order, honesty, respectability, consistent rules and business management into the sport with the organization of the National Association for Stock Car Auto Racing, which he based in Daytona Beach. This company, known in racing circles by its acronym, NASCAR, is now the dominant figure in stock-car racing, stronger even than the National Football League in its domain.

There are four basic forms of stock-car racing. The three lowest levels form the pyramid that supports the top level. This broad base is essential: The thousands of bread-and-butter shows of 25 and 50 miles on the half-mile "bull rings" bring substantial revenue from sanctions (permits) to NASCAR, and they train young drivers for the big time.

At the bottom of the pyramid are the jalopies, euphemistically called "cadet" and "hobby" cars, that are so familiar in the boondocks. Next up are the modifieds, highly imaginative re-creations of cars originally produced 15 or 20 years ago. Then there are the sportsmen, conventional-looking sedans more than three years old.

At the top of the structure are the late-model sedans, steel-bodied machines based on cars of the three most recent production years. This late-model category, called the Grand National, is the showcase offering, the most glamorous, with the biggest purses, best drivers and TV coverage.

The Grand National series runs 30 to 32 races a year on asphalt-surfaced tracks ranging from a half-mile long to "superspeedways" of 1 mile to 2.6 miles. Superspeedway events generally run 400 to 600 miles, with purses up to $150,000. Among the superspeedways are tracks at Daytona Beach; Charlotte and Rockingham, North Carolina; Darlington, South Carolina; Hampton, Georgia; and Talladega, Alabama. There are others in California, Pennsylvania, Michigan, and elsewhere, but the truly authentic local-color races—with beauty queens, parades, politicians, invocations, high school bands—are in the South.

The fans come to see thrills and skillful driving, to marvel at how close Pearson or Baker can come to the brink of disaster. They love the violent, close-action racing that involves occasional car-to-car contact, or "bammin' and frammin'."

In any race, two strong competitors may swap the lead two or three times in one lap, with positions changing in the blink of an eye. Every so often you'll see a strong driver hang back, catch up and pass the leader, and then drop back again. What he is doing is testing: he wants to be certain he can pass later on in the race, when positions are critical. It also serves to "psych" the driver he passes. Another way of unnerving a leader is to "dive" under him on the left side as the two cars enter a turn.

One of the most spectacular maneuvers is drafting, or slipstreaming. A driver tucks in behind another driver and tailgates him lap after lap. The car in front is pushing through the air, using up fuel and imposing wear-and-tear on its engine, its slipstream is like the V-shaped wake of a boat. The driver who is drafting simply stays in that V-shaped slipstream for a free ride, or "tow." He is getting the same 165 miles an hour, say, as his benefactor, but he is using only three-fourths as much throttle. So he conserves fuel and engine stress. Petty says he can begin to feel the draft 100 yards back, "but it don't start to free up your car until you get within a couple of car lengths. For a perfect draft, you've got to stay within a car length."

Not only is it awesome to see the drafter maneuvering a two-ton car within a couple of feet of a car ahead. It is also impressive to see six, seven, or more cars drafting as though they were part of a wagon train.

The draft leads to another maneuver, the slingshot. When the drafter decides he wants to pass, he breaks the suction by steering left or right. The front car is running flat out—at maximum speed —but the drafter, having had the benefit of a tow, has some power in reserve. Now out of the slipstream, the driver floors his accelerator and slings—or slingshots—past his competitor. "When you get even with his door," as Petty explains it, "you start hitting about as much wind as he is. But you've already got your momentum built up, and even though you hit it and feel it, you'll sail right on by."

The slingshot is used throughout the race, but most theatrically on the very last lap, the sprint to the finish line, when the challenger is harassing the leader with a well-executed draft. He sets up his man for the slingshot close enough to the finish line so that his victim does not have enough time to set up his own draft and rearrange the chase. It's an art form.

For all practical purposes there are two groups racing out there. The more important one consists of the handful of "hot dogs," who are the best drivers with the best equipment. They run by themselves on the "high groove," an imaginary lane next to the outer retaining wall. The lesser racers and cars run their own race in the lower grooves for the money that is paid for 10th place, 11th place, and so on. They are there to fill out the field and make it look good.

A race of 400 or 500 miles works out to a series of sprints. The intervals between sprints are the pit stops. These are made necessary by the fact that the fuel limit of 22 gallons is enough for only 80 to 90 miles and because the right-side tires, which take the most friction in constant left-turning, need to be replaced every 100 miles or so.

Most pit stops are related to accidents on the track—collisions, blown engines, spinouts against the wall, tire blowouts and the like —that spill debris and oil on the pavement. That stuff is dangerous, and it has to be cleared by the track safety workmen. During these minutes when the workmen are tidying up, race officials flash yellow caution lights around the track and wave a yellow flag, which slows down the pace to half speed or less. The cars then bunch up into a sort of train, tooling around the track.

The significance of the caution period is that no driver may improve his position—no passing is allowed. So, with the cars going slow "under the caution," it is advantageous to come into the pits for fuel and tires, dash out onto the track and resume position in the slow-moving procession. Although a driver may not pass another car, the caution period does make it possible to close up a gap because of the way the cars bunch up.

When the debris is cleaned up and everything is "sanitary" again, the green lights flash, the starter waves a green flag, and the race starts anew, with a mass of drivers, closely packed, breaking out of position and fighting to get ahead in the traffic. The restarts are hairy and exciting.

What happens if there are no accidents? This makes the pit stops even more exciting, because the drivers have to come in for fuel and tires while their competitors are racing flat out. Races can be won or lost in the pits, and the length of a pit stop is of overwhelming interest. The track announcer makes a point of calling out the time for each—16 seconds, 18 seconds, and so on.

There can be five or six men in a pit crew, but only four are permitted (depending on their specialities) to jump over the wall at any one time to work on their car. The basic pit stop entails jacking up the right side of the car and changing the two right-side tires; at the same time, at the left rear, a crewman is swiftly decanting 22 gallons of gasoline blend into the fuel cell. He sloshes the stuff from two 11-gallon "milk cans" designed for this operation.

In stock-car racing the chief mechanic is often the owner of the race car. The mechanic is almost as important as the driver, even though he doesn't get anywhere near as much public attention. Pit stops are pure show-biz, like a ballet. The men are colorfully uniformed, and they do their work with speed, grace, and precision. The best of them can manage a two-tire change plus fuel in 15 1/2 seconds, others do it in 17 to 20. A four-tire change takes 30 to 32 seconds. Oh yes, they also wipe the windshield and extend the driver a cup of water on a long pole.

The interior of a stock car is like nothing familiar to most people. No upholstery, no door handles, no window cranks, no radio, no heater, no speedometer. There is no door, because the door is welded shut. There is no window glass—only a window opening through which the driver climbs. There is only one seat, a bucket seat stoutly secured to the frame of the car.

The materials that go into the car are built for strength, durability and precision, either from scratch or from "pieces" that originate in Detroit. They come from a relatively narrow supply system. Richard Petty and his family are the exclusive distributors of Chrysler parts and equipment to the racing community. Holman & Moody, in Charlotte, have the same arrangement with Ford and Mercury. Bobby Allison distributes Chevrolet pieces, but he does not have a monopoly: There are other Chevrolet distributors in the field, and racers can also buy materials through ordinary Chevy dealers. Petty Enterprises sells a basic racing car called the Saturday Night Special for about $10,000 (minus engine), which can also be purchased, at less cost, in kit form.

The most conspicuous installation inside the car is the roll cage, an intricate network of 250 feet of steel tubing, 1 3/4 inches in diameter, that forms a protective cocoon around the driver. This is the strongest part of the race car, and its purpose is to prevent the car from being mashed into a ball and crushing the driver.

I have seen dozens of spectacular crashes from which the driver emerged only "shook up," or with some bumps and scratches. In the 1971 Daytona 500, Maynard Troyer caromed off the outside retaining wall and became airborne. What followed was a series of barrel rolls and end-over-end loops that were difficult to count even on the movie films. After a seeming eternity, Troyer's car stopped bouncing and landed on its roof, and safety workers pulled him out. The only treatment he needed was a brief stay in the hospital to get his plumbing system back into phase.

In the 1972 Daytona 500, Walter Ballard's car hit the wall and began flying just like Troyer's. It struck the ground four or five times. Each bounce sheared off windshield, fenders, engine parts, wheels, trunk and engine lids, body panels. Then the car slid about 100 feet on the pavement upside down, until it reached the grass border on the inside of the track and flipped once again, landing on its wheels. Ballard's only injury was a scratched forearm.

What saved these two drivers? First, neither car stopped abruptly; rather, each had a sequence of "stops" that absorbed a share of the violent force against the car. The second reason is the construction of the race car, which is designed to dissipate violent impact by sacrificing pieces. When the front end shears away and the wheels fly off, those pieces are taking the initial force and diverting that force from reaching the driver in the roll cage. The crucial thing is that while pieces of the car are flying off, the core holds together and the driver is not crushed.

There's a lot of superstition and psychological warfare in stock-car racing. Hence "the tip," some esoteric little secret that gives a team an advantage. Often it is something trivial, but many crews treat it seriously until it is tried and discarded.

At Rockingham the tip is to inflate the inner liner with 85 pounds pressure. But use six pounds less at Darlington—"I'll guarantee that's the tip." Overinflate at Charlotte, underinflate at Hickory, switch right-side tires to left at Martinsville, front tires to rear at Bristol. At Greenville, use a soft compound on the left front.

A tip at qualifying time is to wait for clouds to cover the sun—tires run cooler and therefore quicker. In the pits the tip is to glue lug nuts in place on the spare wheels so that no time is lost during tire changes. Another tip is for a mechanic to hold five lug nuts on a wire in his teeth—that way he doesn't waste time looking for them.

Obviously, if the tip is any good it will be kept secret. But quite often a team plants a phony tip as a red herring to confuse the enemy or waste his time. Freddie Lorenzen qualified fair and square for the pole—the No. 1 starting position—by running the fastest car. His tires were the same as everyone else's, but he conned the opposition into believing they were different and therefore had something to do with his speed. Instead of white code dots on the sidewalls, Lorenzen's dots were red. So red-dot tires were the tip, and everyone demanded red-dot tires from the tire supplier. The company had no red-dot tires and it was accused of playing favorites. Of course, Lorenzen had merely painted his dots red.

A few years ago at Daytona, the Petty family let it be known that the roof of Richard's Plymouth was painted in a rough texture to alter the flow of air over the top of the car. That was the tip because it added a couple of miles an hour in speed. Well, it turned out the roof was a cheater, illegally thin to save weight. How did they thin the roof panel? By dipping it in acid.

Then there was Lee Roy Yarbrough's tailpipe. Normally the exhaust system is short, with the exhaust pipe terminating about halfway back on one side or the other. When Lee Roy won the Daytona 500 in 1969, he was driving a Ford with an exhaust pipe that reached all the way to his rear bumper. His chief mechanic, Herb Nab, answered questions with an enigmatic smile. By the next race, at Atlanta, six other cars appeared with long tailpipes even though, as Nab noted, "the mechanics didn't know why they had them." Eventually NASCAR prohibited the long pipe. "And NASCAR never knew why they banned them," Nab says.

In a world so competitive and with rules so complex, cheating is inevitable. But evasion of the rules is so common that nobody thinks of it as cheating. They tell you, seriously, that cheating is the old-fashioned American way of staying competitive. Richard Petty has a homely tip: "Cheat neat."

There are no moral stigmas, no hard feelings, no big deals in penalties. Cheating is a game of wits between the tech inspectors and the mechanics. Each time the inspectors "ketch" a rule infraction, the mechanics invent something more esoteric that will get by for a while. One hoary trick is to overwhelm the inspector with a dozen obvious violations. He is so busy pouncing on them that he fails to notice a more subtle goody somewhere else.

There are countless ways of cheating, depending on what the mechanic is trying to accomplish—more efficient aerodynamics, greater horsepower, better tire adhesion.

One rule requires a clearance of at least 4 inches between the front end and the ground. But mechanics can get more speed if they can get the car lower than 4 inches. The classic way is to secrete a couple of wooden shims, camouflaged with paint, into the springs. At inspection, the shims hold the car up to proper height. But during the race, vibration and friction dislodge them or wear them out, and the car "drops" maybe half an inch. There are variations, such as a hidden cable release to lower the car or fine steel pins in the shock absorbers that break under racing stress.

A race car is required to weigh at least 3,800 pounds, but it has a mysterious way of getting lighter by race time. The trick is to sneak a heavy object into the car before inspection and remove it before race time.

Obviously there is a competitive advantage in streamlining a car more than the original Detroit model. The way to do it is to reduce the height of the car and "flatten" the slope of the windshield. To detect such distortions, tech inspectors use a series of metal templates, or patterns, that outline exactly the original shape of the car. Some years ago a clever mechanic created an optical illusion. He built a car precisely three-fourths the size of its original, and for a while it escaped notice.

There are ways of getting around the rule limiting fuel capacity to 22 gallons. You can get a bit more mileage between pit stops, for example, if you lengthen the steel casing of the fuel cell by just a quarter of an inch. That's good for an extra gallon of gas. If you are very clever, the way Smokey Yunich was, you can hide an extra fuel tank that holds a couple of gallons somewhere in the body work.

For several years NASCAR required the installation of a steel plate with holes of a prescribed size to limit the amount of fuel-air mixture from the carburetor to the intake manifold. The mechanics devised so many ways of enlarging or bypassing those holes—and camouflaging the results—that NASCAR gave up on the plates.

Some years ago, under different weight rules, mechanics substituted aluminum for steel. Aluminum is still illegal and inspectors carry magnets to detect its presence—a magnet does not cling to aluminum.

Stock-car racing's healthy economic base—the box office—is enhanced by solid sponsorships. Racing is a merchandising tool that sells not only automotive products, but also beer, cigarettes, soft drinks, insurance, air-conditioning, variety stores, cities, moving and trucking companies, clothing, and so on. The time is long past when a race track was just a li'l ol' race track: Today it is a "marketing area." And so there are sponsors for race teams, for individual races and for racing series. Every car is a colorful array of advertising decals, a rolling billboard. And on top of the sponsorship structure there is television money, lovely loot that enriches everyone.

The promoters have strong and useful political connections in the South. Like several other sports, auto racing occasionally skates on the thin edge of antitrust laws, and NASCAR has a potent law firm in Washington looking after its interests.

More significant, Bill France, founder of NASCAR and president of the two largest tracks on the circuit—at Daytona Beach and Talladega, Alabama,—cultivates powerful Southern politicians like the late Representative L. Mendel Rivers of South Carolina, former chairman of the House Armed Services Committee, and Representative F. Edward Hebert of Louisiana, the present chairman. France is an old friend of Governor George A. Wallace of Alabama and served as Florida campaign manager in Wallace's 1972 campaign for the Democratic Presidential nomination. When France's superspeedway at Talladega opened in 1969, it had a four-lane access road from Interstate 20 to the front gate.

Friendly state and local politicians can be helpful in other ways, such as favorable tax arrangements, the assignment of massive numbers of state and county policemen to maintain order at the track on race day, and coping with any subversive talk about antinoise legislation.

There is an all-American irony in the stockers' ethics and their politics. On the one hand, there is the free-and-easy acceptance of cheating and, on the other, this cozy relationship with law-and-order politicians like Wallace. It's not a contradiction that seems to bother the sport's multitude of fans.

The World Series

A RARE DISPLAY OF CAMARADERIE

(WORLD SERIES GAME I)

By Phil Pepe

From the New York Daily News

Copyright, ©, 1974, New York News Inc.

Peace, it's wonderful.

Togetherness, it's Beautiful.

In a rare display of camaraderie, the battling A's of Oakland stopped their bickering, their intramural squabbling, and their family feuding long enough to beat the docile Dodgers in the first game of the first all-California World Series here today.

Not a lawsuit was filed, not a punch thrown, not a stitch taken, not an ounce of blood spilled in a 3–2 victory that was, if Charles O. Finley, Catfish Hunter, Rollie Fingers, Blue Moon Odom, Reggie Jackson, and Bill North will pardon the expression, a team effort.

Ken Holtzman was helped out by Rollie Fingers, who was helped out by Catfish Hunter. Bert Campaneris got together with Ken Holtzman to pull off a vital squeeze play. Reggie Jackson helped everybody with a tremendous home run his first time at bat, then spent the last two innings helping to position Claudell Washington, his defensive replacement in right field.

The A's were so helpful toward each other you might think the milk of human kindness had replaced the venom that usually pours out of the water cooler in the Oakland dugout.

There was an irony in the way the game finished, with Hunter coming out of the bullpen to strike out Joe Ferguson for the final out and save Fingers, a man-bites-dog story. Normally, it's Fingers who saves Hunter . . . when he isn't fighting with Blue Moon Odom, that is, or going off to a hospital to get five stitches taken in his head.

But it was ironic that Hunter and Fingers would figure in this victory, the first step in the A's bid for a third straight world championship. For it was Hunter and Fingers who made news yesterday, the Catfish claiming to be a free agent and Fingers tangling in the latest clubhouse fight of the Oakland weirdos.

They proved that when it's time to stop battling and start playing, the A's are not weird at all: they can play the game with the best of them.

Reggie Jackson got it all going in the second inning, Reggie Jackson who had been the center of some doubt because of a pulled right hamstring that reduced him to a designated hitter for the last two games of the American League playoffs.

While many wondered if Jackson could play, there was never any doubt in Reggie's mind. He'd play if he could walk. He would have pain, especially when he swung and missed and landed on his right leg, and he'd have trouble pulling the ball. The solution was obvious —don't miss and hit the ball to the opposite field.

That's exactly what Jackson did against Andy Messersmith in the second. He hit the ball to the opposite field, halfway up the stands between the 370- and 385-foot markers, "about as good as I can hit a ball."

Holtzman was unsteady early, but good when it was required. He stranded one Dodger in the second, two in the third, and two in the fourth and his friends, his pals, the lovey-dovey A's, went out and got him another in the fifth.

Of course, Holtzman contributed to it with his usual World Series double inside the left field line, his third double in his last four at-bats in the Series. After a wild pitch put Holtzman on third, Alvin Dark called for a suicide squeeze on a 2–2 pitch, taking the gamble because "Campy's a good squeezer."

"I surprise," said Bert Campaneris when asked what he thought of the bunt sign, then he executed it perfectly, pushing an inside pitch to the right of the mound as Holtzman scored with a "banzai" to make it 2–0.

The Dodgers had scored their first run, ironically on errors. Campaneris booted Davey Lopes' roller and Lopes came around to score when Bill Buckner's single to right was bobbled by Jackson, who tried to make a bare hand pickup. When Holtzman walked Jimmy Wynn, Alvin Dark's mind was made up. He felt he had to stop the Dodgers, right here, right now, and he brought in Fingers.

The peerless reliever fanned Steve Garvey, star of the playoffs, and Dodger hearts sank. But they beat again when Fingers nicked Joe Ferguson with a pitch, then soared briefly when Ron Cey hit a drive to left field, and dropped again when the ball nestled into Joe Rudi's glove.

That might have been it right there, baseball fans, all 50 million watching on television and the 55,974 plus one mule that made up the largest crowd in Dodger Stadium history.

But it wasn't. There was more excitement to come. And while it seemed inconsequential at the time—and was to be meaningless in the end—the Dodgers came up with a big defensive play in the eighth. It was the defensive play of the game and it almost proved fatal to the A's.

Campaneris had singled, moved to second on Bill North's sacrifice, and scored when Cey threw Sal Bando's bouncer on a hop past Garvey at first. Bando went all the way around to third and the A's had a 3–1 lead, which looked safe with less than two innings left.

A 4–1 lead would look safer and that's what the A's thought they had when Jackson drove a ball to the right center, maybe 300 feet away. The A's thought they had another run. Jackson thought he had another RBI. No way a guy can throw a man out from there: No way.

It should have been Wynn's ball, but Jimmy does not throw very well. And Ferguson came over and took the ball out of Wynn's glove. Ferguson is the right fielder against left-handed pitchers, giving way to Steve Yeager behind the plate because Yeager is considered a better catcher, a better thrower, as he proved when he shot North down on an attempted steal in the fifth.

Now, Ferguson had the ball 300 feet away and Bando was tagged up and Jackson was standing near first base with his bat in hand, knowing right away that Bando would be out. "I knew it," said Jackson, "watching him do his thing."

Ferguson caught the ball and Jackson knew as soon as he cut loose and the ball was over Lopes' head.

"It was a super, super throw," said Jackson, "the kind of play you see in a World Series. The man just made a great throw."

That's what Jackson said, not what he was thinking, standing there near first base with his bat in hand watching Ferguson do his thing.

"I thought, 'Oh, sh—' "

Bando came in hard and knocked Yeager over, but the catcher held the ball.

"He may be the best defensive catcher I've ever seen," said Bando. "I said to him, 'are you all right?' I wanted to let him know I don't intentionally hurt anybody."

No matter, a 3–1 lead with Fingers pitching was safe enough and he proved it when he beat back still another Dodger challenge in the eighth. He walked Cey with one out and gave up a pinch single to Willie Crawford with two outs, then got pinch hitter Von Joshua on a bouncer to end the challenge. Was it the Dodgers' last?

Hardly. They had one more in the ninth after Fingers got the first two batters.

Then Rollie threw a 2–2 breaking ball to Wynn "that had neon lights on it" and Jim hit it over the wall in left center as Rudi and North both went up for it and collided. North got his glove on it after it was over the fence and thought he might have caught it if he hadn't got bumped by Rudi. In his frustration, he kicked the wall.

When Garvey followed with a single to right, Dark made his move. He had been saving Catfish Hunter for this situation. In the sixth, he sent Catfish to the bullpen and Hunter said, "I couldn't have pitched then, my heart was beating so much."

In the eighth, Hunter got up for the first time.

In the ninth, he was in, to face Ferguson with the tying run on base.

THE DODGERS EVEN IT UP

(WORLD SERIES GAME II)

By Jim Hawkins

From the Detroit Free Press

There were ironies all over the place. Don Sutton, the pitcher Charles O. Finley personally scorned nine years ago, returned the favor Sunday afternoon, overturning Charlie's Oakland A's, 3–2, on behalf of the Los Angeles Dodgers to even the World Series at one win apiece.

Meanwhile, Mike Marshall, the kinesiology professor from Michigan State, treated former pupil Herb Washington, the A's professional pinch runner, to a painful lesson in humility.

So, the Series shifts to Oakland Tuesday evening with the Dodgers looking very much alive again.

It was a game the Dodgers simply had to win. None of them ever tried to deny that. And Joe Ferguson's mammoth two-run homer, plus the pitching of Sutton and Marshall made it possible.

For Sutton, a 19-game winner during the regular season and definitely the Dodgers' best pitcher, Sunday's success was particularly satisfying.

The way the 29-year-old right hander had it figured, he owed Finley one.

Sunday, for the first time, Sutton revealed the story of how he almost signed with the A's in 1964, when they were still quartered in Kansas City.

Whitey Herzog, who was scouting for the A's at the time, offered young Sutton $20,000 to sign with Kansas City. They shook hands and called it a deal. "But we ought to call Mr. Finley to get his approval," said Herzog.

Well, it so happened Finley had just finished signing Catfish Hunter, Blue Moon Odom, and Jim Nash—all for sizable bonuses —and his bankbook apparently was depleted.

"When we got Mr. Finley on the phone, he asked me what people called me," recalled Sutton. "I said, 'Just Don, that's all.' And he said, 'I just signed three guys named Catfish, Blue Moon, and Jumbo Jim and if you can't come up with a nickname like that for yourself, I don't want you.'"

So Sutton signed with the Dodgers and, until Sunday, he kept his secret inside.

The reigning world champs got just five hits off Sutton—and only two through the first seven innings while the Dodgers were building up an adequate three-run bulge against Vida Blue.

Ron Cey walked, went all the way to third on Bill Russell's bloop single and scored on Steve Yeager's base hit up the middle for one run in the second inning and Ferguson's HR, some 400 feet to dead center field with Steve Garvey aboard in the sixth, gave them the two more they were to need.

Helpless for the first seven innings, the A's loaded the bases against Sutton in the eighth but an extremely close double play, made possible by first baseman Steve Garvey's brilliant grab, got LA out of the inning unscathed.

Sutton wasn't so fortunate in the ninth though, when he hit Sal Bando, then watched Reggie Jackson loop a check-swing double to left.

Marshall, the Dodgers' man of steel, made his entrance at that point. And while Sutton watched nervously from the dugout, Joe Rudi singled, driving home two Oakland runs.

Then Marshall went to work.

First the former Tiger struck out the dangerous Gene Tenace. . . . Then he skillfully set up Washington, who had been sent in to run for Rudi, and picked him cleanly off first base. . . . Then he struck out pinch hitter Angel Manguel to end the game.

But the pickoff of the speedy Washington, just as he was about to take off for second base, qualified as the key play of the inning.

It was only the third time the A's base-stealing specialist and one-time sprint star had been picked off all year—and the first time since May.

And it was, as Washington admitted, "a helluva time for it to happen."

Washington was a student of Marshall's at Michigan State in a class on child growth and development. Sunday he recalled how he had convinced Marshall to change his grade from a C to a B.

But, so far as baseball is concerned, he conceded, "My education continues."

Marshall, who acts as if playing baseball was beneath him, at first refused even to acknowledge the fact that Washington was in his class. And he claimed the two men had no special relationship, even though they're both prominent athletes.

"I was the teacher—he was the student," he said curtly. "I don't pay any attention to what goes on in the athletic department up at State. I don't go to sporting events."

Garvey's attitude was exactly opposite.

The Dodger first baseman, who was a senior at MSU when Washington was a freshman, exchanged comments with him on Saturday's Michigan–Michigan State football game, when Herb arrived to pinch run.

But that was where the sympathy stopped.

"We had him frozen for an instant—there was no way he was going to finesse me and get back to the bag," explained Garvey. "We know he's a world class sprinter, but it's another thing to be able to play baseball."

"We all knew he had been sent in there to steal a base," said manager Walter Alston. "Marshall did a great job of setting him up and a great job of finishing him off."

"We needed this win awfully bad," said Sutton. "It would have been tough to go into their ball park down two–zip and still expect to win.

"This Oakland ball club is the kind that kills you if you make a mistake. Fortunately, I made as few as possible. I took the scouting report home last night and studied it. I guess my final exam will be coming up this weekend."

"Now we go to Oakland knowing it's all even," added Ferguson. "We start all over again. We've got as good a chance as they do now."

THE ATHLETICS LEVITATE INTO THE LEAD

(World Series Game III)

By John Owen

From the Seattle Post-Intelligencer

Copyright, ©, 1974, Seattle Post-Intelligencer

They say that magic acts are making a big comeback in show-biz these days, quite possibly because of the Oakland Athletics, who levitated to a 3–2 victory over the Dodgers here last night to take a 2–1 World Series lead.

During the regular season the Athletics were last in the American League in hits—215 behind the Twins—yet ranked third from the top in runs scored, just seven behind the Red Sox. This is baseball's equivalent of shoving Snow White into the box and sawing her up into Seven Dwarfs.

Last night the A's put Superman into a phone booth and a few innings later out walked a goat . . . by the name of Joe Ferguson.

Credited with the defensive play of the Series in the opening game, a thrown strike to home plate on a fly to right center, Ferguson became the offensive star of the Dodgers' second-game victory, with a two-run homer.

Last night, Ferguson tied a World Series record, becoming the first catcher since the 1928 play-off to commit two errors in one game. Fame is fleeting and the A's were almost as quick in converting the bobbles into runs with just three assisting waves of the wand, all resulting in singles.

It added up to a pair of runs in the third inning, a single tally in the fourth for a 3–0 lead. The Dodgers made it close, with solo homers in the eighth by Bill Buckner and in the ninth by Willie Crawford. But all three of the games have been tense right up until the final out and have all ended by the same 3–2 score.

The only thing we don't know about tonight's fourth game is which team will win, when Andy Messersmith of the Dodgers goes against Ken Holtzman of the A's.

Catfish Hunter was the winner last night, yielding only five hits and Buckner's homer in the eighth. Rollie Fingers replaced him, was roughed up by Crawford in the ninth and then watched Ferguson get on bases because of Bert Campaneris' error at short. But Fingers retired Ron Cey on a strikeout and got Bill Russell to bounce into a game-ending double play that touched off the Oakland Stadium fireworks.

Bill North, the A's center fielder from Seattle, got his first World Series hit with one away in the third. And Bill broke from first just as Campaneris swung at an Al Downing pitch. The ball went to Cey at third, he made a fine stop and the throw to first, but North went all the way to third. After Sal Bando walked, Reggie Jackson came to the plate and hit a little bouncer in front of the plate that had him cussing before he'd taken his second stride.

Ferguson palmed the ball, dropped it like it was an overripe mango and North scored. A single by Rudi plated Bando with the second run.

An inning later Oakland's Dick Green walked and was sacrificed to second. Campaneris rapped the ball through the hole, the play went to the plate and the ball got past Ferguson as Green scored and Campy went to third. At this point Downing left the game and Jim Brewer fanned Bando to prevent further bloodshed.

In the fifth inning Ferguson was at first charged with a passed ball trying to handle the knucklers thrown by the third Dodger pitcher, Charlie Hough. It was later changed to a wild pitch, possibly because the scorer decided Ferguson had had enough grief for one night. Mike Marshall finished the game for the Dodgers.

It was announced to reporters before the game that A's owner Charles O. Finley was poised with a telephone in his box next to the Athletics' dugout and that he planned to call and invite President Ford to throw out the first pitch here today or tomorrow. The call was apparently made but the President said, Gee thanks, anyway, but he had to mow the White House lawn or something.

The timing was probably a coincidence but when the A's had forged their 3–0 lead a release was circulated throughout the press box, officially denying rumors that the shift of the Athletics' franchise might be contemplated after this World Series.

"Mr. Finley vehemently denied the reports and I can certainly understand his irritation," the statement quoted R. T. Nahas, the president of the Oakland-Alameda County Coliseum, Inc.

"Neither Mr. Finley nor the American League have ever indicated to us by word or deed their desire to move the team. Unfortunately, however, these irresponsible reports worry and concern many loyal A's fans," Nahas continued.

"In order to assure the fans and press of the stability of the franchise in Oakland, we want to repeat that our long-term lease with Mr. Finley . . . continues through the last day of the 1987 season. In addition to this firm, unconditional period of 20 years, there are additional options which could extend the lease through the year 2,007."

Gee, if that's true, think how many more presidents Charlie will have to work on!

THE SPOILED BRATS TAKE IT ALL

(WORLD SERIES GAME V)

By Maury Allen

From the New York Post

Reprinted by permission of the New York Post

© 1974, New York Post Corporation

They shake, rattle, and roll. They hold rumbles in the clubhouse. They are spoiled brats with big mouths. They hate their fiefdom, hate their owner, have no respect for their manager.

Then comes the game.

They long-ball and short-ball you, they bunt and belt, they swing from the heels and run on their toes, they play the game of baseball as well as it has ever been played.

They don't have the thunder of the Ruth and Gehrig Yankees or the depth and skills of the DiMaggio-Keller-Henrich gang but they play this old game better than anybody else in the world playing it for pay today.

The Oakland A's beat the Los Angeles Dodgers 3–2 last night to win the 1974 World Series four games to one and moved deep into the baseball annals. They have now won three straight championships.

The Yankees did that on their way to four from 1936–1939 and the Yankees did it again on their way to five in 1949–1953 and nobody else ever won three in a row.

"We are the best," said Reggie Jackson, the best of the best, in the champagne-covered, shaving-creamed Oakland clubhouse. "We'll be going for four in a row. We are young. We win that, we'll be going for five and then six. I want six."

It was Jackson's arm on a throw to second baseman Dick Green that set up a game-saving throw to third baseman Sal Bando that ended the last Dodger chance at a 1974 run and closed up the Series. It was a perfect play. It was an Oakland play.

"I never looked at Greenie," said Jackson. "He was just supposed to be there. I just threw it."

The out at third in the eighth was the last chance for Oakland to lose a game this year and they never let it happen. A sign in left field said, "Go A's, moider dem Bums." The A's moidered dem by a run.

Vida Blue, who has never won a Series game in three years, was the Oakland pitcher at the start with a chance to vindicate his past failures and end the baseball summer. Baseball summers always end in fall.

"I knew I couldn't make any mistakes or I'd be out of there," said Blue. "I know how my manager manages and I know how my owner owns."

Blue had his run in the first when Bert Campaneris singled off Don Sutton, who hadn't lost a game in 12 starts, and Billy North forced him. Speedster North stole second, went to third on the catcher's overthrow and scored when Sal Bando hit five fouls on tough Sutton pitches and one fair fly for the run.

"He does," said Alvin Dark, "what has to be done."

Ray Fosse lined a hanging curve into the left field seats for the second A's run. It was now an Oakland laugher. Later he remembered two long foul shots into the stands by Joe Ferguson better than he remembered his own homer.

"Those two Ferguson foul balls," he said. "Two heart attacks."

Ferguson singled after one long foul and struck out after the other one so no damage was done.

The next Oakland problem came in the sixth when Tom Paciorek lined a double to left and Blue walked Davey Lopes. Billy Buckner, who talks good enough to be an A, bunted well as the runners moved up. It was as good a bunt as Joe Rudi's the night before.

Jimmy Wynn got the Dodgers on the scoreboard with a sacrifice fly and Steve Garvey tied it with a line single to left off a tough Blue fast ball.

"He's the best hitter I ever saw," said Jackson, in deep admiration of the Dodger first baseman.

"Now I knew I couldn't make another mistake," said Blue, "or I was gone."

He got two hitters out in the seventh and walked Steve Yeager, the Dodgers' number eight hitter. A bad mistake.

"I told Wes Stock (pitching coach) to watch him after the seventh," said A's catcher Ray Fosse. "He seemed like he was losing his stuff."

Mike Marshall, who had relieved in the sixth inning after Paciorek had batted for Sutton, was the batter. Blue threw two balls.

"I saw the man coming for me so I gave him the ball," said Blue.

"Were you unhappy about the decision?"

"C'mon out early tomorrow morning," said the best left-handed quarterback pitching in the AL, "and we'll throw spirals."

Blue Moon Odom, who had gotten into a "friendly scuffle" with Rollie Fingers that cost Fingers a hole in his head and cost Odom a sore leg, was the pitcher. He finished walking Marshall.

"I was pressing," he said.

"I wanted to get him out and I still wasn't really warmed up."

Odom then got Lopes to ground to short and the inning was over. The score was still 2–2 as Rudi moved to the plate in the seventh against Marshall.

The fans were beginning to get into the game as fans have been doing lately in the World Series and frisbees, some garbage, and a bottle landed in left field near Buckner and in center field near Wynn.

Buckner started to move in toward home plate.

"I'm not going to get killed out there," he told umpire Tom Gorman. "I'm going in."

Walter Alston and several Dodgers, including Marshall, conferred with Gorman for several minutes.

"I told Buckner I would stop the game if it continued. I wanted him back out there and I wanted things to quiet down. It was a big game," Gorman said.

Buckner went out there, Marshall went to the mound and Rudi went back to the plate.

"I knew he hadn't warmed up for some time," said Rudi, "so I expected he would try and sneak a fast ball by me. Otherwise it would have been a screw ball. That was the time to go for it."

Marshall's first pitch was an inside fast ball and Rudi lined it over the wall in left field for a 3–2 Oakland lead. The A's were six outs away from their third title. The first out would be the toughest.

Buckner cracked a single to right as North chased it down.

"I was jogging behind Billy because he doesn't make errors," said Jackson. "Then it got by him and I chased it down and fired as hard as I could."

The relay went to Green, the throw was at Bando's glove and the tag got Buckner by some two feet as he reached for the base with his hand.

"He was out by a lot," said Bill Kunkel. "It wasn't really close."

"It was one of those plays," said Alston, "where if you make it you're right and if you don't make it you're wrong."

Walter Alston, who is unsigned for next year at the moment as is Alvin Dark, was asked to evaluate the Oakland A's.

"They are a top-notch club," he said. "They don't make any mistakes. It took two perfect plays to get Buckner and they did it."

They did everything. They beat the Dodgers in five games and made it look easy. They won three world championships in a row.

"Sure, they don't appreciate us yet," said Reggie Jackson. "Only history will appreciate us."

Other Baseball

HENRY AARON WAS ABLE

By Bob Hunter

From the Los Angeles Herald-Examiner

The ground crew was ready. God was willing and Henry Aaron was able.

And as the Dodgers' Al Downing threw a fast ball from 60 feet, six inches, Aaron drove it 385 feet last night to wipe out 39 years of immortality that had belonged to Babe Ruth alone.

The largest crowd in Atlanta baseball history, a national TV audience, and fans around the globe thrilled to one of the most dramatic moments in sports history.

It was, truly, a shot heard around the world.

It may never cease reverberating through the lore of baseball.

It was home run No. 715 for Bad Henry, a gentle person with lightning wrists, concluding an ever increasingly pressing pursuit of the game's most legendary record.

There is something permanent about Roman numerals, so call him King Henry the 715th for the time being, only make it DCCXV instead of the Arabic.

Henry hit his first one two decades ago.

As recently as five years back he said he never thought he would be in the fishbowl that has been his life recently.

"God must have seen fit for me to do it here," he declared as his new bride Billye snuggled at his side, sharing the glory of the moment.

"I wanted to hit it in Atlanta, but if I hadn't, it would have been some place else."

Henry emphasized his first feeling was that the Braves won the ball game, although it did not detract from the grand feeling of his accomplishment, and what he contributed.

It was a 7–4 victory over the Dodgers, and the fact the losers committed six errors and played a horrible game will be little noted nor long remembered.

The evening belonged to Henry and Billye, and his mother and father, who raised him in poverty in Mobile, Alabama.

History paused for 11 minutes after the colossal stroke to left center field that carried two people into the Hall of Fame, Aaron in the front door, and Downing in the back door.

"I didn't know my mother could hug so hard," said the dewey-eyed Aaron after the mob scene at home plate.

The hardships and struggles of Mobile were erased with that one grand hit.

His mother wept. Her son had more than made up for those uncertain times of 20 years ago.

Just as in Cincinnati last Thursday, when Henry hit the first pitch at which he swung to tie the record, he did the same thing here in Atlanta's circus before 53,775.

You had an excellent view on your TV set of the biggest hit in the annals of baseball.

It was a hummer over the middle of the plate and high—higher than Downing wanted it, but just where Aaron had wanted it.

He had guessed fast ball, because that's what the Dodger left hander threw him when he walked him on five pitches his first at bat in the second inning.

In the fourth, Downing started off with a ball as the fans booed, just as they had done at the four wide ones before.

When umpire Satch Davidson called the only strike on Bad Henry his first at bat, the fans also booed.

It was Henry's night, and the overflow throng already was standing as Downing made his second pitch in the fourth inning.

Aaron swung for the first time all night with that spring steel flick of his mighty wrists.

He hit a baseball that never has been hit before.

It sailed 10 feet over the left center field wall.

It was marked invisibly, and indelibly 12–12–2–2.

It was history at 9:07 P.M. here, 6:07 P.M. in Los Angeles, and forever on Cloud Nine, where Aaron had to be as he majestically toured the bases.

Cloud Nine is where the immortal Babe has been for 25 years—

or six before Henry ever hit his first homer off Vic Raschi in St. Louis—and undoubtedly Ruth was among the first to offer his congratulations.

The Babe, with his beer belly and a hot dog in his hand, would have loved it.

These were the good times. The Babe's times relived.

You saw Bill Buckner race towards the 385-foot mark in left center and drape himself atop the fence, although he never had a chance to interfere with history.

It cleared the fence by ten feet.

"At first I thought I had a chance to catch it," said the Dodger left fielder.

Asked his reaction as it sailed into the rainy night, he answered: "My second thought was to go over the fence after it."

But Tom House, in the Atlanta bullpen which had been switched to left field for the occasion, grabbed it.

Ironically, he had said before the game he was going to grab the homer.

It was the biggest catch of the night, with the Braves relief pitcher from the University of Southern California leaping over the barrier and bringing the trophy in to Aaron.

The invisibly tattooed ball is destined to travel even further than it did last night with Magnavox, the company that Aaron recently joined in a long-term contract.

Four years from now, it will reach Cooperstown.

Maybe Henry can deliver it personally, because he said this would be his last year, so he'll be entering the Hall of Fame just about that time.

"Mr. Ruth held the record for 39 years," Aaron spoke softly, almost reverently. "He deserved it.

"During my career I've been somewhat slighted in the awards.

"As far as the home run record goes, I put it at the top.

"I consider myself one of the best players baseball has had. I won't say the best, because there have been some great ones.

"But I am among them."

There had been thundershowers and tornado warnings in the afternoon and evening with the drops starting to fall on the pageant in the second inning, when Henry batted for the first time.

But it couldn't rain on Aaron's parade last night, even though the drops were heavier as he came to the plate and the umbrellas made the stands look like a circular field of multi-hued mushrooms.

Then, after he delivered what the world wanted to see, the rains pelted even harder. It still wasn't an official game.

Home run No. 715 could revert to No. 714.

"Did the rain worry me?" smiled Hammerin' Hank.

"Only that I would have run out and put the tarp on the field myself."

The 11-minute ceremonial interlude might have been too long, but the ground crew was ready, God was willing, and Henry was able.

The fans, while damp, were delirious when he came up in the fifth inning, not only because the home run was in the books as indelibly as the I.D. on the home run ball, but because he had a chance to do it again.

However, there could be no encore to one of baseball's greatest acts. He grounded out—then bowed out.

However, Aaron is not through.

He says the show will go on, that Atlanta must finish one-two-three, and that he has one more personal goal.

"I would like to break Stan Musial's record for National League base hits," he explained.

The Man has the staggering total of 3,630, but it's a figure that is within reach of the Atlanta gentleman, who needs only 120 in his final five months of competition.

"That record is one I certainly would like," he emphasized as Billye squeezed his hand.

The clubhouse was wall to wall delirium as his teammates turned on the bubble machine.

He was toasted with champagne, and the tears flowed like wine in this hour of triumph and achievement.

It was a time, an accomplishment, a moment never to be relived.

Henry almost was mumbling:

"I just felt if I got a strike to hit, I would hit it out.

"I hit it fairly well, but it really wasn't one of my greater shots."

The world will argue that.

President Nixon was on the horn, but this time Aaron was in the outfield.

At the end of the inning he was able to take the call.

"He invited me to the White House," reported Henry.

When?

"He didn't say when," answered Henry, and everyone laughed.

It was a date to be remembered, though, because April 8 was one of the rare dates on which Aaron never had hit a home run.

It was only his third off Los Angeles pitching in two years—and all came off Downing.

Aaron was not bothered that most of the dampened and freezing crowd left the theater immediately after his act.

They had seen what they had come to see.

Despite the cold and the rain, he had Babe Ruth's number. The dogwoods were in bloom.

It was the climax of Aaron's many-splendored spring—and baseball life.

NOW COMES THE BIG TEST

By Dick Young

From the New York Daily News

Now that he has the job, the question is how long will he keep it? What will Frank Robinson do with it, this first big-league managership entrusted to a black man?

That depends upon things. It depends upon the patience of the Cleveland owners, the attitudes of the Cleveland players, the support of the Cleveland fans, the standings of the American League, and the personal conduct of Frank Robinson.

If he conducts himself with the assurance, the poise, the mature calm in fielding reporters' questions that marked today's inaugural press conference, he not only will make it, he will be Manager of the Year.

If he resorts to the temper flareups of the younger Frank Robinson, or to the needless challenging of his ball players as in the Gaylord Perry incident, then it will be a rocky and short tenure in Cleveland's ball park, where the walls are lined with the scalps of short-termed managers.

Which is the real Frank Robinson?

Right now, it is more the second than the first, more the good than the bad, more the rational, clear-thinking man, approaching middle age, than the hotheaded juvenile who once waved a gun at a short-order chef, a bat at a fan in the stands, a fist at a newspaperman.

Those things were 10, 15 years ago. More recently, he is the Frank Robinson who has gained the respect of ball players, white and black, of fans, white and black, of newspapermen, white and black. Among the telegrams of congratulations he received today was one from the baseball writers of Southern California, where he played the past few years. There was none from the newsmen in Cincinnati, where he played the first ten years.

I hope and pray he does well. Not because he is black, or the first black. I couldn't care less. There will be other black managers. I know lots of whites, players and managers, who aren't worth five minutes of your time. After you have been in this business awhile, you find yourself rooting for the good guys, regardless of what uniform they wear, regardless of what skin they wear. I find Frank Robinson II, the Frank Robinson of recent years, to be a good guy, strong without being nasty, reasonable in conversation, honorable, and willing to express an opinion. Besides, his wife is a doll.

"When he was a player, he never brought the game home with him," says Barbara Robinson. "But in Puerto Rico, when he managed, he'd come home after a tough game and we didn't have a real happy dinner."

When he comes home next season, after a double-dip defeat, manager Robinson will find no shoulder to cry on. "I told him to leave it at the ball park the way he is as a player," she says. "I need Frank's support more at home than he needs mine. I think dinners at home with the kids are so important, so few, they should be enjoyed."

She has a *café au lait* complexion, flowing hair, a petite, ample body, and much nicer legs than Frank. She dressed informally for the inauguration, white long-sleeved blouse, red turtleneck sweater, sleeveless, brown slacks, and a bright smile that won't stop.

She describes herself as a quiet fan. "I pray inside when he's up at bat," says Barbara Robinson. "I can remember yelling at only one player." She recalls it was the 1966 World Series with the Dodgers. Frank hit a home run off Don Drysdale. Drysdale kicked the dust in disgust.

"I yelled, you big hot dog, you." She giggles at the memory. "I'm not emotional," she says.

Her husband is. Most athletes are. It's part of being competitive. Some control it better than others. I guess you can say that of most men. How Frank Robinson masters his emotions, on the field and in the clubhouse, will determine the success or failure of Frank Robinson as a big-league manager. He cannot make many more boo-boos like the one the other day, in the Cleveland clubhouse.

Gaylord Perry had popped off in public about money. Frank Robinson had just come to the Indians with a $173,000 salary that had been upped to $180,000 for the coming season. At this moment, Frank Robinson was a designated hitter, not a manager, although most everyone knew he was to be the manager shortly.

"I deserve more money than Robinson," Perry said. It got into print, with elaboration, the next day. "My stats will stand up better than his," Perry was quoted as saying.

Robinson called Gaylord on it. "I don't mind you using me in your private contract talks to get more money," he said, "but I don't want you dragging my name through the press."

Perry snapped back. Robinson shouted back. It got pretty hot, and might have grown physical if not for other players intervening. Frank Robinson could have blown the whole thing right there.

A better way would have been for Robinson to get off to the side with Gaylord, chat privately with him, quietly. In making a public shouting match of it, Robby was just as wrong as Perry was in putting down Frank publicly.

Many caustic things were said by ball players in the Yankee clubhouse, within earshot of Bill Virdon, when he came as a stranger to New York. Bill Virdon bit his lip and ignored them, and went about his business, acting strongly, saying little. Bill Virdon learned a lot from the year before, when as manager of the Pirates, he challenged Richie Hebner, screaming at him in the clubhouse, "Gutless."

Jackie Robinson was innately a trigger-tempered young man, but when he was given the responsibility of being the first black player in the bigs, he locked his taut emotions in a vault for two years. Times have changed for the better. No man need swallow his pride now. Neither should he go looking for trouble.

"If I had one wish," said Frank Robinson today, "it would be for Jackie Robinson to be here to see this moment."

My one wish for Frank Robinson is that, whenever need be, he can show the restraint Jackie Robinson showed to overcome the natural hostility of man.

TOM SEAVER IN THE LOCKER ROOM

By Aaron Latham

From New York Magazine

I am proposing that sport behavior is functionally equivalent to the hunting pattern. . . .

—Lionel Tiger, *Men In Groups*

Tom Seaver is a great pitcher. He is also a pretty good practical joker. These two talents may not be entirely unrelated. The more Seaver "rags" the boys in the locker room, the more aggressive he may be on the pitching mound. This notion is based on the assumption that a baseball team has a good deal in common with a band of prehistoric hunters. This should not seem too far-fetched, since both ball players and Neanderthals are famous for carrying wooden clubs.

Back in prehistory, men survived because they learned to hunt in bands. The bonds which developed between males supposedly made them better hunters—the stronger the bonds, the more aggressive the men; some sociologists believe that the same general rule holds true for the modern equivalent of hunting bands such as fraternities, political clubs, armies, the Hell's Angels, the Ku Klux Klan, and baseball teams.

If the sociologists happen to be right about baseball, then the stronger the ties in the locker room, the fiercer will be the team on the field. In the clubhouse, there is always a kind of ritual courtship in progress which is largely based on ragging. One player will pay attention to another by tying up his clothes or stuffing Tampax in his locker. When Tom Seaver takes to the mound for the Mets to slay the opposing side, he will presumably have a more deadly fast ball if his dressing room courtship of other players is going well. This theory could help explain the apparent contradiction between the seriousness with which he approaches pitching and the foolishness with which he approaches locker room life.

Of course, one does not quite know how seriously to take these sociological hypotheses. After all, most of the studies of "male-bonding" have been based upon the observation of monkeys, not men. It is irrefutable that in the locker room most baseball players act like baboons. On the field, many of them play like apes. But that does not prove that ball players are actually some sort of missing link—not even Yogi Berra.

During spring training, I went down to Saint Petersburg, Florida, to see Tom Seaver, who stands 6-foot-1, weighs 206 pounds, and is nicknamed "Big Boy." In the dressing room, it seemed to me that there was a special bond between Seaver, shortstop Bud Harrelson, and right fielder Rusty Staub. It did not take long for the monkey business to start.

One morning, when Seaver was getting dressed, he took time out to pin a clipping to Rusty Staub's locker. The eight-column front-page headline read: PLANE CRASH IN FRANCE KILLS 345. The story went on to say that a Turkish DC-10 had gone down near Paris, setting a new record for carnage, surpassing the old record of 176 held jointly by a Jordanian 707 and a Russian Aeroflot airliner. Baseball players are very interested in records.

Seaver said, "Staub hates to fly. During takeoff you don't see him. He puts his head down between his knees and says his Hail Marys. I think he's in the wrong business."

Rusty Staub, wearing only beige slippers, walked up to his locker looking like Desmond Morris's "naked ape." He read the headline and started cursing.

Bud Harrelson asked Staub, "Three hundred forty-five—how many teams is that? It's over half of baseball."

Seaver said, "Rusty may retire."

Staub wiped his nose, shook his head, wadded up the paper, and threw it at the wastepaper basket. He missed.

Jim Beauchamp, a utility infielder, told Seaver, "You're a sick bastard."

Staub, who is a gourmet cook, turned to Seaver and said, "You did it, didn't you, bastard? I was trying to think who was sick enough. You'd better check your food when you eat at my place again."

Tom Seaver, who once wanted to be a dentist, is good at hitting nerves.

> Human males appear to be adapted to a throwing motion closely
> related to the one universally used by hunters in spearing game.
> —*Men in Groups*

Seaver, 29, who was born several thousand years too late to be the greatest spear-thrower that ever lived, loves to talk about pitching. One morning while he was getting dressed, Seaver said, "I had an experience three springs ago that sent chills up and down my spine. I could feel what my hand and body were doing when I delivered the baseball. I could tell if my hips were too far ahead, when my hand was cocked, when it was just right. I could tell where my timing was off just a fraction. Many pitchers have no idea what the parts of their body are doing."

Seaver feels that from that point on his control improved and he became a more consistent pitcher.

"I get down lower on my right leg than most pitchers," said Seaver, who wears a pad on his right knee because he gets down so low that his knee often bumps against the ground. "I use my legs because they contain the biggest muscles of the body—the adductor longus, the sartorius, the semitendinosus. I let the legs absorb the strain. That takes it off my elbows and shoulders. Mechanically, I feel I use my body better than most pitchers."

Sometimes when Seaver talks about pitching, he makes it sound like a martial art. One day he said:

"Watch a pitcher's opposite side. Some carry their glove hand in close. As a result, they are just arm-throwing, not using their body. I reach out with my glove hand and pull back almost like a karate movement, as if popping someone behind me in the chest."

> Outside of eating and sleeping, grooming takes up more time than any
> primate activity—far more than sex.
> —Lionel Tiger and Robin Fox, *The Imperial Animal*

The spring training workouts started every morning at ten o'clock. Seaver would arrive in the locker room at 8 A.M. Baseball players dress as slowly as Zsa Zsa Gabor. It takes Tom Seaver, who approaches everything meticulously and systematically, 90 minutes to put on the following items in the following order: jock, jockey shorts, second jock, cup, USC T-shirt, sweatshirt with blue sleeves, white legging on right leg, second white legging on right leg, blue legging on right leg, right garter, white legging on left leg, second white legging on left leg, blue legging on left leg, left garter, knee-pad, baseball pants, baseball shirt, right shoe, left shoe, cap. In journalism, only sports reporters regularly see their subjects dress and undress. One wonders how it would affect political reporting if the White House press corps occasionally saw the emperor without his clothes.

One day pitching coach Albert Bluford (Rube) Walker took an especially long time getting dressed. The problem was that some-one had tied up his clothes and put tape all over his locker.

"When something like this happens, two guys always get blamed for it—Koosman and I," Seaver said. Turning to pitcher Jerry Koos-man, Seaver asked, "Koos, did you screw up Rube's locker yester-day? Who did it?"

Koosman, who had a comic Linda Lovelace mouthwash advertise-ment pinned to his locker, admitted that he was the culprit.

Rube Walker walked up and Seaver told him, "I couldn't sleep all night thinking about somebody screwing up your locker."

Koosman said, "Yeah, who did that? Did it teach you a lesson? Next time we'll burn your clothes."

To top off his dressing ritual, Tom Seaver stuck a wad of Red Man ("America's best chew") tobacco in his cheek. Now he was ready to go to work.

Last year, when the Mets were playing the Reds for the pennant, a fight erupted at second base between Pete Rose and Bud Harrel-son. The Met bullpen emptied as even pitchers joined the fray. Only a couple of men remained on the sidelines. One was Tom Seaver. He was probably protecting his arm.

Seaver guards his arm constantly. He coddles it the way a parent coddles a child. An important part of taking care of that arm is trying not to wear it out prematurely.

Most starting pitchers pitch every fourth day. Tom Seaver pitches every fifth day. All the Mets' starting pitchers do. The Mets' theory is that if a pitcher is on the mound only every fifth day instead of every fourth day, then, in the long run, the pitcher's arm will not wear out quite so fast. Seaver hopes that, pitching every fifth day, he will be able to go on playing for another seven years, until he is 36.

Systematic Tom Seaver has worked out an elaborate routine

which he follows on the days he does not pitch. On his first day of rest after a game, he runs fifteen wind sprints, but not hard. On the second day of rest, he throws for eight to ten minutes in the bullpen and then runs hard wind sprints. On the third day of rest, he does no throwing but runs 18 to 20 wind sprints all out; then that night he tries to get 12 hours' sleep. On the fourth day of rest, he runs 12 easy wind sprints and that night tries to get nine hours' sleep before pitching the next day. One day last season, Seaver got to bed about five o'clock in the morning, slept very little, and then pitched great the next day, allowing only one run. But he still believes in his routine.

The five-day rotation schedule is only one line of defense for Tom Seaver's arm. There are many others. Caring for his arm is a 24-hour job. He always sleeps with it under the covers. The right-hander always tries to sleep on his left side because if he sleeps on his right side he wakes up in the night with his pitching arm aching. He performs such acts as petting dogs and reaching into his shaving kit with his left hand.

In spite of all the care he lavishes on his arm, in spite of the money value of his pitching hand, Tom Seaver still cannot resist a joke. One evening he was having dinner with Rusty Staub. The main course was barbecued beef. The star pitcher of the Mets kept picking up the barbecue grill with his right hand just to drive Staub crazy. When Seaver would grasp the grill, Staub would look as sick as if he were in a plane that was just taking off.

Sal Marchiano, who reports on sports for Eyewitness News, walked up to Tom Seaver in the locker room.

Seaver said, "Hi, dago."

Marchiano said, "You can call me anything but dago."

Seaver said, "You're getting to be a fat dago."

Marchiano said, "You Wasps are all alike." Irritated, the newsman asked Seaver if he had seen a UPI story which maintained that the pitcher could not win important games, a reputation which had plagued the Mets' star ever since he won one and lost one in the 1969 World Series and won none and lost one in the 1973 World Series. Marchiano chided, "UPI says it has documentary proof that Seaver can't win the big one—names and dates."

Jon Matlack, who may eventually challenge Seaver's position as king of the mound, said, "Sounds official."

Seaver said, "It'll probably end my career."

Changing the subject, Marchiano asked a cliché question: "How much bigger is your pitching arm than your other arm?"

Seaver joked, "I can't tell. They're both so f—ing massive."
Marchiano said, "They're the only thing on you that is big."
"Except my ego," Seaver replied.

He might have included his salary. This year the Mets agreed to pay Seaver a reported $172,000, which makes him the highest-priced pitcher in baseball. Last year, Seaver pitched 290 innings. If he pitches about the same number this year, he will earn about $600 per inning, or $200 per out.

Jim Bouton walked into the locker room. He is supposed to be something of a pariah around baseball because of what he exposed about players' sex lives in *Ball Four,* but no one in the Mets' dressing room seemed concerned about his presence, no one except Sal Marchiano. Bouton and Marchiano passed within a few feet of each other, but each pretended not to see the other. Last year, ABC let Bouton go and replaced him with Marchiano. Now Bouton works for CBS.

Joe Durso of *The New York Times* sat down on a stool beside Seaver and launched into an interview. Seaver, who reads a lot and is always interested in self-improvement, asked Durso if he could set up a lunch with James Reston. The pitcher evidently wanted to get to know a higher class of reporter than normally hangs out in a base-ball locker room. Durso said that he would do what he could.

Seaver asked, "If we did have lunch with Reston, could I call him Scotty?"

Durso said, "Do you mean 'Mr. Reston' does not come easily to you?"

Seaver asked, "What do you call him? Dad?"

Durso said, "Gramps."

Sal Marchiano reappeared and handed Seaver the UPI story he had been talking about earlier.

Seaver read aloud, " 'The conclusion is inescapable. Seaver is yet to be as effective on the mound as he is in salary negotiations.' " The pitcher looked up and said, "Holy s—, it's the end of the world!"

He tossed the wire copy at a wastepaper basket. He hit it dead center.

Born in 1944 in Fresno, California, where his father worked for a raisin-packing plant, Tom started pitching at age 9 as a member of the North Fresno Rotary Little League team. He wasn't very good. Seaver went on to pitch for North Fresno High School, but he didn't make the varsity squad until his senior year, and then his record was a disappointing 5 wins and 4 losses.

"I matured late physically," Seaver said one morning. "I wasn't a phenomenon like Matlack who had 8 no-hitters in high school."

When he graduated from high school, Seaver took a vacation from academia for a year to think about what he wanted to do with his life. After sitting around for several months, he joined the Marine Corps reserves because his older brother had. Seaver credits the leathernecks with turning him into a good pitcher. The Marines transformed him from a 160-pound weakling into a 195-pound strongarm. And the Marines made him want to go to college.

When Seaver finished his six months' active duty, he enrolled in Fresno Junior College, where he discovered a new power on the mound. His freshman year he won 10 games and lost only 2. That season, Fresno played Vallejo Junior College in the Northern California State finals. Seaver pitched in the next-to-last game and won, but Tug McGraw pitched for Vallejo in the deciding game and beat Fresno.

For his sophomore year, Seaver transferred to the University of Southern California because he had heard a lot of good things about its baseball team and its school of dentistry. His first year at USC, he won 11 games, lost 2, and gave up the idea of becoming a dentist.

Tom Seaver did not have a junior year. Instead, he signed with the Mets organization, which sent him to Jacksonville, Florida, to play Triple-A ball. Living in the Roosevelt Hotel in Jacksonville, the young pitcher grew more and more miserable. When he could stand solitary hotel life no longer, he called a girl named Nancy whom he had met in junior college and asked her to come to Florida and marry him. She did. Soon Tom Seaver had acquired a car, an apartment, and a wife. He felt better.

The year was 1966. Seaver won 12 games in Jacksonville that season, but he also lost 12 games. The next year he moved to the big leagues.

In 1967, his rookie year, Seaver won 16 and lost 13 for the Mets. In 1968, he won 16 once again and lost 12. In 1969, the miracle year, he won 25 and lost 7. During the off-season, Tom and Nancy had been going back to USC to study during the winter semester. The winter of '69 should have been Seaver's last semester at USC, but instead he ended up in the World Series. The Mets' world championship cost him his degree, at least temporarily.

In 1970, Seaver won 18 and lost 12; in 1971, he was 20 and 10; in 1972, 21 and 12; in 1973, the year of the near miracle, he went 19 and 10. And this year, just before spring training started, he finally finished up his college studies. He did a lot of correspondence work, some of it tailored especially for him, including such catalog courses as baseball broadcasting, geology of infields, and the geography of baseball. He would like to go to graduation but he will be unable to. Graduation exercises are set for June 6, when the Mets have a day game scheduled at Cincinnati.

Seaver holds all kinds of Met records, including most complete games (121), most shutouts (24), most strikeouts (1,655), and most victories (135). Seaver also owns another Met record of which he seems proud: most money.

"Presenting" is a gesture usually involving an exposure of the hind-quarters to a dominant baboon. The gesture is important in "ritualizing" social bonds.

—Men in Groups

One morning, Frank Edwin (Tug) McGraw walked into the locker room and took off his pants to reveal an extraordinary pair of shorts. They were bikini style, made out of net, and trimmed in blue.

McGraw yelled, "Hey, Seaver, do you think Rusty will like these?"

Seaver said, "Yeah."

Proudly modeling his transparent underwear, McGraw told Staub, "If I get in a hurry I can slip it out through the net."

Seaver said, "McGraw only has about 48 cards in his deck. I'm not quite sure which ones are missing."

Staub lost interest in McGraw's shorts and turned his thoughts once again toward what often seems to be his first love, cooking. He sat in the macho dressing room talking about recipes.

"You heat the water slowly to 104 degrees," Staub explained to one of the pitchers. "The crabs die between 104 degrees and 113 degrees."

Tom Seaver is the Mets' Player Association representative. With that job comes a number of unusual duties. One morning, he said that he had some "paperwork" to do. He asked to borrow my pen. I asked why.

Seaver said, "Last year the players bitched about the crummy signatures on their bubblegum cards."

He took my pen and went around the locker room getting all of the players to sign their names five times on a sheet of paper.

"Get your asses over here!" Seaver yelled. "Just sign it the way you want it on your bubblegum card. Big goddamn deal!"

The collection of signatures was temporarily interrupted as the locker room rocked with giggles. A streaker wearing only bright red shoes and a bright red hat raced the length of the dressing room and then raced out again. He streaked toward the locker room door, beyond which a crowd of spectators waited, but he stopped just short of the exit, sparing the people outside. The man in the red hat and red shoes then ran up to locker number 33 and sat down. He was Ray Sadecki, the veteran Met pitcher, whose age is the same as in the number on his uniform, 33. Sadecki bent over. Third baseman Wayne Garrett pretended to "goose" him.

A pretty girl stuck her head into the locker room. The players squealed as if she were the vanguard of a jock raid. The girl looked around and then ducked out again. The players spent several minutes speculating on how much of whom their visitor had seen.

Tom Seaver's best pitch is his fast ball. That makes sense. He is that kind of guy. On the mound or off, he seems to believe that the best way to get what he wants is to aim directly at the target. On the field or off, he does not favor curve balls or screw balls.

Seaver is very goal-oriented. One of his goals was to have a family. He got married early, when he was just 22. Now he has a pretty blond daughter who is 3 years old. He keeps her picture in his locker, next to his chewing tobacco. Seaver seems to be very proud of his family.

Another of his goals used to be to become the best pitcher in baseball, but that seems to have changed. Seaver says that now he simply wants to become the best pitcher that he personally can be. At first, that sounds like the old rationalization for not making it to the top. Seaver goes on to say, however, that he thinks it would be too easy to settle for being the best pitcher in the game. Forcing himself to be the best pitcher he can be is a higher goal.

Seaver's friends say that one of his goals used to be to become the highest-paid pitcher in baseball. He has attained that. Making money has always been a good all-American goal. To flesh out his income, Seaver works in the off-season making television and print ads for Sears, a company that is a lot like him and also a lot like baseball: all-American and a little square.

Seaver says that after he retires as an active player, he would like to manage a team. He is getting a taste of managing while he is still pitching because Met manager Yogi Berra is too shy to do his own managing. Berra, who is too scared of his own voice ever to raise it, will often come up to Seaver and ask him to tell the players this or that. Tom Seaver then raises his voice and passes along the order that the manager is too timid to give.

Seaver's friends say that some day his goal is to be commissioner of baseball, but right now his goal is to play as long as he can.

In the dressing room one day, 24-year-old Jon Matlack told 29-year-old Tom Seaver, "I see a gray hair."

Seaver said, "I had one the other day. I pulled it out."

Seaver's major-league career, now that he's 29, is at least half over. It may be even later for him than that. He still enjoys the game, but at the end of last season he was tireder than ever before. His wife was tired, too.

When Tom Seaver first started pitching for the Mets, he would come home from night games and find his wife waiting up for him. Now when he comes home after a night game, Nancy is asleep when he crawls into bed.

> Dominant animals are not necessarily the ones that can win the most fights, but often those than can get the rest to pay attention to them. . . . Rather than sex, this may be the clue to the cohesiveness of primate groups.
>
> —*The Imperial Animal*

This seems to hold true especially for baboon troops and baseball teams. In the Met locker room, Tom Seaver is unquestionably one of the dominant animals, probably the dominant animal. He gets the attention of the press, but he also gets the attention of the other players. They watch him much more than they watch Yogi Berra. And the very attention that they pay him helps define them as a team. Throwing on the mound or joking in the locker room, Tom Seaver has an importance to the Mets far beyond his won-lost record: he is the team's head monkey.

DON'T JINX THE NO-HITTER

By Hal Lebovitz

From the Cleveland Plain Dealer

Copyright, ©, 1974, Plain Dealer Publishing Co.

In the sixth inning a fan poked his wife and said, "Look into the Cleveland dugout. Nobody's sitting near Dick Bosman."

"Why?" she asked. "Is something wrong with him?"

"No," he replied knowingly. "He's pitching a no-hitter. Nobody wants to talk to him. Nobody wants to jinx him."

From then on the wife kept watching Bosman's every move as did the other 24,302 fans.

"Look," she said as the innings progressed. "They're moving even farther away from him."

In the seventh inning a grown man in the upper deck yelled agonizingly, "I can't stand it."

Bosman kept taking deep breaths, studying each hitter as the moments between each pitch became intolerable. The A's went down in order in the seventh.

The man shouted, "I can't stand it. I really can't stand it."

A lady with a cast on her arm moaned, "I want to bite my nails but I can't. I'm so nervous."

The pressure grew.

Fans couldn't forget that the Indians had been folding in the late innings. Just two nights earlier they had blown a 5–0 lead. Could Bosman make the 4–0 lead he had stand up? Could he do what Gaylord Perry had failed to do in his last two outings—beat the world champion A's? Could he—don't say it—pitch a no-hitter?

In the eighth he got them out again one-two-three. The emotional fan behind moaned, "Why did I come?"

It was delicious.

Bosman ran out to the mound to start the ninth inning. Reggie

Jackson, the A's great hitter who had battled Bosman three times and failed, stopped at the rubber on his way in from right field and patted Bosman on the rear, then continued to the A's dugout.

It was an unusual gesture of congratulations, good will and sportsmanship.

Yet it wasn't over.

The fans stood up as the ninth started. Then they settled back to boo Dick Green, the A's first hitter. He bounced out quickly.

Next came pinch-hitter Jesus Alou, a veteran with fine bat control, a tough hitter. The fans booed louder. The A's and their manager, Alvin Dark, were conceding nothing. Alou stretched his muscles, waited an interminable time before getting into the box as the fans agonized. Bosman seemed to wait patiently. Finally Alou was ready. On the third pitch he grounded to Brohamer.

One out remained between Bosman, victory and the—don't say it—no-hitter. The fans were on their feet now in anticipation. Tom McCraw came in to talk to Bosman.

"Stay away from him," shouted a worried fan.

Bill North was at bat, swinging determinedly as he stepped into the box.

He hit the first pitch solidly. A slice foul. Whew!

Then another strike. Not a fan was seated.

North swung. Strike three. The shouts of exhilaration, relief, and joy were uncontrolled. The players mobbed Bosman. They hugged him. For a moment it appeared they would kill him with joy.

It was bedlam.

I have seen several no-hitters. This was the most exciting, the most enjoyable. It came against the A's. It was pitched by a man who had been relegated to the end position on the pitching staff. He never moaned. He almost was given away. He kept working. He was thankful when this corner wrote, "Don't give up on Bosman."

He said, "I haven't given up on myself."

If all this sounds corny and trite, so be it. That's the way Bosman's no-hitter made every fan feel. Good.

Said a fan, "What a way to break a slump."

When Bosman finally was able to move clear of his howling, hugging teammates he walked toward the dugout. Just before he stepped in he raised both arms, like a victorious fighter—which he was—to the fans.

Then he went into the dugout, for interviews. The fans sought more of him.

"We want Bosman, we want Bosman," they shouted continuously.

Finally he came again. He went to the microphone and spoke briefly. What he said wasn't heard. The crowd noise was overwhelming. He had won. He did it. The dream. The no-hitter. His words were unimportant.

My wife said, "I'm glad we decided not to go to Musicarnival tonight."

REGGIE JACKSON: BLOOD & GUTS OF THE FIGHTING A's

By Murray Olderman

From Sport

Reginald Martinez Jackson didn't mind posing for the cover of *Sport.* He didn't mind putting on the olive-drab helmet with the four stars of a full general. He didn't mind slipping into the leather holster belt with its dangling unmatched pair of pearl-handled revolvers. He didn't even mind holding the high-powered binoculars and staring, thoughtfully, into the distance.

But when the World War II jeep was rolled in, and Reggie was asked to stand up in it, symbolically commanding his troops, Jackson rebelled, "Hey, man," he said, "I don't want to be that far removed from my peers."

Reggie Jackson's peers, for four or five hours a day, seven or eight months a year, are his teammates on the world champion Oakland A's, and it is one measure of Jackson's curious personality that he is reluctant to do anything—such as posing in a jeep—that would make it seem as if he were acting superior. It is another measure that Jackson willingly donned the helmet, holster and pistol that George C. Scott wore in the movie, *Patton.*

Like Patton, Jackson seems to think of himself both as soldier and general and, inevitably, the two roles sometimes conflict. Like Patton, too, Jackson can be utterly charming or maddeningly harsh, depending on the situation, depending on his mood. And like Patton, Jackson has more than a little ego, more than a limited belief in his own glorious destiny. He wants to lead the Oakland A's to a third straight world championship every bit as much as Patton wanted to roll into Berlin at the head of his troops.

Eventually, of course, the comparison breaks down. Patton was Patton—he could quote the classics and envision himself in an earlier incarnation—and Reggie, for all his uncommon gifts, is only a baseball player. Jackson is not the tactician of his team, not the strategist, not even the captain of the club.

He is, however, the most potent weapon the A's possess, and a perfect symbol of their power. Just as Patton personified American tank warfare in World War II, Jackson personifies Oakland's unique brand of internecine warfare: the Fighting A's fight endlessly among themselves, and their opponents wind up with all the bruises. In that sort of battle, Jackson is a champion: he throws jabs at his teammates, and knocks out the enemy.

The internal combustion of the not-so-model A's has been recognized nationally for about three years, ever since Oakland won its first Western Division title and demonstrated that a successful team doesn't have to be a mutual admiration society. Jackson was ahead of his time. He was ready to slug it out with a teammate three years before baseball realized that family squabbles can be good for you.

One day during the 1968 season, Jackson and Sal Bando, the third baseman, were sitting on the bench, chatting amiably, and suddenly, both were on their feet, fists up, prepared to destroy each other. "That was the only time we ever got mad at each other," Bando now says. "I don't even remember why."

Reggie's first serious fraternal battle came in 1972, and he didn't pick on a set-up. His opponent was Mike Epstein, the A's 220-pound first baseman. Oakland was playing in Dallas, and Epstein had left four tickets for the game for friends of his father. Jackson, prowling the locker room, looked over the pass list and spotted the name "Berman," down for four tickets. The A's, in their infinite generosity, had decreed that to prevent ticket abuses players could provide passes only for their immediate families. So far as Reggie knew, there was no one named Berman on the roster.

"Who put down for these?" Jackson called out.

"I did," said Epstein, "and it's none of your business."

"I'm appointing it my business," said Jackson, who took seriously his position as the A's assistant player representative (he later was promoted to the top job).

"Don't buy more than you can handle," warned Epstein.

Jackson crossed out the name. Epstein wheeled and threw a punch which connected, then threw four more punches. The other players stood around watching, presumably cheering silently for their favorite, until manager Dick Williams barged into the room and broke it up.

Not too long after that, Williams himself was Jackson's target. After a game in Boston, the manager challenged Reggie for holding the ball while the tying run scored. "What were you doing out there?" Williams demanded.

"None of your goddamn business," Jackson replied.

"I'm running this ball club," said Williams.

"You are like hell," snapped Reggie. "We all know who's running this ball club." If Charlie Finley himself had thrown the punch, Williams couldn't have been more stung.

Jackson celebrated the Fourth of July, 1973, by exploding against the entire Oakland coaching staff. He dropped a fly ball during a game, and when he heard that the coaches had criticized his effort on the play, he struck back. "The way these guys criticize you," Reggie announced, "you'd think they were all Babe Ruth when they played."

Obviously, Jackson's tongue is a potent weapon in itself, but he is willing to back it up. Early this season, teammate Bill North, who had hung around with Jackson during spring training, hit a sharp ground ball right back at the pitcher. North, bothered by a pulled groin muscle, didn't bother to run hard to first base. When North got back to the dugout, Jackson openly criticized him for not putting out.

"You're not number five," North shouted. "I only take orders from number five." Alvin Dark, the pious manager who succeeded Dick Williams this year, wears number five. North stopped talking to Jackson, but in early June, in Detroit, their uneasy truce flamed into a brawl. After a hostile exchange of words, Jackson jumped North. Pitcher Vida Blue and catcher Ray Fosse charged in to separate them. The floor became a melee of bodies. Fosse was bumped against a locker; he later went on the inactive list with a slipped cervical disc and pinched nerve and missed half the season.

The fight got so much publicity that owner Charlie Finley huddled with the two men and Dark when the team reached Milwaukee. According to one inside account, Finley put most of the blame on Jackson. Reggie was floored by the failure of most of his teammates to side with him in the dispute. He reacted by pouting.

"It was hurting the team," says North. "Hell, the man wasn't hustling or really swinging the bat. He missed a couple of diving catches. So I went to him in Boston and said, 'Hey, let's go talk for a minute.' We went into the manager's room. Reggie didn't say a word, but when it was over, he said, 'Thank you.' That's all." North and Jackson soon resumed talking.

In all fairness, Jackson fights for his teammates as well as with them. When Finley embarrassed Mike Andrews last fall by placing the second baseman involuntarily and inaccurately on the disabled list, Jackson was Andrews' most vehement defender. And when it became obvious that Finley's interference was forcing manager Dick Williams to resign, it was Jackson who praised Williams most vigorously. Jackson has practically made it a religion to stand up to Finley. The Oakland star is in the process of writing three books— a diary of his 1974 season, an autobiography, and an instructional work—and it is safe to say that Finley will not emerge as the hero in any of them.

"The confrontations on our club come because of the owner we have," says Jackson flatly. "Other persons wouldn't believe and couldn't play under the conditions we have on this club. We have cold weather, a bad ball park, lack of attendance, unbelievable cheapness and a tense air between management and players. To survive, this has become a very loose ball club."

"On this team," says Catfish Hunter, the A's top pitcher, "when you look over in a corner and you think, 'That sonuvabitch is loafing,' you tell him. You don't sit around acting moody. When I speak at banquets, I tell people, 'We've got long hair, so we think like women. No wonder we talk and fight so much.' "

The A's with whom Jackson has fought talk freely about him. "He's probably the most insecure person I know," Bill North says. "The more success he gets, the more insecure he gets, because he doesn't know how to accept his success. He's a very confused young man. He does some strange things for a person of his stature and intelligence. I was his only friend on this team, and he messed that up."

Mike Epstein is out of baseball now—he says he was offered a chance to rejoin the A's when he became a free agent last spring, and refused—but he remembers Jackson well. He recalls a conversation with Jackson that took place late in the 1972 season, after their fight, but before Epstein's battle with Dick Williams, a loud verbal battle on a plane trip during the World Series, a battle that led to the trading of Epstein after the season. Epstein says the dialogue went like this:

Jackson: "You hate my guts, don't you? You ignore me."

Epstein: "I just don't want to have anything to do with you."

Jackson: "It bothers me that you don't like me."

Epstein: "It's not that I don't like you. I tolerate you."

Jackson: "Well, that's not enough. I really want to be a leader on this club."

Epstein: "There are no leaders here. We all play to win."

Jackson: "Being a leader on this club is the most important thing in the world to me."

Nobody won the debate.

The nominal leader of the A's is Sal Bando, the team captain, who can match Jackson in batting average, runs batted in, and candor. After one tough defeat early in 1974, Bando banged a wall in disgust and muttered, "That guy couldn't manage his way out of a meat market." Alvin Dark summoned Bando into his office, and Bando later apologized. The captain can be a diplomat.

Bando has known Jackson longer than anyone else in the Oakland organization. They were schoolmates at Arizona State; Bando, a star on the baseball team, was two years ahead of Jackson, who arrived with a football scholarship and, as a sophomore, was defensive captain of the team. Bando didn't even know for a while that Jackson was a baseball player. "I remember him as a quiet kid," Bando says.

Jackson has been called some terrible things in recent years, but quiet isn't one of them. "At times, we need Reggie to speak up," says Bando. "When nobody else is willing, and something has to be said, Reggie has the guts to say it. I admire him for that. I also think he may speak up sometimes when nothing should be said."

Bando diplomatically softens that needle. "Reggie is such a physical person," he says, "and it comes out in his personality by being a little abrasive. He may rub people the wrong way, but if you can see Reggie in the light we see him, he's a very likable person. You know, when he gets off the trip of being Reggie Jackson, the star."

Reggie Jackson is a star, a superstar, beyond any question, no matter what Dick Allen, the Chicago superstar, once said: "Why so much fuss about a guy who's never hit .300?"

Allen's comment was sharp and funny and accurate and—quoted all by itself—unfair. Going into 1974, Jackson never had hit .300 in one season of professional baseball—not even in 1966, playing in Lewiston, Ohio; not even in 1973, when he won the Most Valuable Player award in the American League. His career batting average through 1973 was .264, and not until 1973 did he ever lead the American League in home runs or runs batted in.

Yet Reggie's talent is so obvious, so awesome, he deserves all the fuss. He hits with power. He runs with a sprinter's speed. He throws hard. He's 6 foot and 207 pounds, with 27-inch thighs bulging through his uniform, and yet he moves with a panther's quickness. When he whips a bat around and lashes into a ball, people notice. He received more votes for the All-Star team this year than any player in history.

He has a star's personality, too, a complex, almost unique personality. He can be glib and charming and witty and spirited, and he can be sullen and evasive and quarrelsome. He is totally unpredictable. "He's hot and cold," says Monte Irvin, one of the earliest black superstars, now an assistant to the commissioner of baseball. "One day, Reggie's gung-ho. The next day, he might not even talk to you."

Most of all, Reggie Jackson lives like a star. At the age of 28, one-eighth Spanish on his father's side, Reggie is a paper millionaire fully capable of indulging his passions for cars (four), women (more), and the high life. His total income, with his Arizona real-estate investments added to his $135,000 baseball salary, approaches a quarter of a million dollars a year. He isn't reluctant to admit that he carries $1.8 million worth of insurance on his bachelor's life.

He lives in Arizona during the off-season, and in a new $85,000 condominium from April to October. His condominium is in a development called Hiller Highlands, high on a hill above the exclusive Berkeley Tennis Club, and it offers him a magnificent view of Oakland, San Francisco, and the bay. It is a long way from Wyncote, Pennsylvania, on the north side of Philadelphia, where he grew up, the son of a tailor who had to sell numbers on the side to raise three sons.

"Ain't nobody lives like I do," Reggie said one night this season, jiving with John Mayberry of the Kansas City Royals. "I'm the only black in my neighborhood. Before I moved in, they told me I could only go out at night. And I had to ride in a black car and keep my head down."

Jackson can talk like that with fellow blacks—"Can't hurt a nigger's hide," he tells a brother who wants to know how he feels—and he says he takes all his meals at a soul-food spot, Lois the Pie Queen on the Oakland-Berkeley border. He may push his soul a little hard; at times he has been criticized by blacks because most of his social life is with whites. (Vida Blue once pointed to the A's outfield—

white Joe Rudi in left, Latin Angel Mangual in center and black Reggie Jackson in right, and said, "There are three cliques on this team, and you can see all of them out there." And some people wondered which clique Jackson belonged to. Reggie said, not surprisingly, he transcends them all.)

"Reggie's Place!" A trim brunette named Marlene answers Jackson's home phone. She is his private secretary; she sorts out his bills, handles his phone, and each day sends out 75 postcards, bearing Reggie's picture and autograph, to his fans. "I pay $4.50 an hour to get my mail answered," Jackson says, "and put my own stamps on the letters."

The A's, unlike some teams, do not provide a fan-answering service for their players. In fact, they charge the players $4 a copy for the team picture, which is not so surprising, considering that they haven't bothered to paint the tarpaulin that is stored in center field for seven years.

One of the A's economies did not turn out badly for Reggie. A young blonde named Mary, who has a friendly smile and a stunning build, used to be one of Oakland's two ballpersons, stationed in right field to chase down foul balls and, occasionally, to dust an umpire's shoes. Charlie Finley dismissed the ballpersons this year to cut his expenses. Mary, chased out of right field, now does the next best thing; she spends spare hours with the right fielder. The day I visited Reggie's Place, he and Mary sat and talked for a long time. She looked lovely in a lotus position and a green bikini.

Reggie had told me we needed a lot of time to talk—"I want to talk about my peers, and I need a lot of time to do them justice"— but somehow, I didn't get much of a chance at his place. Instead, I thumbed through his *Penthouses* and his *Playboys,* glanced at his color TV set with a Holy Bible and a pistol on it, listened to the sounds of the Carpenters and the O'Jays on his stereo, and wondered, quite seriously, what his peers were doing right then

THE LONGEST ENTRY IN "WHO'S WHO"

By Steve Jacobson

From Newsday

Copyright, ©, 1974, Newsday, Inc.

The moral of this story is, don't buy drapes in Cleveland the day before the trading deadline.

MILLER, ROBERT LANE
Born, St. Louis, Mo., Feb. 18, 1939. Bats Right. Throws Right. Height, 6 feet, 1 inch. Weight, 195 pounds.

The longest entry in "Who's Who in Baseball" is under the name of Bob Miller. He's on his second time around with the Mets, his twelfth stop on 10 different teams in the major leagues. That's his record. Somebody always wants him, or somebody always wants to get rid of him, depending on the date, town, manager, or phase of the moon.

He's also appeared in more games than any active pitcher, which means he certainly is experienced. Some day his grandchildren will mention the name of a famous player and Miller will be able to say, "Hey, I played with him." About almost any player. He's appeared in 35 different major-league ball parks—four in New York—which probably is another record, if anybody's counting.

"Maybe there's another trade," Miller said recently, "I haven't read the papers yet."

Signed as bonus player, St. Louis Cardinals, June 20, 1957.

"Stan Musial was like a god," Miller said. "He was the first man to walk over and introduce himself, like I needed to be told who he was." Robin Roberts of the Phillies was Miller's idol as a pitcher, also the first man Miller beat in a big-league game.

One of Miller's lasting memories of St. Louis came on the day

he saw Pittsburgh broadcaster Bob Prince dive from a third-floor window into the pool of the Chase-Park Plaza Hotel. Fully clothed.
Drafted by New York Mets for $125,000, Oct. 10, 1961.

He saw Frank Thomas, recovering from a shattered thumb, catching barehanded the best throw from any challenger. "Either he was crazy or he had the toughest hands in the world," Miller said. Casey Stengel called Miller "Nelson" after some old associate. The first day, trainer Gus Mauch told Miller not to cut his toenails in the trainer's room.

"It was amazing how bad we were. I didn't think anybody could be, especially with the names we had. We really believed we would be better than the Cubs and Phillies."

Miller was the losing pitcher the night Sandy Koufax pitched his first no-hitter and was the winning pitcher in the 40th and last victory of 1962.

Traded to Los Angeles Dodgers for first baseman Tim Harkness and second baseman Larry Burright, December 1, 1962.

He was coming out of a show in a Las Vegas casino when a pit boss told him he'd been traded. Stayed with the Dodgers for five seasons and three pennants.

He saw Koufax pitch his perfect game and his second no-hitter: "He's probably the finest pitcher who ever lived. . . . I saw his elbow swell and turn black and blue when he pitched. He threw a 'second-deck curve ball.' It started up there and broke across the knees. . . . I imagine he's very happy living in Maine. Being a celebrity was not his bag." Miller also recognized Maury Wills's genius. "If I saw him make one mental error, it was the only one," Miller said.

It was the first of three associations with Buzzy Bavasi running the ball club. "He's the greatest man I've known in baseball," Miller said. One year he sent Miller a contract calling for a 60 percent cut, which was illegal. When Miller phoned, Bavasi said he'd held an office pool on what time Miller would call.

"He would put three pieces of paper on his desk in front of you and tell you to pick one, which would be your salary. You'd pick one and he'd crumble the others and throw them in the basket. He'd say, 'I'm glad you didn't pick the other two.' They were probably all the same. We never knew."

Like so many players who've passed through the Dodger organization, Miller says, "I feel I'm still a Dodger."

Traded to Minnesota Twins with catcher John Roseboro and pitcher Ron

Perranoski for pitcher Jim Grant and shortstop Zoilo Versalles, November 28, 1967.

If he were still a Dodger when he had his best years, Miller thinks he'd have made a lot more money: "Nine out of ten times you get a token raise when you're traded. If you've had a good year, it isn't enough, but you don't want to start out arguing with the new club."

He says he enjoyed playing for Billy Martin at Minnesota: "If it was a big game to win, he gave me the ball." That included the game that put the Twins in first place, the game that clinched the pennant and, "over somebody's objections" the third game of the play-off. Baltimore beat him.

Traded to Cleveland Indians with pitcher Dean Chance, infielder Craig Nettles and outfielder Ted Uhlaender for pitchers Luis Tiant and Stan Williams, December 11, 1969.

He was a stockbroker in Portland and got a letter requesting his autograph on a baseball card. The letter said the fan was starting his Cleveland Indian collection early. That's how Miller found out.

Cleveland, Miller says, was the only city he didn't like. "Alvin Dark was the one manager I didn't get along with. He used to call the pitches for me after ten years in the big leagues. He wanted to rule everything," Miller said.

Miller's wife, Susie, joined him from California on June 14 and bought drapes for their apartment.

Traded to Chicago White Sox with pitcher Barry Moore for outfielder Buddy Bradford, June 15, 1970.

"I left Susie in Cleveland and went to Chicago. . . . She's adaptable. She went to 12 schools as a child. We had her horse, Peacepipe, in four cities," Miller said.

"It hasn't been easy for her. She never can have anything that's her own where we are during the season."

Sold to Chicago Cubs, September 1, 1970.

Miller flew from Chicago to Oakland with the White Sox, then was told to fly back to Chicago to join the Cubs. "I felt uncomfortable with the Cubs for some reason," he said.

Released by Chicago Cubs, May 10, 1971 and signed by San Diego Padres, May 11, 1971.

While waivers were clearing, Don and Ginger Drysdale gave a retirement party for Miller in Los Angeles. Then Miller went out and wound up the season with the best earned-run average in big leagues, 1.64 in 56 games. It was his second experience with Bavasi, and he decided he wanted to live in San Diego.

Traded to Pittsburgh Pirates with cash for outfielder John Jeter and pitcher Ed Acosta, August 10, 1971.

"The Pirates were so noisy. They were always swearing and yelling in the clubhouse and it was all in fun." Got a first-hand look at Roberto Clemente. "He and Mays, they broke their ass for nine innings. They could hit a home run or get a runner to second," Miller said.

The team won one division championship and one World Series in two seasons and, Miller says he reached his peak in earnings, $60,000, including Series share.

Released by Pittsburgh Pirates, April 2, 1973, and signed by San Diego Padres the same day.

Third term with Bavasi.

"I want to beat the Cubs and the Pirates more than anybody else. They released me. They told me I couldn't play baseball any more. That's a slap in the face," he said.

With the Pirates he was closest to Dave Giusti, also a relief pitcher. "I'd feel for him if I beat him in a game that meant something, but I'm in the game to win. Other teams talk to me on the mound all the time. They're friends of mine, but I'm a good competitor. . . . I feel the outside three inches of the plate are mine. I have to move hitters back even if they're friends."

Awarded to Detroit Tigers on waiver claim, June 22, 1973.

Second time with Billy Martin as manager.

He was in the clubhouse when [coach] Joe Schultz asked, "What're you putting that uniform on for?" Miller said, "We have a game tonight." Schultz said, "You got one someplace else."

Sold to New York Mets, September 23, 1973.

"I got to be on the same team as Mays for ten days," Miller said. He also got to be on the same team as Tug McGraw who lives in the next house in Poway, California. Miller says he's seen McGraw hitting tee shots off his lawn across the road, over men nailing roofing tiles on a new house. "Something goofy happens every year. I try not to be the one to do it," Miller said.

Coach Joe Pignatano calls Miller "Nelson" after a 1962 association.

Susie and daughter Krissie, in kindergarten, won't be joining Miller until June. "I don't think all the trading is good for [them]. Most of the time when [they] see me, it's on TV."

The greatest contrast he sees between these Mets and those Mets, he says, are these Mets are thinking about winning another pennant, and "the uniforms fit."

The last time he looked, his uniform still said Mets on the chest. But it's still early in the year.

Football

THE DOLPHINS WIN A GAME OF INCHES

By David Casstevens

From The Houston Post

Copyright, ©, 1974, The Houston Post

Through a thick sleepy fog Sunday, the Miami Dolphins shone like a lighthouse, a landmark of power, precision, and pride once again unequaled in the National Football League.

Ever so convincingly, they won Super Bowl VIII, 24–7.

This was to be a titanic struggle, a game of inches between the Dolphins and a game-hardened band of Minnesota Vikings, those purple ogres from the Northland who this year have lived by piracy and plunder and even been accused of offering prayers to Thor.

It wasn't that way at all, though.

With unvarnished strength, behind an undeniable wall of blockers Larry Csonka made the Dolphins' second straight world title victory a game of yards—and yards and yards.

The way he ran rattled the china at the Shamrock Hilton.

Before 68,142 Rice Stadium spectators and television viewers from Berlin to Caracas, Csonka's performance was awesome in any language—145 yards rushing on 33 carries, including touchdown runs of five and two yards.

He wasn't fancy, just effective. So is a street sweeper.

Almost before Viking coach Bud Grant took his stoic stance on the sideline, Csonka set the tone of this glitter and glamour game by running for 16 yards, then five, and finally five more for the opening touchdown on the first series.

On his last two steps, Csonka carried with him Minnesota's Paul Krause and Jeff Siemon—430 pounds worth—into the orange-and-aqua splashed end zone.

Somewhere Eric the Red spun in his grave.

The Dolphins, 32–2 over the last two seasons, spun their offensive machinery for 259 total yards, 196 of that by overland express. In addition to Csonka's two scores, his bearded and now sometimes forgotten sidekick, Jim Kiick, punched over from one yard—his first TD this many-splendored year.

That was it, almost.

A Super Bowl without Garo Yepremian just isn't quite so super, so the little balding kicker from Cyprus bumped through a 28-yard field goal in the second period, with his size 7 1/2 left shoe.

No, he didn't throw a pass this year, but who needed to pass this time?

Bob Griese didn't.

The Dolphin quarterback passed only seven times and completed six of them. With his team holding a 17–0 half-time lead, Griese threw but a single time after intermission and that was a 27-yarder down the sideline to one Paul Warfield, a well-executed prelude to Csonka's second touchdown.

For the Vikings, this gray chilled day naturally was as joyless as Mudville.

In Super Bowl IV they were badly beaten by Kansas City and in Super Bowl VIII again their golden dreams tarnished badly—like Stassen, every four years seems to be a predictable disappointment.

Francis Tarkenton tried gamely to play catch up.

That the Viking quarterback scored himself on a four-yard end run in the final period was an obvious point of irony—for indeed Minnesota found that running against the Dolphins' swarming defense was like running on Johnny Bench.

Miami was always waiting.

A total of 44 minutes, 17 seconds elapsed before the Vikings, with Oscar Reed and Ed Marinaro and the darting Tarkenton and NFL Rookie of the Year Chuck Foreman could manage a single first down rushing.

Reed finished with only 32 yards, Foreman 18 and Tarkenton 17.

How gritty was Miami's defense?

For example: Trailing 17–0 with a minute left in the first half, the Vikings had fourth down and one from the Dolphins' 6-yard line when Tarkenton slipped the ball to Reed.

As he hit the right tackle area, middle linebacker Nick Buoniconti darted in, jarred the ball loose, and Jake Scott alertly recovered at the 6.

Viking misfortunes came in quick-step.

(1) Twice Tarkenton was jerked down like a cork, first by Vern DenHerder and then by Manny Fernandez.

(2) The drive that led to Yepremian's field goal was set in motion by a 15-yard unsportsmanlike conduct penalty on Wally Hilgenberg.

(3) John Gilliam returned the third quarter kickoff 65 yards but the ball was returned to the Viking 11 due to a clipping penalty on Stu Voigt.

(4) On third and four from the Minnesota 5-yard line, the Vikes sent a white-shirted avalanche after Mercury Morris. The eight-yard setback, however, was negated by a holding penalty on Hilgenberg and two plays later Csonka scored.

(5) Following Tarkenton's fourth-period score, an onsides kick was successful when the ball glanced off Bob Matheson's foot and Terry Brown jumped on the ball near midfield. An offsides penalty on the Vikes' Ron Porter, though, extinguished any comeback flicker.

Tarkenton found few teammates reliable, but Voigt did his duty.

Fran's tight end caught third down passes of 17, 16, and 14 yards, the final reception a key play in the Vikings' only drive that produced points.

It required ten plays for Minnesota to travel 57 yards and prevent a first, and worst possible, Super Bowl footnote—a shutout.

Borrowing time with his backfield floating, Tarkenton managed to complete the short pass against Miami's 5–3 defense and finish with 18 of 28, for 182 yards. He also was almost able to even the total offense ledger, too—after a totally barren first quarter (25 yards), the Vikings finished just 21 yards behind the winner and still champion.

Still, it was a far cry from what many anticipated.

As they left the field, the Vikes, with their purple helmets complete with pointy horns, brought to mind their namesakes and the prayer of the European churches long, long ago: "God, deliver us from the fury of the Northmen."

Obviously, back then they didn't have a Csonka.

NOT JUST ANOTHER PRETTY FACE

By Jim Murray

From The Saturday Evening Post

Copyright, ©, 1974, The Saturday Evening Post Company

When the Los Angeles Rams proudly announced their new coach, Chuck Knox, was "the best-looking young coach in the league," everybody thought they meant his blue eyes. They thought he was just another pretty face. He would get the girl in any movie you ever saw. Robert Redford would play his best friend. He might not win the Super Bowl, the wits wagged, but how about the Academy Award?

As it turned out, the best-looking thing about Chuck Knox was his record—12–2. He missed the 1974 Super Bowl by a field goal or two. The Rams knew what they were doing. They got a Paul Brown, not a Paul Newman.

Nobody would admit to being surprised but, frankly, when the new coach's pre-season record was 0–3–1, the press-box survey was that the owners should have picked someone with glasses and buck teeth. The guess was that Chuck Knox had too much hair and too many teeth to make it. Football coaches are supposed to be broken-nosed, bald-headed old gaffers like Knute Rockne or gap-toothed disciplinarians like Vince Lombardi. Knox looked too much like a collar ad. "Show 'em your profile, Chuck!" screamed the fans in the early, losing exhibition season.

The players were as skeptical as the rest of the town. "To tell you the truth, when the guy walked in the door, I thought, 'Oh, no! We need a Vince Lombardi and we get a Guy Lombardo.' The guy looked like a 'Y' instructor, y'know what I mean?" summed up one lineman who doesn't want to be memorialized for his feelings.

The Rams Knox took over were not quite a demoralized crew.

They had too many holdovers from a set who had barely missed the Super Bowl a few years earlier. They had nearly as many All-Pros as the Miami Dolphins. But the coach who had put them together had been thrown out by the late owner, Dan Reeves. Dan's dislike of George Allen was so cordial, he had once fired him on Christmas morning.

The Rams' next mentor was Tommy Prothro, a stoical type from the college ranks (UCLA), who thought the pros should be treated as grown-ups—and other mistakes. Tommy spent most of his time putting in playground plays like the Statue of Liberty and everybody-out-for-a-long-one. Evenings, he attended a nightclub where his star defensive end was performing. Not surprisingly, the team settled gradually into a 6–7–1 record.

When Carroll Rosenbloom, a Baltimore millionaire and probably the most successful owner in the history of the game, traded the Baltimore Colts for the Los Angeles Rams, it was clear Prothro was not his idea of a dashing leader. Noted for his uncanny ability to spot youthful coaching talent, it was evident he regarded Prothro as possessing neither. Prothro, a glacial, monolithic man of owlish imperturbability, always seemed to be standing in the midst of disaster eating a banana. Rosenbloom wanted men of perturbability and he was so impatient to unload Prothro that he inspired a lawsuit when he did so. Which surprised everybody. They didn't think Prothro cared that much.

Rosenbloom found Chuck Knox buried in the middle of a Detroit Lions staff that could mercifully be described as mediocre. Imprisoned by his good looks or the unimaginativeness of his superiors, Knox was a not-so-secret success in the private councils of the league. (When Vince Lombardi heard George Allen described by his aggrieved boss, George Halas, on whom he had jumped a contract, as "unprincipled, dishonest, opportunistic and word-betraying," Lombardi leaned over to Dan Reeves, the party of the second part, and whispered, "Looks like you got yourself a good one.")

Carroll Rosenbloom got himself a good one. Charles Robert Knox has been preparing himself for an NFL head coaching job all his life. He came up from the hard rock country of Sewickley, Pennsylvania, where they treat the coal better than the people. He had come up a long hard way from a company town knocked flat through the long hard Depression. You might say he came up through the school of hard Knoxes. Mom was born in Scotland, Dad in Ireland and the Knoxes never took the United States of America or its opportunities for granted. He was, and is, one of the hardest-working in a hard-working profession.

Initially he took jobs for learning, not money. He went from high school to assistant at Wake Forest. He went to Kentucky to learn under Blanton Collier, to the New York Jets to absorb what Weeb Ewbank knew. By the time he went to the Detroit Lions, people had begun to learn gridiron techniques from him.

When he came to the Rams, his reputation had preceded him. Which is to say he didn't have any. When he confronted the Rams, he was like a shavetail right out of West Point taking command of an outfit that had been on the line for thirty months. They were all too aware of the press-box gag, "Knox, Knox, who's there?" "Chuck." "Chuck Who?" "Exactly."

Rosenbloom, who had hired a young Weeb Ewbank and a young Don Shula for his Colts, both Super Bowl coaches, thought he saw something of the same fire in Knox. Football is not a game. It's an emotion. Teams are as sentimental as a Corsican wedding and games are played by 280-pound brutes whose feelings are more easily bruised than their noses.

The Rams were a confused team when Knox took them over. For one thing, the ownership had just traded away their longtime quarterback, Roman Gabriel, and installed John Hadl from San Diego in his stead. Now, a quarterback is the wheelhouse of a football team. An uncertain or unfamiliar hand in there and you're aground. Jimmy the Greek thought the Rams looked about as poor a betting proposition as the bull in a bullfight.

The Rams had always been a team trained to venerate its old, a form of ancestor-worship in the best traditions of the British Peerage. Suddenly, not only the coach was young, so were the players. George Allen had always revered experience, even to the point where it interfered with team speed and quickness—and even eyesight. Prothro wasn't committed one way or the other. He was more interested in plays than players.

Knox swept out veteran defensive players like Jimmy Nettles and Gene Howard. They flunked their screen test. Like aging movie stars, they were betrayed by a projector.

The veteran linebacker, Marlin McKeever, something of a sentimental favorite in L.A., was swept along with them. Marlin had been kept on not so much for his athletic ability, which was waning, as for his ability to call defensive signals. "We felt like we'd rather have a better athlete in there; we didn't put that much reliance on defensive signal calling, the so-called coach on the field concept. We didn't need a coach on the field. We had five of them on the sidelines. We said we'd let them call them and get somebody in there who could carry them out," said Knox.

In all, Knox installed a rookie at cornerback and substitutes at middle linebacker and defensive end, an audacious move that didn't go unnoticed in the press when the pre-season started badly. "The worst Ram team we've seen in years!" harrumphed two of the most prestigious local critics.

But the team was finding that this was, indeed, a hard Knox. "I remember our first meeting when he called the whole squad together. I remember thinking, 'Oh-oh. I hope he's as good as he sounds,'" recalls the 14-year veteran and greatest defensive tackle in the game today, Merlin Olsen. "He had a very confident approach," recalls offensive guard Joe Scibelli. "But, y'know, Napoleon was optimistic, too, at Watcrloo."

If Chuck Knox ever had a self-doubt, no one knew it—least of all Chuck Knox.

"He was, like, a pro, y'know. We spoke the same language," adds Scibelli, a 15-year veteran who had been chafing under Prothro's college-holdover habit of "flip-flopping" his guards. "Flip-flopping" is a complicated technique which calls for the guard who plays the "strong side" (the side of the center which has the most players on it in the unbalanced line) to remain on that side even if it means changing from right to left guard periodically to do so. Pro players hate it. Accustomed to playing their positions like chess-set pieces, they hate to be put in front of unfamiliar opponents and unfamiliar defenses; it's an arhythmic choreograph of the game which, they feel, makes them look bad. When Knox was asked if he intended "flip-flopping" his guards, he only smiled. He made friends with his offensive line before he even met them. "Flip-flopping never even came up," recalls Scibelli with contentment.

With a new coach, a new quarterback, and five rookies, two of them free agents in the starting grid, the Rams seemed like a troop of Boy Scouts setting out for Indian territory with a flashlight and a penknife. The initial results were disastrous. They lost three out of their first four pre-season games and tied the other one.

Knox refers to this period of his career as "a gut check." "We took a reading of the intestines," he says. "We knew what we were doing was fine and right. But the public said, 'Who the hell is Chuck Knox and why is he doing those terrible things to the Rams?' If I hadn't been raised by some good coaches, I might have put in some finesses and things right then that would have looked good but wrecked the whole program."

Scibelli and Olsen agree. "I was pleased he stood by his guns," recollects Olsen. "He did what he said he would. He didn't panic. I really admired his confidence in himself in the face of some very pointed criticism. The man stayed constant."

Agrees Scibelli: "He didn't panic. He was very confident. The team wasn't concerned because we knew that whenever we had eleven starters in there, we did pretty well. But you watch for a man to crack under the boos. He didn't. He did it his way."

"Lots of people were bailing out on us," remembers Chuck Knox. "We ran into a lot of flak. I looked around the boat and there was no one in it. I was rowing an empty boat."

Football, it has been said, is no place for democracy. "You don't get to vote here, son," Vince Lombardi is supposed to have said to a disgruntled aspirant. "If you want to get back to the free world, take your things with you."

Knox did not exactly restore the secret ballot. But he appointed co-captains (Scibelli and Olsen) and then appointed an "executive committee." The bottom line on a committee is that "a camel is supposed to be a horse that was designed by a committee," but the Knox committee (Scibelli, Olsen, Guard Tom Mack, offensive tackle Charlie Cowan, receiver Harold Jackson and quarterback Hadl) worked very well. "Together with the associate captains I appointed each week, I had an eight-man decision-making board. The guys felt involved."

The team was free but not anarchical. "I kept curfews and bed-checks (something Prothro had foregone). You have to have a disciplined team. Lack of discipline shows on the field, too. Football is not an ad-lib game. It's not a series of solos like baseball. We wanted mistake-free football and we felt a mistake-free lifestyle would help. The previous year, this team had 103 penalties. Last year, we had 66, second lowest in football. Know who had the lowest? Right! The Miami Dolphins. The Super Bowl champions. They had 63. Know who had the third lowest? Yep! The Minnesota Vikings, the other team in the Super Bowl. They had 69. And we were the only three teams in football with 12–2 records."

Knox had a subtler form of team discipline. Traditionally, Monday has always been an off day in football—no practice, no team meetings, no drills, no films. Teams which build all week to the climax of Sunday afternoon habitually blow off steam Sunday night in an ocean of beer, booze, or broads—or all three—after the game and are accustomed to sleeping it off on Monday. The Rams work Monday. They get Tuesday off.

"Players who play on Sunday are anxious to see the films as soon as possible," explains Coach Knox with a perfectly straight face. "If they make mistakes, they're anxious to face up to them as soon as possible, get it behind them. If they have to wait for Tuesday, that gives them two days to brood about it."

He pauses, then adds: "Of course, we run twenty 50's [50-yard dashes]. Boils 'em out." And a slow grin crosses his features.

The first act was good. It's a John Wayne production so far. The town now knows Chuck Knox is the guy in the white hat. But will there be a happy ending? Does he get to kiss the Super Bowl in the fadeout?

Tex Schramm, general manager of the Dallas Cowboys, is one who doesn't necessarily think the Bad Guys are out of it. "Sometimes," he says cautiously, "you win in the first year under a new coach on enthusiasm and vitality and newness alone. It's a kind of high unto itself. But, then, you have to find a way to keep it up when the romance is tailing off. That's the hard part. In football or any other marriage."

The Rams came up a touchdown and a field goal short last year. They missed a perfect regular season by a total of three points. That calls for a pretty tough encore. If Knox caught the league by surprise last year, he won't have the advantage of that element this year. Still, the owner is convinced. He tore up the old three-year contract and gave the coach a new one (for five years). Knox got to six figures faster than any coach in history.

The hair is grayer and thinner. New lines are etched around the eyes. But, so far as L.A. and ye olde Rams fans are concerned, the "best-looking young coach in the business" gets better looking by the day.

A LONG CHANCE LOSES

By Sam Blair

From the Dallas Morning News

Copyright, ©, 1974, Dallas Morning News

It was the sixth minute of the fourth quarter. By now the oddsmakers of America had a splitting headache. Unbeknownst to anyone in a packed Cotton Bowl, however, the long-shot Longhorns were just about to join them.

Oklahoma was supposed to be leading from here to Red River but weird things had been happening all afternoon. The Sooners only recently had managed to scrap back and gain a 13–13 tie in a football game so keenly fought that you wondered if Texas secretly had suited up the junior varsity for its previous four games this fall.

Now there were the Longhorns at midfield, facing fourth down and needing about two feet to keep possession. They could try to make it, or they could punt. If they executed well on the punt the Sooners would have been looking at what seemed like several acres of Astroturf between them and the goal line.

Darrell Royal decided to keep on bucking.

A week before this game the Texas coach had stressed how his guys must play inspired football and not make any errors. "And running three times and punting is not an error," he noted. But time and conditions had changed a lot of things.

The fourth-down play would be the fifth for Texas in this particular possession. Marty Akins had kept on the first and skipped for 12 yards to the Texas 40. Obviously the yards got tougher from there but the Longhorns had held their own in crucial moments all day.

And they did once again. Trouble was Earl Campbell didn't hold the ball.

The freshman fullback tore into the teeth of the Sooner defense, right into the middle where the Seimon brothers and all those other bad dudes hang out. He made the needed distance with maybe a half-foot to spare but then fumbled. The ball fell free just inside Oklahoma's side of the 50 and LeRoy Seimon jumped on it.

So with 8:59 left to play the Sooners had all they could ask for—the ball and an opportunity to win. They did what they had to with both and thus they went home with another victory over Texas.

The 16–13 decision, achieved on a 37-yard field goal by second-string kicker Tony DiRienzo with 5:25 left and some swarming defensive play the rest of the way, obviously was hardly the classic stampede some had expected. It will be worth just as much in the record book, however, as OU's 52–13 humiliation of Texas a year ago. Now the Sooners have won four straight in this ancient rivalry but you might ask if they would be celebrating once again if Texas had punted.

You might, but Royal wouldn't.

"I would go for it again if I had it do over," he said.

Keeping the ball and moving at least close enough for one more shot by Billy Schott, who had boosted Texas' lead to 13–7 in the third quarter with his second field goal, overshadowed anything else from Texas' viewpoint. The Longhorn defense had played nobly most of the way and it was conceivable they might have made the most of one more modest lead.

Well, so much for what might have been. What happened was Oklahoma played well enough to win under tremendous pressure, a condition the Sooners hadn't known in a long time. And Texas lost with dignity—a bruising, grudging dignity.

It was an afternoon filled with suspense and Oklahoma faced some more when it left town. What will this squeaker do for the Sooners' standing in the Associated Press's national rankings?

After averaging 584.3 yards total offense and 54.3 points in three previous victories, tops in both categories on the NCAA chart, they stood No. 2 behind Ohio State. They may sag some now in the eyes of the sports writers across the land who vote in that one.

They're not sweating the UPI poll, of course. The national board of coaches which votes in that one refused to consider the Sooners because they're on probation. For most of Saturday afternoon though, they were much more disturbed about being in bad with the Longhorns.

Oklahoma came into this one favored by three to four touchdowns but soon realized it was not facing the sluggish Texas team which had lost to Texas Tech, 26–3, two weeks earlier. The Sooners quickly received two great opportunities when cornerback Eric Van Camp grabbed fumbles which snuffed out Texas' first two possessions at the Longhorn 35 and 27. But each time the Texas defense, less distinguished but obviously just as determined, got the ball back the same way.

Joe Washington, the wondrous halfback who was to spend a hard afternoon gaining 122 yards on 26 carries, broke for his biggest run of 13 yards on that first Sooner possession but lost the ball to linebacker Bill Hamilton on the Texas 6. Next time it looked like Oklahoma was for real when it punched to a first down on the 3. But Steve Davis, the usually smooth quarterback, was blasted loose from the ball by Hamilton on the next play just before he reached the goal line. Longhorn halfback Sammy Mason chased it down in the end zone and suddenly Texas was taking over again out at its 20.

If the Longhorns had needed another shot of inspiration in the early minutes, keeping the Sooners off the scoreboard this way did it. From there on most of the first half was closely fought with neither offense receiving much encouragement until the Sooners got the ball on the Texas 43 after a 15-yard penalty against Raymond Clayborn, who interfered with Washington's fair catch of a punt.

Davis began to move the Sooners then. Three plays later he tore toward his right from the Texas 22, broke free on halfback Grant Burget's block and fled for a touchdown. John Carroll, the old reliable kicker, converted for a 7–0 lead and the crowd wondered if Texas might falter now.

Nope, instead Clayborn raced 57 yards to the OU 38 on a crisscross kickoff return and Texas had its best field position of the first half. The Steers pushed to the 22 but there on third-and-six Akins was thrown for a two-yard loss by end Jimbo Elrod and linebacker Rod Shoate, two of those OU numbers you saw plenty of in this one. That left it to Schott to kick a 41-yard field goal with 16 seconds left and the Sooners found themselves pondering a nervous 7–3 half-time lead.

Texas turned the game in its favor with a big third quarter. Carroll somehow sliced a punt only 13 yards upfield and the Longhorns got the ball on the Sooner 33. Campbell contributed the key yardage from there, making nine on a third-and-six from the 29 and wrapping it up three plays later when he burst up the middle from the 12 and scored easily with tackle Rick Thurman and guard Will Wilcox throwing key blocks.

The Steers gained steam from there. Late in the quarter they launched their longest drive, from their 20 to the OU 23, but LeRoy Seimon and Elrod tossed Campbell for a two-yard loss on second-and-four and Texas ultimately settled for Schott's 38-yard field goal.

Then Oklahoma, which hadn't trailed in the fourth quarter since it was forced to come back for a 24–20 win over Miami over a year ago, came on strong. The Sooners staged their best drive, a 66-yarder, for the tying TD. Billy Brooks scored it from 49 yards out on a slick end-around on third-and-seven which saw him escape down the right sidelines after some nifty execution, blocking, and footwork.

Then Carroll, a senior and the regular kicker for the past two seasons, sent the ball wide to the right on the extra-point attempt. It was 13–13 and Texas came back for that push to the moment of decision at midfield. That's where the Longhorns saw in one play what this whole game would wind up meaning to them. They got what they were going after, then they lost it.

HE'S A THROWBACK—WAY BACK

By Joe Soucheray

From the Minneapolis Tribune

Copyright, ©, 1974, Minneapolis Tribune

Ohio Stadium sits on the east bank of the brown Olentangy River like an old factory. Two smokestacks from the Ohio State Power Plant building rise up behind it and pennant poles around the horseshoe top look like lightning rods. The stadium is greasy factory gray, with ugly black water stains drooling down its stone sides. The cathedral front is dished out and frescoed with flowers from the Buckeye tree.

It is a period piece, from the Roaring Twenties.

If you put a steamwhistle up there and blew that whistle at four o'clock, it would not look strange to see 1,000 men with pug caps trudge out with black lunch pails and blink in the sunlight.

The last man out would be a bull of a white-haired man with a white shirt rolled at the sleeves and a green eye shade like foremen in factories wear. He would blink in the sun with his men and tell them all they had done a good day's work. The men would nod and filter through the gates to go home to their families.

The man in the eye shade then would worry about his men because they would be out of his control. Only superfluous things are accomplished in a superfluous world. Production, fulfillment of goals, sweat, teamwork, these are the elements of a wholesome and spirited life.

The men would return day after day, year after year, building, learning defeat, loving victory. Dedicated to their leader, to their work and to each other.

What else is there?

Woody Hayes says that football is the perfect anachronism. Because he believes football is the last look at what's right with America, it is football that gives him his purest pleasure and it is through football that he acts out a life of values that he fears are disappearing from society.

"Football is unique and good," Woody says. "Where else in life do you see dedication and teamwork and spirit? People enjoy it because it is reassuring to them to see good things."

In 23 years as head coach at Ohio State, he has raised football to an institution unsurpassed in Columbus (Ohio State has led the nation in 21 of those 23 years in home attendance). He has disciples, and to him and the true believers football isn't even a game any more. It's a function, as natural and necessary as breathing.

"Now do you know what our governor (John Gilligan) told Gerald Ford when Ford became president?" Woody says. "Governor told him, 'Sir, don't you think foreign policy is going to change. No sir. Foreign policy is still to beat Michigan.'"

Every Saturday, nearly 88,000 strong, the fans march into that old gray period piece to delight in fresh victory brought to them by a period piece named Wayne Woodrow Hayes.

Woody Hayes was born in 1913 in Clifton, Ohio. He lived through stern times. He played tackle and earned an English and history degree from Denison (Ohio) University. He joined the navy. He became a war historian, and says World War II was too dull, as wars go. He coached, first at Mingo Junction then New Philadelphia High then back to Denison and then to Miami of Ohio and finally to Ohio State in 1951. His Buckeye teams, going into this season, have won 159, lost 49 and tied eight. He has won nine conference titles, three national championships and four Rose Bowl victories.

His teams are fueled by an efficient and far-reaching recruiting machine that dumps blue-chip players at his door every year. He chews them up and spits them out, men enough to lick the world.

If you talk football with Woody, you talk good things because that is all he admits to knowing. He works out of Room 147 in the Ernie Biggs Athletic Training Facility over on the north side of the campus near the agricultural buildings at the edge of the Buckeye Village, where married students live. Ernie Biggs was a trainer at Ohio State.

Woody's office is nondescript, windowless with a small chalk board, some books and a red leather cot where Woody sleeps the deep hours of the night away, too busy to drive to his home in the suburbs. He can step into the hall and be in touch with his assistants.

Across from him is a training room and equipment room, where men sit at a row of old Singers repairing shoulder pads and uniforms.

Woody doesn't look like a football coach. His voice is soft. He is fleshy. His sportcoat sleeves are too long and his fingers work nervously at the end of the sleeves. His lips curl and his head lists to the right as he speaks.

"You know," says Woody—who has a habit of saying "you know" —"Young people, these young writers particularly, they want to tear down and destroy institutions. They want to twist things. You know what this is? This is permissiveness. These young people who want to destroy are unloading their own guilt feelings and this is destroying our country. Now, you know, you don't see this with our young people in football."

There is a knock on the door. Woody pauses and shakes his head.

"Open it," he says.

"Hey coach, you have my tickets for the game?"

Woody looks at the player and clicks his tongue. He stares up at his blackboard, as if he doesn't believe he promised this player some tickets. He sees his name.

"Well dammit, then," he finally says. "Here." But he is smiling.

"I am close to my players," he says when the player departs. "Now you take your old-time coaches, your Bernie Biermans, your Colonel Blaiks, your General Neylands, your Knute Rocknes. No, not Rockne, I don't know about him. These old coaches held players at an arm's length. They didn't have to get close to them. Today in our changing society the greatest assurance people have in life is keeping in touch. It reassures me to know my players, to keep close to them.

"I like to sense the kids. You know, I go to all the training table meals with the kids. Now, I don't eat, but I'll have a cup of coffee and talk and listen to the kids. I like to know what they're thinking. You know, I can eat a kid out on the field, just chew him up every which way, but I can take that same kid and soap his back in the showers. And I've done it many times.

"The other day I asked a kid a question and he didn't hear me and says 'What?' I said to him, 'What did you say?' Then I cracked him across the belly. . . . Then I told him, 'Now you start that question over again.' He said he was sorry and began more politely.

"You know, you don't put up with bad manners. You let a kid get away with bad manners and he'll try you again. You see, every organization needs discipline and formality."

On the Friday before a recent home game Woody steps into the hall to herd the players to the bus. When Tyrone Harris walks past him, Woody looks puzzled.

"Who's that guy?" Woody demands of an assistant.

"Ty Harris," the assistant says.

"Ty, Tyrone," says Woody. "Now don't you have a better coat than that?"

"Whatchamacallit went to the dorm to get it, coach."

"What?" Woody asks.

"Uh, whatchamacallit went to the dorm to get it for me."

"Well goddamnit then, here, wear one of mine." Woody and Tyrone go into Woody's office and Tyrone comes out wearing a genuine Woody Hayes sportcoat. Tyrone almost rips it in half every time he takes a breath.

On the Friday nights before home games, in a bar called the Grog Shop, in the very hotel where Woody and his men sleep, a not very good group sings of the superfluous things of life. But as if on cue, the hairy singer wraps his sweaty hands around the microphone and breathes into it, "Well how about O-Hio State, they gonna win?" Everyone freezes, but then the waitresses in the micro leatherette skirts and the boys in the group and the people at the tables sing out in boozy unison, "Oh, yeah, we will. We."

On Saturday Woody's Ohio Stadium is a phantasmagoria of past and present glories. Pennants fly from their standards. Gray doesn't look gray intermingled with the colors of the rainbow. Rah-Rah college fight music sings from sideshow bullhorn speakers on concession stands from which hustle Buckeye buttons and Buckeye flags and Buckeye seat cushions and Buckeye Buckeyes.

The Olentangy sparkles, people line its banks to watch the Ohio State marching band work out on the regulation football field marked off for them on the parking lot. The unlucky, who want to be disciples, walk aimlessly with two, three, four fingers raised, silently hoping for a ticket score.

The afternoon flies. The Buckeyes whip Wisconsin 52–7 and Woody again delivers his followers from the pain of Watergate and inflation and war and confusion.

The people leave. The stadium takes on a gloomy factory air. The players leave, step outside with their tote bags and check the sky.

Woody is the last man out. Before he leaves he revels in the victory, talks for an hour to sports writers who will transcribe every single word for Sunday editions.

"Ah, football," he said. "You know what's most interesting about football besides the people playing it? The action, the reaction and the hit-em'-where-they-ain't."

"What about losing?"

Woody cuts a look to kill. His eyes burn, he clicks his tongue. He can't believe the question. Losing is the destruction of production, the unfulfillment of goals and, yes, a breakdown in teamwork.

"Losing," Woody sputters. "Losing! Jesus, we don't talk about losing."

The last man out almost gags.

MADDEN SENDS IN A PLAY

By Glenn Dickey

From the San Francisco Chronicle

© Chronicle Publishing Co., 1974

Trailing by four points with no time-outs left and 96 seconds remaining, the Raiders marched 52 yards for a touchdown to beat the Cincinnati Bengals, 30–27, before 51,821 at the Oakland Coliseum yesterday.

The Raiders used all but eight of the seconds allotted them, scoring when Charlie Smith swept right end from two yards out on a third-down play, diving into the end zone when it seemed he might be stopped.

The play was sent in by coach John Madden, and it was a risky one, because the Raiders would not have been able to get off another had Smith been tackled in bounds. "Smith got the game ball," said Madden after the game, adding after a dramatic pause, "for not being tackled."

This game was an improbable one from the start. Helped by Raider mistakes (including a fumble that set up a touchdown and a whopping five offsides penalties in the first half), the Bengals swept to an early 14–3 lead, only to see the Raiders come back for a 20–14 lead in the third quarter.

The Bengals came back to take the lead at 21–20, the Raiders hit a field goal to make it 23–21, but Cincinnati scored again to make it 27–23.

Then, it really got interesting.

With eight minutes remaining after the final Cincinnati score, the Raiders moved from their 30 to the Bengals' 31, and seemed on their way to a go-ahead touchdown. But a third-down pass from Ken Stabler to Cliff Branch mysteriously missed at the 15, Branch moving one way and the pass going another, and they had to kick.

Only a little more than three minutes remained by this time, and the Raiders used up some more—and got a delay of the game penalty—to make sure they knew what they were doing. What they were doing was punting.

"Fans think of that as a give-up play," said Madden after the game, "but it really isn't. We had to figure that our defense could hold them and we could get the ball back."

Punter Ray Guy did his job perfectly, putting the ball out at the Cincinnati eight, and the Bengals took over with exactly three minutes remaining. The Bengals got a first down at the 18—which was not in the Raiders' plans—and then the Oakland defense took charge.

On first down, Boobie Clark was smeared by Gerald Irons and Dan Conners, and time was called—1:54 remaining. On second down, Clark got three, and time was called—1:49. On third down, Clark got two, and another time—1:43.

Then Dave Green punted, George Atkinson took a fair catch at the Oakland 48, and it was the Raiders' ball, with 1:36 left.

Stabler threw to Fred Biletnikoff for 12 yards on the right sideline, with only four seconds elapsed. Then, with the Cincinnati defense looking for more sideline passes, Stabler twice hit tight end Bob Moore, first for 14 and then for 12, the Raiders each time going to the line of scrimmage without a huddle.

With a first down on the 14, Stabler twice threw incomplete, and time was no longer as much of a factor as the downs. Then, Stabler hit on perhaps the key play of the drive.

"I was looking for a pass down the middle," said Stabler, "and I took a long time, because I knew the Cincinnati defense was dropping deep. Then I saw Mike Siani at the right sideline, waving his arms like crazy."

Siani was waving his arms because he was open, and Stabler quickly threw his way. Siani caught it at the five and was run out at the one, and the Raiders had first and goal with 33 seconds left.

Suddenly faced with a situation where they had enough time, the Raiders decided to run, but Marv Hubbard was stopped for a yard loss by outside linebacker Al Beauchamp, and then Stabler threw incomplete for Branch, and the officials missed what seemed to be an obvious pass interference call on Branch.

Then Madden sent in the sweep, reasoning that it would take that to get outside the Bengals, who had massed six men on the line of scrimmage, and also that Smith might also be able to get out of bounds if he didn't get into the end zone. But Smith was determined to get into the end zone. He leaped over a Cincinnati defender at the goal line, and that was it.

The Bengals had enough time to get off one play after the ensuing kickoff, but the Raiders deployed most of their defense just short of their own goal line and Skip Thomas intercepted a desperation pass by Ken Anderson.

And that kept the Raiders, now 5–1, in first place by a game and a half in the AFC West.

The early going gave no hint of the final outcome as it seemed for a time that the Bengals might run away from the mistake-prone Raiders. After George Blanda opened the scoring with a remarkable 49-yard field goal—by far his longest of the year—the Bengals came back to score two first quarter touchdowns in impressive fashion.

The first came immediately, as the Bengals drove 72 yards in seven plays. The biggest play was the first one, a 60-yard pass play from Anderson to rookie John McDaniel, making his first catch of the season a beauty.

McDaniel got behind Willie Brown on a fly pattern and would have had a touchdown if he had kept his feet on the slippery turf, which was a day-long problem for everybody. Instead, McDaniel fell down making the catch at the 20, then got up and ran to the 12 before Atkinson caught him.

It took the Bengals six more plays from there, but they finally got in when fullback Doug Dressler skirted left end from a yard away. Brown hit him at the goal line but Dressler's momentum easily carried him in.

The next Bengal score was a direct result of Raider generosity. First Moore fumbled after catching a Stabler pass and Sherman White recovered at the 34. The Raiders later were detected offside on a play in which Anderson was sacked and fumbled, with Horace Jones recovering.

Given that reprieve, the Bengals went in to score, again in seven plays, with Clark getting the final three yards.

The Raiders closed to 14–10 with Blanda's 31-yard field goal just three seconds before the end of the half, and then went ahead in the third quarter with two touchdowns. The first was set up by a Jack Tatum interception, which brought the ball to the Cincinnati 4, and the Raiders scored two plays later when Hubbard went over from the 1.

The second TD was on a 61-yard drive in seven plays with Pete Banaszak getting the final yard.

But then, just when the Raiders seemed to be taking command,

Stabler was sacked by Mike Reid and fumbled, White again recovering, this time at the 35, and the Bengals took the lead by going for the touchdown in seven plays, Anderson hitting Bob Trumpy with a 10-yard pass for the score.

The Raiders took the lead on an 18-yard field goal by Blanda, and then Cincinnati scored again—the big play being a 47-yard Anderson pass to Isaac Curtis, and the touchdown a two-yard run by Dressler—to take the lead at 27–23 and set up the closing heroics, and a long, long plane ride home for the Bengals.

WHAT GOES THROUGH A FIELD GOAL KICKER'S MIND?

By Doug Mintline

From the Flint Journal

Copyright, ©, 1974, Booth Newspapers, Inc.

Mike Lantry
University of Michigan
Ann Arbor, Michigan

Dear Mike:

I've often wondered just what goes through a field goal kicker's mind, especially when a game hinges on whether the ball splits the uprights or misses.

I have had many chances to chat with football players in that position and it seems to me nothing can produce a greater thrill than to win a game in such a circumstance or a greater sense of sadness in failure.

Yet it seems to me the final feeling is one of having attained the position of being called upon in just such a situation. Certainly percentages figure in the ultimate result, good or bad, but the long-range assessment is what really counts.

It is with this in mind that I agree with your coach, Bo Schembechler, who said last Saturday that nobody should place the burden of Michigan's 12–10 defeat on you just because your 33-yard field goal attempt with 16 seconds remaining barely missed.

I've had a full day to think about the game and the position you were placed in to determine the outcome. I wondered what has been going through your mind, your wife's mind. I wondered what your son might think some day when he's old enough to understand.

There are some, Mike, who don't realize you weren't recruited for football at Michigan. There are others who don't realize you are 26

years old and a Vietnam veteran. There are still others who don't
realize how you walked onto the U of M gridiron, proved your ability
and then went on to become the greatest extra point and field goal
kicker in Wolverine history.

Perhaps that's little consolation at this moment, when all of your
friends, the M seniors, are lamenting the fact they went 30–2–1
without ever getting a chance to play in the Rose Bowl. It just
doesn't seem right, does it?

Yet things don't always turn out the way we dream. Even the goals
we work so hard for, we sometimes don't achieve. It's so easy to say
an inch here or there could have made the difference, because that's
true.

Certainly there are things of far greater importance in our lives
than football games, and it's my guess your experiences, both good
and bad, will serve you well in preparing to meet more serious
things ahead.

I even wonder if the things you learned in Vietnam aren't more
important than whatever feeling results from making or missing a
field goal.

Certainly Coach Schembechler has endured some difficult moments because of an inch here or an inch there, yet he also has
learned through the hardship of a heart attack that life is a constant
challenge worth facing, no matter what the disappointments along
the way.

It's my feeling that once the bitterness of being so close to an
outright Big Ten Conference championship, a Rose Bowl bid, a
perfect season, and a national championship has passed, you will be
able to look back on these few dark days and understand the loss
of such goals weren't your fault.

Sure, the opportunity was there. You'll never forget that, trying
that kick over and over again, wishing and hoping it traveled just a
little more to the right. It's my guess there'll even be some kidding
about such a sad moment once it finds a rightful place in history.

Yet much more important is that you realize now and savor later
the fantastic record. How about those 50- and 51-yarders that did
go through?

There has to be a deep sense of satisfaction about kicking 113 out
of 118 extra points and 21 out of 45 field goal attempts for 186
points during an era matched by no other major college team in the
nation.

Hopefully, that strong left leg of yours will provide an opportunity with the pros and, as such, another chance for glory with a kick here or there that not only helps a team win, but actually provides the winning margin in the last few seconds.

It could be you aren't even interested in the pros. Even if you are, it could be you won't make it.

That's not the point.

What does matter is how on this day, when Ohio State has been selected as the Big Ten Rose Bowl representative, that you don't try to shoulder the responsibility for the Wolverines being left as co-champions for three straight years without a Pasadena trip.

The pressure of standing before 80,000 to 100,000 spectators and having to attempt such a field goal as you faced last Saturday and other times must be tremendous. Yet so many times, luck and skill were with you. The snap from center was just right, the placement just right, the swing of your leg just right. What a thrill when it works that way.

The point is it doesn't always work just right and on this occasion, by ever so little, an important kick missed, I feel so very much that a little of all of us who wanted Michigan to win and you to succeed went out to you in that terrible moment of despair.

History will ease that despair, Mike, but nothing can tarnish your outstanding career during a three-year stint that saw you and your teammates lose only twice and then by a total of only five points.

Best of luck to you and your family in the more important days ahead.

THE FIRST YEAR

By Ron Martz

From the St. Petersburg Times

They've been slandered, libeled, heard words they never read in the Bible. They've been stabbed in the back, cheated, lied to, and kicked from Washington, D.C., to Annapolis, Maryland, to Norfolk, Virginia, to Orlando and still no one wants them.

The Florida Blazers' first season in the World Football League has been an artistic success, an artistic success which took place in the midst of a colony of muggers and thieves and morons.

No one knows the trouble they've seen, Lord, no one really knows.

And it all ended with as much uncertainty as it began.

Enter laughing.

First, Florida's Miller Farr kicked Birmingham's Jimmy Edwards in the butt.

Then, Florida's Billie Hayes stole the ball game.

Hayes was chased into the Florida locker room by Birmingham's Paul Costa.

Costa was chased into the Florida locker room by the Florida Blazers.

Outside the Birmingham locker room the doorkeeper and a television cameraman began fighting.

Inside the Birmingham locker room, where winning players of the first-ever World Bowl were standing in athletic supporters pouring champagne over one another, team president Mrs. Carol Stallworth, a buxom, charming blonde, walked around and hugged the players who had been caught with their pants down. . . .

While a Jefferson County deputy sheriff waited to confiscate their pants because of delinquent payments on bills.

Welcome to the World Football League.

Exit laughing.

World Bowl I was an ignominious end to an ignominious first season for the World Football League, a first season in which a dozen starry-eyed investors had plunked down a few hundred dollars each, bought themselves professional football franchises, dubbed it all the WFL and went on to lose $20 million.

What had been so nobly launched on July 10, 1974, so ignobly ended on December 4, 1974, in this city [Birmingham] of soot and smog and steel in a tragic-comic game filled with errors, brawls, pathos, vainglorious attempts at heroism, true heroism, good football, and a touchdown that was but wasn't.

It shall be recorded in the archives of football that on December 4, 1974, in Birmingham, Alabama, that the Birmingham Americans beat the Florida Blazers for World Bowl I by the score of 22–21.

The touchdown that was but wasn't.

It was a victory in spirit only. There is no money in the league. The Americans have not been paid for nearly two months. The Florida Blazers have been without pay for 14 weeks. Neither team wanted to play.

If all they had to play for was pride or the spirit of winning or perhaps for each other, the Blazers were denied the first two. Denied even their pride. The touchdown that was but wasn't.

Exit crying.

On January 28, 1974, Jack Pardee accepted the head coaching job with the Washington Ambassadors of the new World Football League. Pardee, a large, kindly man who had been an outstanding linebacker with the Washington Redskins of the National Football League (NFL) and who had overcome a mild form of cancer during his playing career, was ready to coach.

Pardee saw the job with the WFL team as a chance to introduce himself to the job of coaching, to get in on "the ground floor of a new league, to build my own team the way I think a team should be built," as he so often put it.

So Jack Pardee became the first man to jump from the NFL to the WFL.

For some time Gary Davidson had been thinking that the National Football League was monopolizing professional football. He was convinced there was room for competition, provided the new league was established properly. A Newport Beach, California, lawyer, Davidson had been instrumental in the formation of the American Basketball Association to rival the National Basketball Association and the World Hockey Association to compete with the National Hockey League.

The same thing, Davidson thought, could be done in football.

On October 2, 1973, the World Football League officially swung into operation. It was to be a textbook study on how to develop a profit-making corporation from the ground up. It would study mistakes of other similar corporations and benefit by those mistakes.

The uniforms would be stylized and color coordinated.

The team nicknames would reflect items indigenous to particular franchises. No "Bears" or "Lions" or "Eagles" for the WFL. Instead, there were the Chicago Fire, the Portland Storm, the Philadelphia Bell and the Southern California Sun.

In an attempt to inject some change into what was becoming a very staid game in the NFL, Davidson decided there would be some changes made in the rules, like . . .

Kickoffs from the 30-yard line. Goal posts moved to the back of the end zones. Missed field goal attempts returned to the line of scrimmage. No fair catches on punts. Touchdowns worth seven points. Extra point kicks eliminated and action points worth one point gained by running or passing after a touchdown.

And there would be no perfunctory exhibition schedule as in the NFL. All 20 games on the schedule would count in the WFL. And those games would be played on Wednesday nights with one game nationally televised on Thursday nights. No sense in bucking heads with the NFL the first year. Maybe next year.

The first inkling that perhaps all was not as well as it appeared with the WFL came with Pardee and the Washington Ambassadors. When the Ambassadors found they could not play in Washington, D.C.'s, Robert F. Kennedy Stadium because the Redskins played there, the Ambassadors tried to move to Annapolis, Maryland.

The "No Vacancy" sign was out in Annapolis.

They tried to move to Norfolk, Virginia, and became the Virginia Ambassadors.

Another "No Vacancy" sign.

About this time, the NFL was meeting in Miami to consider expansion possibilities. Rommie Loudd of Orlando, a black man who had once played the part of a slave in the movie *The Ten Commandments* and had ferried Moses around Egypt, was ferrying the hopes of pro football for central Florida much as he had done Moses in the movie. When it became apparent Tampa was favored over Orlando, Loudd was miffed.

"The NFL is still in the eighteenth century," he said. "They awarded a franchise to a city, not to a group of investors."

So Loudd looked north where the Ambassadors were looking for a home and with a group of investors purchased the team.

And they became the Florida Blazers.

In late March, 1974, Larry Csonka, winner of the Most Valuable Player award in the Miami Dolphins' second straight Super Bowl victory, stood in the men's room of a Toronto restaurant, talking to his lawyer Ed Keating and doing what comes naturally.

When the two left the men's room, the WFL was off and running.

A multi-million-dollar deal would bring Csonka and Miami teammates Paul Warfield and Jim Kiick to the Toronto Northmen for the 1975 WFL season. The WFL quickly became a bargaining lever for other NFL players who were having problems with their contracts. Lured by big money talk, such players as Calvin Hill and Craig Morton of the Dallas Cowboys, Ted Hendricks of the Baltimore Colts, Ted Kwalick of the San Francisco 49ers, and Ken Stabler of the Oakland Raiders signed WFL contracts for future seasons.

Somewhat later, an aging Leroy Kelly was cut by the Cleveland Browns and Oakland Raiders and signed with the Chicago Fire of the WFL.

"I don't look at playing in the World Football League as a comedown," said Kelly. "What brings me to Chicago? Money, dough. The 'Mean Green,' my man, is where it is all at."

Kelly, like so many others, has yet to see the "Mean Green."

But the WFL training camps opened with much optimism because of the signings. When those camps opened in early June they became havens for every NFL castoff, misfit, miscreant, crumbum, or armchair quarterback who wanted a shot at the bigs. Some teams opened camp with more than 300 people on their rosters. Some of them were players.

In Harrisonburg, Virginia, the Blazers, already three times moved, opened camp and nobody showed up. Directions and airline tickets had not been properly disseminated. Besides that, electricity in the dormitories and offices had been turned off.

And away we go.

The Blazers arrived in Florida by Auto-Train, a 17-hour trip from Virginia to Sanford, with stops in picturesque towns such as Rocky Mount, North Carolina, Florence, South Carolina, and Savannah, Georgia. Seventeen hours.

When the train stopped in Sanford, linebacker Billy Hobbs

opened his weary eyes, stepped off the train, sniffed the air and proclaimed: "Fellas, we made it to the big time."

Hobbs thought he was in Texas.

At 8:07 P.M. on July 10, 1974, the Florida Blazers kicked off to the Hawaiians in Orlando's Tangerine Bowl to open the first game of the World Football League. The game was played 15 minutes from Disney World. Disney World is the home of Mickey Mouse. Mouse did not attend.

The Blazers still won 8–7.

On July 11, 1974, the Sharks beat the New York Stars 14–7 in the first nationally televised WFL game.

Shortly before 2 A.M., after the Sharks game, WFL Commissioner Gary Davidson was dancing on top of a table with a lissome blonde in a downtown Jacksonville nightclub. His baby had been born.

The afterbirth was still to come.

But attendance reports for the first week were more than encouraging. Philadelphia reported 55,534 in attendance, Jacksonville 59,112.

That same morning in that same nightclub, Bud Asher, the head coach of the Sharks, who in one magnificent leap had gone from high school coaching to professional coaching, strode to the bandstand, unceremoniously dropped his pants and revealed a silver shark sewn on the butt of his underwear.

Welcome to the World Football League.

Welcome to the big time.

Those were weeks of contentment, of happiness and hopefulness for the WFL. Attendance figures remained encouraging. A Lou Harris poll revealed 41 percent of those surveyed thought the formation of the WFL a good idea. The NFL players were striking and the WFL was the only game in town. The WFL players and coaches were talking about being on the same level of ability as the NFL. And they laughed and danced.

Then something happened. The WFL became an illusion.

In Philadelphia where 55,534 people were reported on the Bell's opening night and 64,719 the next week, it was revealed that only 20,000 of those people paid to get in.

The joke was not so bad in Jacksonville, where of the more than 100,000 people reported for the first two games only 44,000 were admitted free under one pretext or another.

The yellow brick road had ended.

When the free tickets declined, attendance declined. Owners began searching for new investors because without money from ticket sales they could not cover expenses. When investors couldn't be found in one area, a franchise moved.

The Houston Texans moved to Shreveport, Louisiana, and became the Steamers.

The New York Stars moved to Charlotte, North Carolina, and became the Hornets.

In Detroit, the Wheels ran out of money. When the team ran out of adhesive tape it was not until a medical supplies salesman donated a case of tape that the players' fragile joints could be taped. One player on the Wheels asked for a shoelace and was denied.

Unable to operate on or off a shoestring budget, the Wheels struck their tents and died an ignoble death.

In Jacksonville, owner Fran Monaco borrowed $27,000 from Asher to meet a payroll. Payroll met, Asher, who had been described as a combination Don Shula, Knute Rockne, and Vince Lombardi, was kicked out the first available door by Monaco. But his demise was followed closely by the team's. Monaco, the 5-foot-2 owner who loved to roam the sidelines and give instructions to his players, then shower with them after games, capitulated.

And then there were 10.

In Portland, Oregon, a Storm fan attended a Sunday practice, then took the players to lunch, lighting up a bulb in a front office man's brain.

"We need local businessmen to take our players to lunch," said the front office man.

In Charlotte, the Hornets had their dirty uniforms confiscated by sheriff's deputies until they promised to pay some of their bills.

The deputies returned them as they found them—dirty.

No place were the league's problems more evident than in Orlando, where the Blazers were doing terrific on the field, rotten at the gate, and worse in the front office.

Loudd was having problems getting the city of Orlando to help with minor things at the decrepit Tangerine Bowl. Nobody wanted to take any responsibility. So the crowds stayed away. And racism began to creep into discussions.

In provincial Orange County, everybody huffed and nobody moved. Loudd wanted to move to Atlanta. There was no field available. He wanted to make the team public property, like the Green Bay Packers. Nobody wanted the team. And the Tangerine Bowl decayed.

After a late August game against the Houston Texans, a Blazer coach picked up his right shoe and was about to put it on when he saw a frog in it. When he looked around there were frogs all over the semi-underground locker room. Some were hopping madly. Some were hopping slowly.

"Hey!" said the coach. "What the hell's this frog doing in my shoe? There's a frog in my shoe. What the HELL's this frog doing in my shoe?"

Welcome to the big time.

Welcome to the World Football League.

Midway through the 14 weeks of going without paychecks, the Blazers voted not to play unless they were paid. The league obligingly sent along the checks, the team played, and the next morning the checks bounced all the way back to Newport Beach.

All over the World Football League, players were sending wives and kids home to mother. Cars were being repossessed. Back rent of several months was being demanded. Bills were piling up and piling up and credit rapidly was dwindling.

Gary Davidson was ousted as commissioner of the WFL in a power play move by Chicago Fire owner Tom Origer. Origer later pulled his team out of the league and is attempting to sell the franchise. The WFL was in chaos.

Things got so bad at the Blazers' office that the Xerox machine to duplicate statistics broke down and there was not enough money to have it repaired. But it didn't matter. There wasn't enough money for postage.

Still the players persisted.

"It was a week to week thing," said Florida running back Tommy Reamon. "There was never any one point where we got together and said we're going all the way with this. But I figure I've got a product to sell and that product is my body. That's the way a lot of the young guys on the team feel. I've got my body to sell and I've got that TV exposure so I'm going to go out there every week and do the best I can and know that somebody is going to see me. Somebody."

Larry Grantham played for the New York Titans when the American Football League was started in 1960. Those were not good years. In 1969, he played on the New York Jets' Super Bowl champion team. That was a good year. Now he plays for the Florida Blazers. He doesn't know what to think of this year.

"I don't think I've learned a lot about cashing checks this season, but I've learned a lot about football from Jack Pardee and I've learned a lot about people. It's been one hell of an experience," said Grantham.

And so it goes among the Blazers. They speak in the trite and corny phrases athletes use when they are winning. They speak of love for one another and admiration for one another and a genuine respect for the coaching staff. Somehow, after 14 weeks of not being paid, after losing World Bowl I by a touchdown that was but wasn't, after front office mismanagement and league foulups, they seem to feel something unusual for one another.

Could this be love?

"I can't really put my finger on it," said quarterback Bob Davis. "This is an incredible bunch of people. I mean they have to be to put up with the things they've put up with this season."

Florida defensive back Ricky Harris said, "After ten years in pro football I've found out what the game is all about with these people. I love these guys."

Exit querulous.

These feelings of togetherness led the Blazers through play-offs that almost weren't and to World Bowl I which almost wasn't. The players originally wanted to give the title to Memphis and its 17–3 record outright. But insaner heads prevailed.

The original eight-team play-off format was scratched for three teams which was scratched for six teams which was kept. The Monday before World Bowl I, the Americans voted not to play. The next day, they relented. The play-offs and the World Bowl were to have been the epitome of the WFL's first season, the showcase event, complete with Don Perignon, dancing girls, colored lights, and hoopla that would make the Super Bowl look like Ted Mack's Original Amateur Hour.

And, in keeping with the poverty of the situation, a tax man was at Legion Field in Birmingham to skim off the top that which he could in order to help pay off the more than $100,000 in back taxes owed by the Americans. So the 70 percent share for the players— 60 to the winners and 10 to the losers—apparently will be minuscule. They couldn't even get 35,000 people out for the game.

Welcome to the World Football League.

Welcome to the big game.

What went wrong with the WFL?

What happened and why?

"I think the prime reason for our financial problems was the overoptimism of the owners," said Chris Hemmeter, the new president of the WFL. "Our problems surfaced around September or October because the owners had run out of season ticket money by then and didn't have any other revenue coming in."

Hemmeter has called for a financial restructuring of the league, better knowledge of who is buying into the league, more competent leadership, and expansion into major television markets.

"The ultimate survival of the WFL will be determined in February or March of next year," he said. "Whenever we talk about options that [dissolving the league] is one of the options. I don't foresee it at this point in time. Two weeks ago I did. If the program is there, the sport will carry itself. The sport will market itself. But from now on we'll play a little game called pay as you go."

Hemmeter was also the president of the Hawaiians and lost $3.5 million on his franchise, one of the league's more solvent. He told a news conference the day of World Bowl I he is ready to stick it out. All the way with WFL.

As Hemmeter outlined some of his plans for the league, his wife sat in the back row, busily doing a large green flower in needlepoint. A blond, vivacious woman, she was quite confident of her husband's abilities.

"If anybody can do it, Chris can," said Karen Hemmeter. "I think he can put this league back together again."

And all the king's horses and all the king's men . . .

The first year of the World Football League, a year of hard times and confusion and $20 million lost and a touchdown that was but wasn't and no one knowing for sure if there will be a WFL in 1975, is over, all over.

Like an expensive toy, it looked great at first, great before the rigors of everyday life and reality wore it down. And in the end there was nothing but confusion, and the future of the players was as nebulous as the future of the league.

Mike McBath, a defensive tackle for the Blazers and a Ph.D. in business, feels most of the players will have their lawyers try and get the money owed them. McBath will return to work for General Development "taking money from old people" and using "caviare helper" because times are tough but not that tough for Dr. McBath, who will worry about next year next year.

Bob Davis will write a book which he says will be the World Football League's *All the President's Men.*

Tommy Reamon, a rookie and one of the league's three most

valuable players, will go home and think of what has happened and hope somebody out there was watching.

Somebody.

Jack Pardee almost assuredly will not return to coach the Blazers. Detroit, Baltimore, and Atlanta of the NFL have all expressed an interest in his coaching ability. And although the work is more hazardous there, there's a paycheck every week.

The other Blazers will try to find work to pay off some of those long overdue bills and remember to forget what has gone before.

And so it ended in Birmingham, with Miller Farr kicking Jimmy Edwards in the butt and Paul Costa chasing Billie Hayes into the locker room and people fighting and a good-looking woman walking in on a bunch of near-naked men and hugging them and the deputies waiting to take *them* away, ha ha, and clowns laughing and people crying.

Nobody knows the trouble they've seen, Lord, nobody really knows.

DEAR MR. GARVEY

By Dave Klein

From the Newark Star-Ledger

Copyright, ©, 1974, Newark Morning Ledger Co.

Edward Garvey
NFL Players Association
Washington, D.C.

Dear Mr. Garvey:

As someone who used to play a little touch football on Saturdays, I feel I am eligible to join your union. I sure would like to, because you seem to be offering more to the players in your league than John D. Rockefeller made available to his children.

Recently, a copy of the NFL Players Association demands fell into these hands, and an immediate perusal of same left me with unbounded respect for your aims, objectives, and optimism.

First of all, I'd like to compliment you on certain phrases you used in your introduction to the team owners. Those that really stick out are "we accuse you of ignoring the injustices occasioned by head coaches and general managers who fine indiscriminately and who threaten disciplinary action if players exercise their first amendment freedoms" . . . "you are guilty of indifference to societal changes" . . . "the suffocating paternalism and suppression of constitutional rights in the NFL."

They were just great, Ed. Keep up the good work.

Then, in the part of your paper titled Demands, I just loved almost every one of them. I was particularly smitten by your proposed elimination of the option clause, the player waiver system, the commissioner, all fines, reserve lists, the commissioner's authority to discipline players, and all psychological and personality testing of players.

But all the good stuff is still to come. I was absolutely entranced by your training camp demands. No camp earlier than July 20 . . . no out-of-city camp for longer than ten days . . . no curfews . . . not more than three hours on the field per day, and your new pay scale for all players during the pre-season schedule.

You ask for $500 for the first game, $1,500 for the second, $2,000 for the third and fourth, $3,000 for the fifth and sixth and $7,000 for the seventh. That's spectacular. That means the players will get $19,000 before the season even starts. Beautiful.

But what really got it together was point 3 of the pre-season demands. Come on, you know. The one that says "if there is a ten-day training camp, the team must provide the player with the reasonable amenities to which men are normally accustomed." Unreal. If you mean what I think you mean, you can probably organize Xaviera and her group and get them to bring along the bottles, too.

The regular season stuff is pretty good, too. The $20,000 minimum salary for rookies and $25,000 for veterans is OK, but you're pretty sneaky about that, because don't we have to add the $19,000 for the pre-season games? That means minimums will be $39,000 and $44,000. Super.

Oh, yeah, that $30 per day travel expenses is a nice touch. I know some players who could save $27.50 every day they're on the road.

Now, your post-season demands. Masterstroke, if I may say so.

Like conference championships, when each member of winning AND losing teams gets not less than $15,000 or three-game checks, whichever is greater. And the Super Bowl, when the winning players get $25,000 and the losers $20,000. Beautiful. And you're right. I don't think the closeness of the money will take away any incentive, either.

I also like that stuff about a moratorium on synthetic turf fields and their replacement with natural grass when they wear out. And that business about two tickets for away games, four for home games and 500 (to the NFLPA) for the Super Bowl was fine. I especially liked that condition that the Super Bowl tickets be between the 20-yard lines and at least 20 rows up in the stadium.

All those other demands "with respect to other conditions of employment, pension and insurance" were terrific. The one about no player representative or NFLPA officer being cut or traded during the term of his office is a smacko idea. Nah, players wouldn't purposely elect an old friend who can't really cut it any more just to get him another year's salary. Of course not.

All those other points were well-taken, too. You're really doing a fine job for all those underpaid, abused, and exploited players. After all, somebody has to watch out for them or they might wind up playing for nothing, right?

By the way, what are you going to be doing this summer and fall? I know of a super little fishing cabin up in Maine you can rent cheap. From the looks of these demands, there won't be much else going on, you know?

WAS THE TICKET WORTH THE MONEY?

By Hank Inman

From The Daily Oklahoman

Copyright, ©, 1974, The Oklahoma Publishing Co.

So you think you got your money's worth when you saw Oklahoma skin a Kansas State Wildcat last Saturday afternoon?

Ha! Ha! If you paid the normal $7.25 for a ticket, and you think you're a wise spender, read on, brother, you may have been wasting more time watching the 63–0 debacle than you thought.

The late writer-singer Jim Croce exclaimed in one of his hits, "But there never seems to be enough time to do the things you want to do, once you find them." Why Jim even tried to "save time in a bottle," but all he got was a flask of empty dreams. But he didn't see OU play Kansas State in football.

The OU sports information office says the game officially started at 1:30 P.M. and ended at 4:15 P.M. Not being one who adds well, I had Addie Lee Barker figure up the total elapsed time. "That's two hours and 45 minutes," said Addie, "but our official stats say two hours, 15 minutes and they say that includes the intermission."

Fear not, Addie. The official stats aren't as far off as you think— they're farther off!

Being a native of the "Show Me" state, Missouri, I took a stop-watch to the K-State game to see how much actual playing time was involved. The watch was started as soon as Tony DiRienzo kicked off and stopped when the ball was dead.

The watch ran only from the time the center snapped the ball until the play was completed. Sounds simple enough. It is. But here's the shocker.

It took both teams a total of only 15 minutes, 24.7 seconds to run off 177 plays!

Oklahoma ran 94 plays for an average of 4.568 seconds per play, and a total figure of 7 minutes, 9.45 seconds. Kansas State meanwhile, ran 83 plays for a 5.856 per second average and a total of 8 minutes, 15.25 seconds.

The longest sustained drive of the day was Kansas State's opening try. The Wildcats used up 57.3 seconds in 12 plays—including a 7.2-second kickoff and return. The Sooners' most lengthy effort came on its second possession of the second quarter—55.4 seconds worth—but it fell fruitless.

Eight other scoring drives (not including Elvis Peacock's punt return for a TD) were marched off in convincingly quick fashion. Oklahoma scored its 63 points in four minutes, 16.8 seconds—an average of 4.780 seconds per play. By the way, it took Elvis 6.1 seconds to wiggle 54 yards for his TD.

The longest single play of the day, excluding punts and runbacks and kickoffs and returns, was a reverse to split receiver Billy Brooks midway through the second quarter. He covered 31 yards in 9.9 seconds.

The shortest play? Kansas State's Art Bailey fumbled the snap from center and Rod Shoate and Dewey Selmon fell on him in 1.9 seconds. That's movin'!

But back to money well spent. Consider the 15 minute, 24.7-second actual playing time. If you paid $7.25 for a ticket, that averages out to approximately 41 cents per minute. Depending on your financial status, that's expensive at $24.60 an hour.

However, sports fans, it took me considerably longer to add up times, write the story, etc. Four hours, 6 minutes, 53 seconds is what it took, coffee breaks not included.

But this is a triple-option story. Either you: (1) wasted your money at the game; (2) got what you thought was your money's worth; or (3) wasted 2 minutes, 19.7 seconds reading this story.

Basketball

NORTH CAROLINA STATE ENDS THE REIGN OF TERROR

By Dave Dorr

From the St. Louis Post-Dispatch

Copyright, ©, 1974, St. Louis Post-Dispatch

Nothing could be finer than to be in Carolina with David Thompson at the free throw line, staring the mystique of UCLA, the dynasty, the monster, eyeball to eyeball.

Who else but Thompson, the kid who left the dirt roads of nearby Shelby, a tiny mill town, to become a basketball legend? It was David vs. Goliath. It was the Great Rematch, and it was the Bruins who blinked.

UCLA's Decade of Dynasty died Saturday amid the shredded banners, hats, and pompoms that frenzied North Carolina State followers left behind when they chased their heroes to the dressing room.

The Wolfpack's sensational 80–77 victory in two overtimes in the semi-final round of the National Collegiate Athletic Association tournament knocked the Bruins on their NCAA crowns. It crumbled another record for UCLA in a season that has been up and down, in and out for the once-feared Walton Gang.

A season that, except for the final burial rites, is over. The reign of terror has been put to rest.

There was UCLA's shocking collapse at Notre Dame, a defeat that snapped the Bruins' record winning streak at 88. There was the double crash landing in Oregon and a scary triple overtime struggle past Dayton last week in the West Regional tournament.

And Saturday there was the Pack, snarling in its own den, wiping out the UCLA hope of an eighth straight national championship and tenth in 11 seasons. The Bruins had won 38 consecutive NCAA tournament games, another record.

All that's left for UCLA, now 25–4, is Monday night's third place game, an event that's for the birds, according to Bruins coach John Wooden.

North Carolina State, meanwhile, will take a 27-game winning streak, longest in the nation, and a 29–1 record into Monday night's new look championship game against 26–4 Marquette. Neither team has been in the title clash before.

The Wolfpack had been itching for a chance to get UCLA down here in the land of cornpone and grits since December when the Bruins beat NC State in St. Louis, 84–66, in a duel that had been billed the Dream Game.

The Pack, unbeaten last year but ineligible to play for the NCAA crown when the school was put on probation because of recruiting irregularities involving Thompson, now gets at its chance. The Pack is back.

"I thought all along," said NC State coach Norm Sloan, "that there would never be anything to equal our victory over Maryland [103–100 here at the Greensboro Coliseum] in the Atlantic Coast Conference tournament final.

"This game today was not exactly like it, but it was very much alike in tempo and style.

"Our greatest victory ever? No, we've had some great ones the last two seasons. If we win Monday, THAT will be our greatest."

Thompson was magnificent. The 6-foot-4 junior All-America leaper was around the rim all day, scoring 28 points and pulling down 10 rebounds. He scored 12 baskets, many of them on lob passes from 5-foot-5 1/2 guard Monte Towe or forward Tim Stoddard.

One of the differences in Saturday's game from that in St. Louis was the scoring of Thompson and UCLA's Keith Wilkes. Thompson was held to 17 points in December by Wilkes, while the Bruin forward pumped in 27.

Wilkes fouled out of Saturday's game with 34 seconds left in the overtime and finished with 15 points. Tom Burleson, the Pack's 7-foot-4 center, played UCLA's Bill Walton almost even. Burleson scored 20 points and grabbed 14 rebounds. Walton had 29 points and 18 rebounds.

As they have done before this season, the Bruins played erratically, even foolishly. UCLA twice blew leads that could have salted the game away. The Bruins steamed to a 57–46 lead midway in the second half behind Wilkes, Tommy Curtis, Walton, and Dave Meyers and led by 73–67 in the second overtime. But both times, the Bruins let the Pack off the hook.

"I would agree," said Wooden, "if you think we had the game in hand a couple of times. But we made too many critical mistakes. We took shots I didn't think we should have. North Carolina State took advantage of them and had the poise to come back.

"We've had trouble holding this season. We knew the string of titles had to end. It couldn't go on forever. I'm happy we had it as long as we did. We were close again today, but not close enough."

Wooden was asked if Saturday's game was a fair evaluation of the teams' strengths since the game was played in Wolfpack country.

"Well," said Wooden, smiling thinly, "we'd like to play them in Los Angeles, not necessarily at Pauley Pavilion but somewhere where we'd have 90 percent of the crowd for us. We've played them halfway [St. Louis] and now here. The crowd can have a tremendous effect."

The Pack caught UCLA at 63–63 in regulation time and then went to a delay game, stalling almost two minutes away. Walton and Thompson traded baskets to make it 65–65. NC State got the ball with 55 seconds to play and ran the clock down to :03 when Stoddard launched an unmolested jumper from 18 feet that missed.

UCLA called time out with :02 left. The clock had to be reset and a shot by Bruins guard Greg Lee was far too short.

In the first five-minute overtime, Burleson and Lee traded baskets to make it 67–67. They were the only points in the overtime. NC State again went to the delay, taking time out twice, the last one with 16 seconds to go. The Wolfpack played catch with the ball until they could work it to Burleson, whose short shot under Walton's arm squiggled out with four seconds left.

In the second overtime, Walton's two free throws and basket and a three-point play on a lay-up by Wilkes off a super assist by Curtis put the Bruins comfortably on top at 74–67, and it appeared that the Pack would not come back. They did.

Six straight points set up a bank shot by Thompson that got the Pack in front at 76–75 with 53 seconds left. Thompson's two free throws and a pair of foul shots by Towe, the hero of all little guys, clinched it. With the score 80–75, Walton made a meaningless jump shot with five seconds to go.

The final buzzer sounded. Bedlam. Pandemonium. The crowd of 15,829 shook old Greensboro Coliseum almost to its very foundations.

"Don't ask me where this team got its extra drive," said Sloan. "Before the season I said we had a chance to be one of the greatest teams ever. All I know is that pressure hasn't bothered them at all this year. I take that back. Mo Rivers in the first overtime said in the huddle, 'Won't somebody please hit one. I don't think I can go another overtime.' "

And on this day of amazing turnabouts, wonder never ceased. Bill Walton, the Howard Hughes of Los Angeles, talked. A little.

Climbing out of the shower, Walton retreated to a corner in the dressing room to sit down, eat a banana and rummage through his backpack that was hanging on a hook.

Would William the Conqueror play in Monday's consolation game?

"I just don't feel like talking now," he said. "Why don't you talk to those who do. I just want to put on my clothes and go home. I'm due for a rest. I'm a graduate now."

HIS FINAL BOW

By Blackie Sherrod

From The Dallas Times Herald

The greatest college player of all time—at least when the moon is right—closed his career with a masterful flourish.

Bill Walton was hunched under the UCLA basket, back to the net, red hair matted like a rug pad, freckles on his bony shoulders shining through sweat, arms dangling like independent spaghetti, mouth agape in a strangely youthful face on a frame like a fireman's extension ladder. Tom Sawyer, after surviving a giant clothes wringer.

Andre McCarter, a reserve UCLA guard, arched a high lazy pass calculated to drop just short of the rim. Walton went to meet it, skinny arms stretching above the rim beyond him. The ball seemed to hang there for him as it touched his fingertips. With a motion as gentle as a mother feeling for fever, he flicked it backward, never looking. Of course, the mesmerized ball fell through the net and Bill Walton had the last two points he would ever score for a college team.

The second half of the NCAA consolation game (for third place nationally) was not yet midway, but Walton trotted to the UCLA bench, in response to nobody's summons but his own. Teammate McCarter lifted his arms high above his head and started applause, parading around the court and looking up at the stands. Walton is not a popular figure with foreign fans, as few tall men are, but this time he got a standing ovation as if alien witnesses finally acknowledged that they may have been watching the most awesome college cager in history. And that he bowed out with a fantastic shot.

It was a meaningless game, almost embarrassing to play for

UCLA. Third place. Big deal. The Bruins win championships, like seven in a row. They never ask for a doggy bag. But they had been eliminated by North Carolina State in the semi-finals, despite a heroic Walton effort somehow buried in the Bruins' blow of three big leads.

Usually these consolation affairs attract all the attention of a bunion in a nudist colony. Maybe a couple thousand came to the gym early, watching the losers idly while stuffing hot dogs down their necks and waiting for the main event. But this night, there were 10,000 in the stands to see the fallen giants beat Kansas 78–61. They were to stay, of course, swelled by 5,000 more, to watch their darling North Carolina State run away with Marquette for the championship. But now Walton was the focal point.

In truth, there was much curiosity whether he would even stay around for the consolation game. He had never played in one. John Wooden, the coach, seemed almost helpless when he admitted he did not know if Walton and other seniors would even stay in town, after losing to the Wolfpack. Oh, Wooden had tried to cover by saying he always gave his seniors an "option" of playing in a consolation game. But oldtimers reached all the way back to 1963 before recalling UCLA ever playing in another consolation game. It was like Jack Dempsey saying he always gave an opponent 14 counts after knocking him down.

Walton and his friends already had set an NCAA record for individualism this year. At times, they operated independently of their strait-laced coach. Walton, Greg Lee, and Keith Wilkes took a ride Sunday and according to Lee they discovered some valid reasons for not playing. After all, they were seniors; they had no further discipline to heed. It might have been embarrassing to their school, their coach, the NCAA, but what the heck? Youth marches on.

Somebody talked them out of it. Wooden argued their absence would be an affront to Kansas, their third-place opponent. Somebody said Wilkes' parents also were a positive influence. So the trio showed.

"I'm delighted all my players were here and wanted to play," said Wooden, in what must be one of the strangest utterances for a coach ever to make.

Walton was studiedly lackadaisical in pre-game warm-ups, as if to say I'm here, babies, but I ain't straining no gut for no silly third place. He met the Kansas captains at midcourt with a careless slap of hands, looked away in restless boredom as officials gave instructions.

But once the game began, he played savagely, at least on defense. He got six of the first eight UCLA rebounds. Sometimes he didn't bother to follow his teammates' fast break, but for the time he played, about half of each half, he was awesome in his domination of the backboard.

Walton shot but three times, made all three, capped by that showy final goal, before finishing his career as a spectator. In the locker room, he steadfastly refused, as is his custom, to answer any newsmen's questions. He kept repeating, "I don't know." At one point, after he had pulled on jeans, sandals, stuck his tousled head through a T-shirt, he seemed about to say something. A sudden hush struck the attending press-boxers, like the E. F. Hutton TV commercial, when bystanders try to eavesdrop on stock tips. As the silent heads leaned toward him, Walton looked up.

"I don't know," he said again, and vanished into the oblivion he loves and which will be forever denied him.

THE CELTICS SAG TO THE NBA TITLE

By Leonard Shapiro

From The Washington Post

Copyright, ©, 1974, The Washington Post

In the 98th and final game of their 1974 basketball season, the Milwaukee Bucks were forced to scorn the man who had brought them to the brink of a National Basketball Association championship. And so, they lost it.

They lost it today to a Boston Celtics team that sagged every man possible into the middle to keep Kareem Abdul-Jabbar away from the ball, and the ball away from him. The Celtics succeeded beyond their fondest expectations.

When it was over, the Celtics left the Milwaukee Arena with a 102–87 victory in the seventh and final game of a brutally contested series, their first championship ever without Bill Russell playing the pivot, and their third triumph of this series on the road.

Today, Dave Cowens, with an awful lot of help from his friends, was the center in Boston's first championship since the 1968–69 season.

"People said we couldn't win a title with a small man at center," said coach Tom Heinsohn. "We proved them wrong."

The Celtics' strategy was as simple as could be. "We played Kareem differently than when we did in previous play-off games," Heinsohn said. "We fronted him and doubled up on him, and it kept him from getting so many shots."

"We sagged from every which way," said Cowens. "He couldn't do what he normally does. We wanted them to shoot from outside. We created a little bit of havoc."

So Jabbar, who had been averaging 27 shots and 34 points a game in this final series, took 21 today and scored 26 points. He did not score in the second quarter or in the first half of the third period. Good-bye, Milwaukee.

And hello Cowens.

Big Red, although he picked up his fifth foul with 11:47 to play, scored eight of his game-high 28 points in the fourth quarter as the Celtics held off a furious Milwaukee rally and broke things open for good in the first three minutes of the period.

Of course, he had some help. Second-year man Paul Westphal scored five points in the final period and assisted on four baskets. Paul Silas had five critical rebounds, and John Havlicek rectified his worst game of the play-offs by hitting a three-point play with 4:12 to go that finally sent many in the crowd of 10,938 scurrying for the exits, the Celtics ahead, 90–79.

"My body was lethargic and my legs just weren't like they should be," said Havlicek, who won a car for being named the series' most valuable player.

"I felt badly because I couldn't contribute, but when I saw Dave [Cowens] start to go to work, I just said, 'Beautiful, beautiful. The kid can play, can't he?'"

Cowens, making once again like the world's tallest point guard, helped the Celtics take a 17-point lead with 3 1/2 minutes left in the third quarter. The Bucks got within three early in the fourth quarter before Boston ran off eight straight points.

"We just had one more spurt than they did," said Havlicek, who with Don Nelson and Don Chaney were the only 1974 Celtics to play during any of the Russell championship years.

"This one is nicer because I'm older," he said. "All these guys were always reading about the old Celtics. They wanted to start something themselves. Look around. Most of these guys have never had this feeling. It's the greatest thing you can possibly imagine."

Cowens seemed a bit awed by it all as he sucked on a bottle of pink champagne in the sweltering, stuffy, and stuffed Celtic dressing room.

"This is my first championship ever in anything," he said, speaking in a voice barely audible above the din. "I just wish one thing. I wish Kareem wasn't as tall as he is, because then everyone would appreciate him a whole lot more.

"You can't imagine how much I appreciate him. What a player. He could play if he was 6 feet tall."

Jabbar had very little to say in return. "Victory and defeat were in the hands of the Creator," he said. "I just played the game."

"I was proud of them," said Buck coach Larry Costello. "Boston is a great team. They have no weaknesses—at least I haven't been able to find any. They defensed us to death. They took away what we do best. When they do that to you, you are going to lose."

The Celtics, who did not allow the Bucks to break 100 points in regulation play in any of the seven games, returned to Boston tonight, and will be feted by the city on Tuesday.

The Celtics will split the championship share of $100,000, added to the $115,000 they earned for taking their first two series against Buffalo and New York. The Bucks earned $65,000, to go with the $155,000 won against Los Angeles and Chicago.

PRO BASKETBALL REFEREE: JOB FOR A MASOCHIST

By Ted Green

From the Los Angeles Times

The scene: a hotel in Portland. The time: past midnight. A half-asleep Richie Powers is watching a TV movie.

"It's *The Maltese Falcon,*" he says. "I've seen it about eight times."

On his way out the next morning, he turns down the volume but the picture remains. The TV has been on all night.

"Companionship," he says. "It's like having someone to come home to."

The scene: Portland Airport. Richie Powers' flight to Oakland is ready to take off, and a stewardess begins the routine speech on emergency measures.

"The oxygen mask . . ."

Before she can continue, Powers pushes a button above his seat and an oxygen mask drops. The stewardess giggles.

"In the compartment in front of you . . ."

Again, Powers interrupts by holding up an instructional card, then an air discomfort bag. By this time the stewardess is laughing too hard to go on.

"I know the speech by heart," Powers says impishly. "I'm getting tired of it and she probably is, too. Anything to break the boredom, anything for a laugh."

The scene: a hotel in Oakland. Powers has checked in and is walking to his room when he looks at the key and stops.

"Room 180," he says. "I stayed in that one once. Too damn cold. I'll have to get it changed."

At 180 he opens the door, peeks in and turns away.

"What'd I tell you?"

The scene: the referee's dressing room at Oakland Coliseum. Powers and his officiating partner, Ed Batagowski, are taping a sore hamstring and ankle, respectively. Someone is knocking on the door.

"Four minutes," Powers mumbles. "Four minutes to tipoff."

The door opens and a ball boy repeats those exact words.

Powers smiles. "Some places it's five, some four, and some three," he says. "Here it's four. I don't know why they bother to tell me."

Airplanes, taxis, rented cars . . . hotels, coffee shops, bars. Richie Powers has ridden the merry-go-round as a National Basketball Association official for 17 years, city to city, arena to arena, in a lifestyle best described as a tedious, repetitive whirlwind, filled more with loneliness and aggravation than adventure and laughs.

The job requirements go beyond making numerous instant decisions on the play of ten big, fast, strong, and sometimes tricky athletes while being himself in almost perpetual motion (an official runs four to five miles a game); beyond watching, besides those on the court, the two benches, two clocks, a scoreboard and scorer's table, all at the same time; beyond tuning out verbal abuse from players, coaches, and fans who often question his parentage or sexual inclination.

A referee must be willing to be away from his family 80 percent of the time from mid-September to April, while he works about 100 games. Seldom will two in a row be played in the same city. For this reason family and personal affairs are handled by phone or not at all.

All this he must do without praise, for as Dolly Stark, an oldtime official, used to say, "The greatest accolade is silence." And, according to a current NBA coach, ". . . the responsibilities we put on an official far exceed any human's ability."

Since fraternizing is not allowed with players or coaches, an official travels only with his partner. When they are compatible they often dine, drink, and kill the dead hours together. But when interests differ or personalities clash, an official faces the world alone.

It is not surprising, then, that Richie Powers, in his 43rd year, is prematurely gray or that his first marriage ended in divorce. And it helps explain what he calls his "propensity to talk up a storm," the rare times he meets someone new on the road, his zest for reading, and his affinity for TV and for scotch. His nickname is Double D, as in double Dewar's.

But this is to paint an incomplete picture of Richie Powers. For reasons not out of the ordinary—ego, money, and what he calls "the challenge of mixing firmness with compassion"—he loves his job almost to the point of obsession.

He likes to think of himself as the league's "showcase referee," and calls game officials "the cornerstone of pro basketball."

Two things strike you about Richie Powers—the wealth of stories he tells and a pride so fierce that even 7-footers know when to back off.

That this pride has been interpreted as cockiness is understandable. It's evident off court but he positively radiates it on court.

Dick Motta, coach of the Chicago Bulls: "You see him look at you when he walks out on the floor and suddenly you're grabbing your collar and saying to yourself, 'Damn, is my tie straight?'

"Players who haven't saluted the flag in 20 years stand at attention during the national anthem when he's around. Richie's got the timekeeper, the scorekeeper, and the gatekeeper in hand, and I wouldn't be surprised one night if he blew the whistle on the peanut man shortchanging the lady in the 35th row."

To get an insight into the man many consider the best in his business, a reporter spent four days with Powers, who with Ed Batagowski, a second-year ref, worked games in Portland, Oakland, and Los Angeles.

A rainy Tuesday morning in Portland. Powers had arrived late the night before from Philadelphia and "hit the rack immediately."

He had just returned from a shopping spree (long-sleeve shirts) and a ham-and-eggs breakfast. Without prompting, he began talking about himself.

Powers is an Irishman with a Bronx-Boston accent who grew up in New York City and lives with his wife of one year and two stepchildren in Greenwich, Connecticut.

He looks his 43 years, perhaps because of a full head of straight silver hair, but has the vibrance of a man years younger. Barely 5-foot-10, he weighs about 180, thanks to a paunch he blames on science—"Not one of those dummies has been able to invent a low-calorie scotch."

His expressive green eyes light up after a one-liner or funny story and he speaks loudly, in a voice reminiscent of James Cagney. The face is pugnaciously handsome.

"What does it take to be a good referee? Beats the hell out of me," he said. "No one thinks any referee is good. But one who is must be firm, decisive, unflappable, unshakable. I feel like the game rests on my shoulders. No game is going to get out of control . . . that's my main thought. Any one can flare into a war."

The travel?

"I don't like the road better than anyone else. Sometimes it's duller than you can imagine. I'm always thinking about the inevitability of time. That's why I always have that vast wasteland [TV] on. It's noise, it's companionship. I watch it until I get relaxed. It takes me hours afterward to come down from Everest. I guess I look at the TV but sometimes I'm not really watching.

"I suppose the separation from home killed my first marriage. My wife hated my job. But my wife now loves it, which makes it a lot easier."

Perhaps uncomfortable with the subject, Powers held up a book he hadn't started, *KGB*, a tale about Russian spies. "After reading the flap," he said, "I'm not sure I'll get past the preface."

Then he was off again, with a Groucho Marx monologue on technical fouls. ("They say the secret word—usually a 12-letter hyphenated job—and it costs 'em 50 bucks.")

A few yarns later, including one about Phil Jackson disconnecting a wire at a scorer's table so the horn wouldn't go off, Powers said it was time for his afternoon nap. "I don't really sleep," he said. "Can't. Too psyched up. I just close one eye . . . and watch TV with the other."

On the ride to Portland Coliseum, Powers and Batagowski discussed the match-ups. They agreed that neither Portland nor Phoenix is particularly physical, but that Sidney Wicks and Neal Walk merit attention because of their volatile tempers.

"Some referee tandems don't pool their info beforehand and it hurts them," Powers said. "The last time these teams played was there a fight? Did one player really eat up another one? Is anyone trying anything new lately? It takes a while for word to get around that a Don Nelson grabs guys by the pants so they can't move or a Jerry Sloan pulls guys down on top of him to make it look like an offensive foul. Tonight keep an eye on Dick Van Arsdale. He's so intense he doesn't see the people he runs over and can't believe he's been called, even after they're picking the guy up with a blotter."

Sure enough, in the second quarter of a ragged game, Van Arsdale bowled over Portland's Bernie Fryer and provided a typical player-referee-coach confrontation.

"Offense?" Van Arsdale yelled. "What kind of bleep is that Richie?"

Powers calmly signaled a "T." Van Arsdale stomped his foot, and his coach, John McLeod, stormed out.

"What kind of crap is that, Richie?"

"That's a T . . . and sit down."

"Go ahead. Call your crappy T's."

"That's two." Automatic ejection. Exit McLeod.

Later Mike Bantom, a Phoenix rookie, drove the lane and threw up the ball with a grunt. No foul was called. Suddenly, Powers whistled a T and shouted loud enough for almost everyone in the building to hear, "I will not abide that kind of profanity!" (Later, he would say smiling, "It was the 12-letter special.")

Bantom sat down, then yelled to Powers: "Hey, Richie. Can't you do anything besides call T's?"

Powers walked calmly to the Phoenix bench and told Bantom, "That's your second. Now disappear." Exit Bantom.

After the game Powers undressed slowly, savoring the beer a ball boy had brought, which earned a $3 tip. ("My father used to say, 'Throw the cat a goldfish.' ") He unwrapped the thick bandage around his left thigh, stood with eyes closed under the water for a long minute, toweled off, slumped in a chair and rubbed liniment on the sore hamstring.

"Tough business, ain't it," he said.

At the hotel, Batagowski, a good-natured man of 37 with a round face, square shoulders, sad, droopy eyes, and a sense of humor to match Powers', opted for something to eat. But seniority, namely Double D, prevailed.

The bar was busy for midnight, but a waitress recognized Powers and sped the seating process. Four or five Double D's and many stories later, Powers patted his belly and said good night.

"The league keeps telling me to watch my weight," he said in parting. "I keep watching it, and watching it, and watching it. My stomach's getting bigger."

This left Batagowski and the reporter. Like all young officials, he is struggling for the players' acceptance and with the transition from a schoolteacher's life in Connecticut.

"Some kind of life, huh?" he said softly. "People ask me when my daughter was born, and I say, "Philadelphia at Milwaukee. When I look back, if one of my kids [ages 12, 9, 3, and 2 months] has problems I'll invariably link them with this time away from home. Now I just hope my wife is strong enough."

"Then why do it? Richie's making about $35,000 but the younger guys make what, maybe half that?"

"It's not the money," he said. "Sometimes I say to myself, 'Why am I taking all this crap? What am I proving?' I guess it's the insatiable urge to be the best. I want to be as good as Richie or Mendy Rudolph [a 20-year veteran]. If I can't, if the players continue to moan on every call, if they won't let me do it, I suppose I'll quit."

Wednesday morning. After an early breakfast and a flight to Oakland, Powers checked into a hotel near Oakland Coliseum where Golden State was to play Atlanta the next night.

Batagowski used the off day to show San Francisco to a friend from the East. Powers, in 17 years, has had it with sightseeing.

"Not much to do out there," he said. "Most towns have stopped showing matinee movies, and some of the arenas we work in are in a lousy part of town, like Chicago. And Phoenix. There's a strange town. Everyone thinks they're Billy the Kid. They all carry guns. You can walk down the street and buy a Colt .45 with bullets for 35 cents."

So, he relaxed in his room, flipped on the TV and discussed his road to refereeing.

He was the only child in a "WPA-type" family in a melting-pot neighborhood in the Bronx. One boyhood memory is of "a Jewish kid named Irwin who in stickball didn't swing often, but when he did he'd hit it to Brooklyn." Another is the time he was playing marbles and a truck ran over his right foot, crushing the bones.

"My dad wouldn't let me mope after I came back from the hospital. He said, 'Get your fanny back there and play ball.' He believed in perseverance, and when he died after four cancer operations he showed me what guts is all about."

Powers was an athlete of middling ability. He played high school basketball and tried out for the St. John's baseball team ("I was a suspect, not a prospect") but failed. So he began officiating church league and semipro games "to be close to sports."

His reputation (good judgment, feisty disposition) grew, and in 1956 he was approached by then NBA Commissioner Maurice Podoloff.

"What makes you think you can ref in the NBA?" said Podoloff. Powers' reply was characteristic: "What makes you think I can't?"

Seven years later (he was a baseball ump in the minor leagues for a while but quit in 1961 because "they kept me from the big time by claiming I was too short") he left the NBA because of inadequate fees. Also, there was no pension plan, and he was earning $13,000 a year.

He came back in 1965 but was fired two years later for "lack of interest in the job . . . My personal life was screwed up."

In 1969, when four officials jumped to the ABA, Powers called the NBA and asked for his job back. "I needed the NBA," he said. "I was going out of my mind. I wasn't doing the thing I do best in this world. I was vegetating and wasting, working as a salesman. I was 25 pounds overweight."

When Commissioner Walter Kennedy hired him, Powers swore he'd be "the best ref that ever worked the game." And some say he is. Bill Russell, the former Boston Celtics star who coaches Seattle, calls Powers the best ever. And a recent poll of NBA players held similarly.

Now Powers, who two decades ago took home $10 a game, is on the good side of $35,000, has a pension that calls for about $5,000 a year after 55 and has a $5,000 annual allotment for expenses over and above plane tickets, rental cars, and hotel bills, which are covered by credit card.

Because his wife is a successful real-estate broker, they are well off. Richie uses his four-month vacation to play golf (he's a 12-handicap) and rest.

"Who would've ever thunk it?" he said, jiggling the ice in his Double D.

He spent much of Wednesday napping, filling out technical-foul reports, writing postcards, talking long distance to his wife and—what else?—watching TV.

That night it was dinner at an Oakland steak house owned by Jackie Jensen, a former pro baseball player ("I like jock restaurants"), and story time over Double D's. "I never drink on the day of a game," Powers said, "but this is the night. Anyway, it's nice to be sociable."

Thursday night. Oakland Coliseum. The referees' dressing room. "It's no different than the others around the league: two lockers, two chairs, a shower and john, in an area of ten square feet. Not exactly the Hilton," said Powers.

Then he changed the subject: "Once the game is started, I'm really not that concerned over making calls. I seem to have the facility—a God-given gift, if you will—to make instantaneous decisions. Aw, hell. Enough of this seriousness," he said, waving his hand at Batagowski. "As the shepherd said in the lightning storm, let's get the flock out of here."

Watching Powers work, you get the impression his head is ringed with eyes. Or should be. He is responsible, with his partner, for ball-control violations, hidden zone defenses, goaltending, offensive basket interference, and wet spots on the floor. And he must make sure each quarter is 12 minutes long; remember that the foul rules change in the closing two minutes of a period; that the ball must be passed inbounds within five seconds, brought over half-court within 10 and shot within 24; that a man may not stand in the key for more than three. Clocks help with some of this but not all.

Powers said these responsibilities are only 40 percent of the job. The rest involve the unwritten doctrine called "No harm, no foul," which allows a player to commit any atrocity short of manslaughter as long as the referees judge that no undue competitive advantage has been won. His recommendation to alleviate the problem: a third official.

"Away from the ball," said Powers. "That's where the action is. That's where the wars start."

The officials alternate each half as "lead" and "trail." The lead stations himself under the offensive basket. The trail roams near midcourt. Both move constantly, seeking the elusive angles that give the best view. Often they are screened by players' bodies.

Powers makes his calls in a loud, clear voice, and often lets the offender know exactly how he sinned ("Maravich, 44, you yanked Barry!").

During the first half of Golden State–Atlanta, Batagowski apparently missed an out-of-bounds call. A full-scale argument, replete with technical fouls, ensued.

In the ref's room at half time, Powers was waiting. When Batagowski walked in he told him, firmly, that he had stood too close to the play. With a bar of soap, Powers began wildly scribbling diagrams on a long mirror. After a five-minute lecture on referee X's and O's, the mirror was a soapy mess.

Later, Batagowski said: "Sometimes Richie gets carried away . . . he's so emotional. But he's the only one among the experienced officials who takes the time to teach. He seems almost driven to share his knowledge about the game, which is considerable."

Thursday night was a repeat of the night before. So was Friday in Los Angeles. "The days," said Powers, half watching a TV quiz show, "sort of run together. I tend to lose track."

Lakers–Seattle at the Forum. Just another night. Afterward, Powers, drenched in sweat, sat on a stool and pondered a question about retirement. What has he left to prove?

"Everest, my man," he said with his husky laugh. "The job is damn near impossible. And I have a mortal fear of failure, so I'll probably continue this madness until I lose that fear."

GLOBETROTTERS: A RACIST ANACHRONISM

By Wells Twombly

From the San Francisco Examiner

Copyright, ©, 1974, San Francisco Examiner

They come prancing out onto the floor to the tune of an extraordinarily racist piece of music, their eyeballs rolling, their legs strutting, their bodies moving to the rhythm. They jabber like plantation slaves. They act stupid for the palefaces. They are supposed to be comic, but they end up looking grotesque. Their time is long past. They belong to an era when black people had no pride, no dignity, no sense of purpose. They were simply planted in this country to handle menial chores, to tug their forelocks when it seemed proper and to pretend that they lacked even the most modest amount of intelligence.

What stuns the imagination is the fact that the Harlem Globetrotters are still appreciated by members of their own race. They have survived through an era where that most heroic of literary characters, Uncle Tom, has had his name applied to black cop-outs, people who never read the book and never understood Tom's special grace under pressure.

The Globetrotters have survived the purging of Amos and Andy. Remember them? Ah, what small white boy growing up couldn't admire the calm sanity of Amos or be slightly jealous of the Kingfish, the ultimate hustler? They were real people and they were beautiful.

These institutions are dead now. But the Globetrotters linger on. They do their offensive thing and 34,000 people pay as much as $6 each to see them strut at the Oakland Arena on a single weekend. Take a distinguished human being like Nate Thurmond and let him play serious basketball and the Golden State Warriors can't put 3,000 people in the building. Let a muttering clod like Meadowlark Lemon loose and there aren't enough seats available. Why?

"This is good clean fun," said Curley Neal. "It's like the circus. I don't think anybody ever walked away from a Harlem Globetrotter game thinking he has had a bad experience. This team sells fun and people look for us year after year. I don't feel I'm an Uncle Tom at all. I'm not disgracing anybody, certainly not black people."

There's your answer, the Globies aren't hurting anybody. If that is the case, why is their humor so deeply seated in a certain ethnic base? Over the years there have been a few white players who could do the routines as well as any black. It is true that offers have been made to such pale-skinned athletes as Hot Rod Hundley, Pete Maravich, and Rick Barry. They all said no.

Once upon a time, the Globetrotters had a purpose. There were no black basketball players in the lone major league, which seems like an absurdity in an age when only 40 percent of the National Basketball Association is Caucasian. So the Globetrotters gave employment to men who wouldn't get an opportunity otherwise.

In those days, they were undoubtedly the match of any club in captivity. They are no longer. They employ people who couldn't do it with the real professionals. They even have Dave Lattin, one of those Warrior draft choices that somehow evaporated.

It is fun to take your three sons to a Globetrotter game. They believe all the incredible stunts. They even think the Washington Generals, the opposing team, is honestly trying to win. They have no idea that their coach, Red Klotz, was no child when their father was quite small and watched him play against the Hartford Hurricanes in the old Car Barns on Washington Street when the Eastern League and Hitler were both pretty big.

"How come you don't like the Globetrotters?" asked Jason Twombly, who is in the third grade and trying very hard to understand life.

"I don't know, son. I guess it's because I saw Elgin Baylor play too often and because I got to know and respect Bill Russell," his father said.

Behind those charming masks are a group of desperate men. They are not true basketball players. They cling to the edge and pray for survival. Once, when Wilt Chamberlain had to kill a year of eligibility before he could be drafted by the National Basketball Association, he worked with the Globetrotters. It was not a satisfying experience.

One evening he made the hideous mistake of upstaging Meadowlark Lemon. Wilt happened to be in a playful mood and the good times just started to roll. Afterward, Lemon went berserk in the dressing room. He charged Chamberlain in what must have been one of history's greatest overmatches. All Wilt could do was grab him and hold him high over his head.

"I had him up there like a barbell until he stopped screaming," he said. "Lark honestly thought he was a real basketball player. He was jealous of me because he knew I could play the game and he couldn't. I only played with them one year, but that was enough."

In recent years, the Globetrotters have tried to soften their image, to make it less racial and more universal. Somehow, it doesn't work. When Lemon starts to babble it sounds disgraceful. He has a "yowsa, boss" look to him that won't go away. And there is a strong sense of bigotry about the entire production.

At half time there was a ping-pong match between an American and an Englishman. When the latter made an astonishingly good play, the announcer said, "Well, that's your typical sneaky English sportsmanship." Let's just knock this equality business off and forget brotherhood. Let's make the Harlem Globetrotters the central point of a carnival that gives the public what it really wants, shuffling Spades, drunken Micks, greasy Dagos, passionate Spicks, dumb Polacks, cheap Scotsmen, inscrutable Chinks, scheming Hebes, aggressive Krauts, and brutal Redskins.

In what is, hopefully, an enlightened era, the Harlem Globetrotters are strictly for Archie Bunker and nobody else. They aren't funny any more. Sorry about that, fellows. Thanks for the free tickets. It won't be necessary to send any next year.

Boxing

ALI—YOU GOTTA BELIEVE!

By Peter Bonventre and Pete Axthelm

From Newsweek

Copyright, ©, 1974, Newsweek, Inc.

Muhammad Ali danced into the ring in full stride, his feet churning across the canvas in the familiar Ali Shuffle, his fists flicking rapid-fire punches into the muggy night air. George Foreman, the fearsome heavyweight champion, was late in arriving, and Ali's trainer Angelo Dundee protested angrily about the delay. But Ali seemed to savor his final moments alone in the spotlight before 60,000 spectators in Kinshasa, Zaire, and millions more around the world. When Foreman did climb into the ring, Ali allowed his hands to quiver in mock terror. During the prefight huddle with the referee, he chattered and baited Foreman. Then, just before the opening bell, Ali pressed his elbows against his ribs and extended his forearms; with eyes closed, he uttered a prayer to Allah.

It was a classic Ali performance—a flaunting of the fleetness, flamboyance, and Muslim faith he hoped would carry him to a victory that he had modestly predicted would be "the most spectacular wonder human eyes have ever witnessed." But throughout his career as hero and martyr, champion and clown, Ali has thrived as much on surprise as on ritual. And while most viewers smiled at the act and wondered how long it would go on in the face of Foreman's destructive blows, Ali was preparing to spring his biggest surprise of all. He alone knew that he would need none of his dancing or shuffling, bravado or prayer to cope with the supposedly invincible champion. With his 32-year-old body tuned to perfection and his keen mind alive with a clever fight plan, the most marvelous athlete of this generation was ready for his proudest achievement.

Mobutu Sese Seko, the President of Zaire, had invested some $12 million in the fight in an effort to put his country on the map; the closed-circuit promoters had hoped for a worldwide gross of $40 million. Then management bungling and a one-month delay caused by an eye injury to Foreman stripped some of the glamour from the proposed extravaganza, and both Zairian tourism and theater attendance fell far short of expectations. But with the magic that he has always conjured up for important occasions, Ali transformed the troubled event into a dazzling moment.

Foreman, 25, had youth, power and an awesome reputation on his side; he had pulverized Joe Frazier and Ken Norton, the only men ever to conquer Ali, and he was a heavy favorite to whip the aging Muhammad. But the underdog countered with a blend of guile, fitness, and will—and this proved more than enough to give Foreman and a lot of experts a painful lesson in boxing.

Foreman sensed his problems soon after he charged forward to begin the fight. George had expected to chase a dancing, retreating opponent. Instead, he found Ali awaiting his blows while leaning back against the ropes—which had been cleverly loosened in advance by trainer Dundee to give his man more room for maneuvering. Dick Sadler, Foreman's manager, had warned his fighter not to exhaust himself by trying for a quick knockout—but Foreman couldn't resist the stationary target offered by Ali. Glaring, snorting, and throwing sweeping punches, Foreman attacked avidly. But Ali deflected punches aimed at his head, shrugged off heavy blows to his taut midsection—and snapped Foreman's head back with sharp jabs. After only a few rounds, the champ looked arm-weary and bewildered.

"Now listen up," Ali told the press during one of his prefight monologues, "because you'll have to write different columns after I teach you the ways of boxing and show you how dumb you are." Just before the third round, Ali seemed to recall his lecture. Leaning over the ropes, he faced the row of writers. "He don't hurt me," he yelled. "I told you he's got no punch."

Unlike most athletes, Ali thoroughly enjoys his animated adversary relationship with the press. "You guys really juice him up," trainer Dundee told *Newsweek*'s Peter Bonventre. "All this arguing and teasing keeps his mind fresh." That mental freshness may have been particularly important last week, because the postponement of the fight and the overall seven-week wait in Zaire had threatened both fighters' concentration and rubbed nerves raw.

Foreman, growing stir-crazy, had moved out of the special training center in the resort of N'Sele and checked into a luxurious hotel in Kinshasa; but even there, the action was limited. Foreman withdrew into himself and limited his recreation to poolside rests and ping-pong. When some of his entourage sought livelier escapes, they were disappointed. One sparring partner, for example, was enjoying an interlude with one of Kinshasa's bargain-priced prostitutes when he noticed a huge butterfly fluttering near his head. To his shock, the girl plucked the butterfly out of the air and ate it. "A delicacy," she explained. The fighter got sick.

Ali had chosen to remain at N'Sele, and while his hangers-on amused themselves with desultory pursuits like betting on the speed at which mud clods floated down the Zaire River, Muhammad fought boredom in his own way. Sometimes he whiled away long hours by listening to tapes of rock music, of Elijah Muhammad—and of himself. When the press arrived, he grabbed every opportunity to entertain the writers. And when the public attended his training sessions, Ali turned them into small circuses complete with dances, speeches, and bongo music. Foreman made one effort to upstage Ali by hiring his own drummer, as well as a team of local cheerleaders. But loner George just wasn't meant to match Ali's showmanship: he fired the girls after he learned that they were leading cheers for Muhammad on their own time. Foreman owned the world championship, but Ali was dictating all the terms of their confrontation—and he extended that control with every round that they fought.

In the fifth round Foreman summoned his greatest effort. Lunging forward and cornering his foe against the ropes, George threw a flurry of the looping punches that had floored 37 other opponents. Ali answered with taunts instead of blows. "Is that your best, George? . . . You're getting tired, George. . . . Go on, take your best shot." Angry and frustrated, Foreman kept charging. Finally, Ali underlined his cool superiority with one quick combination, and both fighters seemed to sense that the issue was settled. "The bull is stronger," Ali would say later. "But the matador is smarter."

As Ali found his target with stunning regularity, Dundee pleaded from his corner, "Take him home, Muhammad, knock him out." But before he unleashed his own attack, Ali wanted to be sure that his victim was physically and emotionally upset. For all his outward derision, he knew that a careless mistake could expose him to one of Foreman's powerful blows. "I can't lie, he shook me twice," Ali said later. "Once, I took a right hand and I could feel my toes shaking. But I have enough sense when I get hit to hold a man and recuperate. So I survived, and after six rounds he was through. I took the heart right out of him."

In the waning minutes of the fight, Ali paused and raised his fist to the crowd as a signal. In response came the rhythmic chant: *"Ali, bu-ma-ye, Ali, bu-ma-ye."* Literally, the words meant "Ali, kill him." But there was more joy than vengeance in the crowd noise. Ali had courted the Zairians assiduously, even going so far as to characterize poor Foreman as a "Belgian oppressor." And while such tactics were unfair, they also succeeded in giving Ali the home-court advantage that he wanted so much in Africa. As the Zairians celebrated, Dundee became alarmed. "Don't play with that sucker now, Ali," he screamed. But Dundee's words were drowned out as the Zairians shared Muhammad's triumphant minutes: *"Ali, bu-ma-ye."*

Again and again in the last few rounds, Ali lured the uncertain Foreman toward him, only to lash off the ropes with fierce combinations of punches. And in the eighth round, he administered the coup. At one moment, Ali was leaning backward, inviting the champion's ineffectual blows. But in the next instant, he was springing forward, smashing Foreman's face with two straight rights and a left hook. Stunned, Foreman staggered away. Then a chopping right caught him on the side of the head and he was down for the count. "A knockdown is something I've never experienced before as a pro," George said later in a wistful tone. "I imagine that the punch that knocks a man down, he doesn't really see. I suspect that he doesn't know anything about it."

In the days after his defeat, Foreman grew more suspicious, accusing the referee of counting him out too quickly and protesting that Ali's handlers had loosened the ropes. (Actually, Foreman's manager, Sadler, had been remiss in failing to check them out.) But none of this could detract from the dimensions of Ali's feat last week: he had earned the acclaim of the sports world.

From start to finish, President Mobutu's endeavor had been beset with problems. Zaire entrusted the tourist franchise to foreigners who proceeded to overprice tours and deceive customers; local bureaucrats made clumsy attempts to censor the foreign press and gloss over the harder realities of Zairian life. Partly because of the postponement, closed-circuit theaters in the U.S. were filled to only about one-third of capacity—and some had to give refunds when equipment malfunctioned. Even the theater men could find solace in the fact that Mobutu, watching on a hookup in his palace, was blacked out during several rounds.

But in spite of such snafus, the bout was a remarkable achievement for Zaire, winning it global attention and respect. Mobutu had called it his "gift to the people of Zaire," but even the national hero was upstaged by Ali: it was Muhammad who provided the real gift.

Each fighter received $5 million for the Zaire event, and Ali thinks he can command twice that figure for his next fight. "Maybe promoters can't afford me," he said, "but governments are looking for me now." Even while he walks with kings, however, Ali insists on maintaining his common touch: "I'm the world champion but I don't feel any different than that fan over there. I'll still walk in the ghettos, answer questions, kiss babies. I didn't marry a blonde or go nude in movies. I'll never forget my people."

With the fearsome Foreman out of the way, Ali was asked if anything at all could scare him. "Yes," he said solemnly. "I fear Allah, thunderstorms, and bad airplane rides." Then the smile flashed across his face and the carefree, egocentric spirit that has carried him throughout this remarkable decade bubbled to the surface again. "But you have to admit it," he said. "If you were flying and the engine caught fire, wouldn't you feel safer with me in the plane?"

MUHAMMAD ALI: ATHLETE, FOLK HERO, WORLD SOCIAL FORCE

By Will Grimsley

From The Associated Press

Muhammad Ali is a man of many faces, but only one mouth. It is a nonstop mouth on a runaway course, and from it resounds the longest-playing record of the electronic age.

Now that he has achieved one of the most phenomenal comebacks ever in sports, the great one has renewed his license to make all the world his stage.

Fasten your seat belts and order more cotton for your eardrums. It is Ali's rostrum now until someone knocks the props out from under it.

He is an engaging, fascinating, mystical man—this superb athlete who has proved to be the best fighter of his time, who has successfully defied a government and charmed the universe.

He has emerged as more than a folk hero in the broad realm of fun and games. He has become a social force around the world.

He has entrees to the palaces and government seats of the world. Presidents and potentates fawn over him, kings embrace him, scholars court him, children tug at him. Little people—from Bangkok to Baghdad—cry out his name.

What kind of person is he, anyhow, this man born of humble beginnings in the Jim Crow South who now wields such a massive influence?

Muhammad Ali at best is an enigma. At once he is warm and outgoing—an effervescent, mischievous boy. Then a switch is snapped somewhere and he becomes a cold, hard militant.

He is the center of every crowd. He has to be the catalyst. One moment he is laughing, jesting, espousing his cornpone philosophies. Then, suddenly, he can turn to ice. He can look at you without seeing. He can melt you with a glare.

He is enthusiastic, exuberant, loud, subdued, pompous, arrogant, sometimes a king-sized bore. But mostly he is charming.

There is no question that he relates. Few if any men anywhere boast a greater identity factor. Ali can walk through the streets of London wearing a bowler hat and carrying a rolled umbrella, the narrow byways of Beirut in a fez, or New York's Broadway in a T-shirt, and he is immediately recognized.

He has a magnetic quality about him. Like a modern Pied Piper, he captures streams of admirers wherever he goes, not because he is a great champion—there have been many—but because he is Ali.

This is true even in the United States, where there is deep-running resentment of the fact that he refused to wear a military uniform and because he knocks his homeland for its longtime subjugation of blacks.

Some say Ali's destiny is attached to a star. Others say he is the pet of some good fairy.

Ali quickly acknowledges in a thousand words and in a thousand ways that his astounding career has a spiritual propulsion, but he insists it comes from Allah and Allah's messenger, Elijah Muhammad of the Muslims.

Ali has used fists and his unfettered tongue to become champion of blacks and the underprivileged in many parts of the world, but he frequently reverts to his Kentucky seeds to put a more realistic tag on his motivation.

He says: "I'm just another nigger, trying to get bigger."

Human qualities frequently seep through his bombast and arrogance, which some associates contend are nothing more than charade in his running drama.

In Kinshasa, while training for his title fight with heavyweight champion George Foreman, he stopped in the midst of a bag-punching routine and pointed to a plump woman on the front row.

"That's my Mama over there," he announced, as Mrs. Cassius Marcellus Clay, Sr., of Louisville, Kentucky, beamed proudly. "Ain't she pretty? That's why I am so pretty, because my Mama is so pretty."

It's hard to hate a man like that.

But Ali just as likely will be making humiliating remarks about an opponent, or spout insults about the U.S.

"America has 40,000,000 of my people in slavery," he told an African workout audience last week.

Ali is hardly a slave, though. He lives in a $250,000 mansion in Cherry Hill, New Jersey. He has chauffeurs for his fleet of limousines and needs a dozen banks to keep all the money he makes.

"I don't want to live next door to somebody who don't want me there," he once said in discussing his view of integrated housing. The Rockefellers might find it difficult to get into Ali's neighborhood.

Ali was born in Louisville 32 years ago, one of two sons of a sign painter. His father proudly gave him his family's former slave name —Cassius Marcellus—and predicted that his boy one day would be famous.

Young Cassius had a normal boyhood, learning to box on the playgrounds and under the tutelage of a Louisville policeman, Joe Martin. He made the U.S. Olympic team and won the light-heavyweight gold medal in Rome in 1960.

Writers who covered those Olympics remember him as a quiet, pleasant youngster who enjoyed crowds, but was neither loud nor ostentatious.

He turned professional in 1960 and his progress, dictated by a group of Louisville businessmen, was steady.

It was not until Cassius, as he was then called, started knocking out little-known opponents with regularity that he burst into the limelight. He promoted his early career by predicting the result of his fights with fourth-grade level poetry:

> Battling Bo is scared of me,
> So my prediction is,
> He will fall in three.

People laughed. But nobody laughed much in 1964 when the handsome, roundfaced kid with those big brown eyes and the trim physique that should be in the muscle-building ads stopped Sonny Liston in Miami Beach, Florida, to win the heavyweight crown.

It was at this time that Clay was converted to the Black Muslim faith. He was the disciple of Malcolm X, a dissident leader. Cassius' brother, Rudolph Valentino Clay, also became a Muslim.

The assassination of Malcolm X cooled Clay's Muslim fervor for a while, but he later became a strong follower of Elijah Muhammad, Allah's messenger in Chicago.

Cassius changed his name to Muhammad Ali. Rudolph became Rahman. Rahman also fights, but not much or well.

Some contend that the Muslim religion is just a fad with Ali, but this has been proven not so. Ali preaches in the temples.

In 1967, when he refused the military oath, Ali sacrificed not only his title, but his fame and fortune as well.

He had to move into a modest flat in Chicago. He was broke. His only revenue came from speaking engagements on college campuses. He was sought widely as a lecturer, and even spoke at Oxford.

Ali was told at the time he was drafted that he could perform in the Special Services, that he never would have to fire a gun or look at an enemy in anger. Ali refused. He said his religious principles forbade it.

They said he was through, he would never come back.

Ali doesn't drink or smoke. He is a reader and a preacher of the Koran, the Islam bible. He believes women should wear long dresses and never flaunt sex, but he has been seen to look twice at a pretty girl in a miniskirt.

"The woman is the fiber of the nation," he says. "She is the producer of life. A nation is only as good as its women."

Ali divorced his first wife and married a faithful Muslim, who has born him a son and daughter.

At the weekend, Ali, invited to make a tour of the black African countries, was rushing home to be at the bedside of his ailing daughter.

"My daughter needs me," he said.

There will be time later for other things, and Ali is looking to an overflowing cup.

"I am going to show myself to the whole world," he said. "I am going to the people who love me. I am the greatest."

ON THE BLOCK: WAY OF ALL FLESH

By John Schulian

From Sports Illustrated

Copyright, ©, 1974, Time Inc.

Baltimore is a gritty old strumpet of a city where unwriten sociological imperatives require a boxing arena to have Polish bakeries on one side, steel mills on another, and redneck bars all around. Steelworkers Hall meets those criteria with the ease that home boy Joe Gans dropped pretenders to his turn-of-the-century lightweight championship.

Gans would have fit in nicely at Steelworkers because, if students of pugilism verité will excuse its newly painted exterior, everything about this unimposing brick pile seems the product of an imagination longing for another chance at yesterday. "Steelworkers," says a fighter who gets work there regularly, "is a little bucket of blood, just like you'd see in the movies."

I. W. Abel, the union boss, peers down from a photograph on the dingy wall, but he can't see the ring for the smoke. There are 1,225 tan metal folding chairs in the arena, and the critics who fill them cease puffing on cigars only to offer such advice as, "Hit him with a coconut, dummy." Everyone is hustling bets, even the housewife at ringside who puts a couple dollars on the red corner for one fight and a couple on the blue for the next. The action is heavier under the balcony, where a betting man can stop a boxer headed for the ring and tell him how many hundred are riding on him. Local fighters get most of the play—a commentary on their opponents as much as it is on their ability—and on those rare occasions when a decision goes against one of them, it rains beer.

"People gonna get excited," sputters resident promoter Eli Hanover, who is always excited himself. "This is a jumping-up-and-down sport. Who jumps up and down when someone carries a football four yards? Who jumps up and down when someone hits a single? Here people jump up and down just watching two guys trying to knock each other on their butt. Y'unnerstand what I mean about a jumping-up-and-down sport?"

If you don't, check out Eli on a fight night. Up to greet an old pug with a roundhouse slap to the shoulder. And down. Up to find out if a preliminary boy has gotten the message that he is fighting. And down. Up to take another shot at convincing the sporting press that several boxers on the card don't belong in a rest home. And down.

Hanover enjoys the luxury of wearing himself out this way because he knows that all the hands in the till are an extension of his. Daughters Jackie and Gail sell tickets, brother-in-law Bernie runs the hot dog stand, and wife Frances counts the money. The family approach helps keep the overhead low, which helps keep Eli in business, something he is very insistent about.

On occasion Hanover seems to have help from elsewhere. Take the time half of a midsummer's night main event decided he would rather stay in Puerto Rico and celebrate his last victory than fly to Baltimore and get beat on. Eli didn't learn of the change of heart until the afternoon of the fight. He sprayed $150 worth of telephone calls around the East, complaining that his stomach was killing him and assuming that everyone knew his wallet was, too. Four hours of trying produced a 33-year-old Hartford, Connecticut, toolmaker named Jesus Alicia who hadn't been in a ring for a month and whose record was 10–20–4—but who was available. When Alicia showed up 30 minutes before the fight, the man filling out a medical examination card said, "What's your address, Jesus?" "Heaven, where else?" replied one of Hanover's cronies.

There is nothing heavenly about the location of the gym where Hanover makes his headquarters. It is perched over a strip joint on The Block, that swatch of East Baltimore Street famed for showing sailors and salesmen a good time and now as wrinkled, fat, and toothless as any atherosclerotic burlesque queen. The strip joint is the Jewel Box, and until last January Eli owned it. He sold out to Lou Barber, who managed several fighters Eli uses on his cards and who was recently convicted as part of a gambling ring that included local cops. So it goes on The Block.

The red door to Sports Activities, Inc., is next to the entrance to the Jewel Box. Anyone who picks the gym over the watered-down drinks and mush-bellied strippers gets a pained look from the Jewel

Box doorman. Yet the gym's occupants aren't removed completely from the house of few lights below. The music from the jukebox pulses through the floor of the gym, massaging the ears and feet of everyone topside.

The Isley Brothers blend a burning question, "Who's that lady, beautiful lady?" into the normal gymnasium cacophony—the beeps and bongs of the automatic timer, the snorts of the sparring boxers, the splat of their gloves, the machine-gun bursts on the speed bag, the frantic lashes of a rope-skipping fighter struggling to keep pace with his trainer, who is singing "Tea for Two."

Up front Eli Hanover is talking. As usual. His audience is a man from the outfit that made the gym's ring. Like the one at Steelworkers, it is 18 by 18, smaller than the standard 20 by 20 because, Eli says, "I don't like to see nobody running away." The ring's size, however, doesn't keep Eli from telling the man, "All that canvas, sheesh, you guys must be making a fortune."

The man laughs. "You haven't paid for it yet," he says.

"It's better to give than receive," Eli replies.

Eli's klaxon voice oogahs forward on the square wheels of a nasal Baltimore accent, grating to the uninitiated. The body is middle-aged Mickey Rooney. The head is Humphrey Bogart. But the dark brown eyes are strictly Eli. They dance like a nimble fighter stalking a night's prey. They take in all on the street below, from the wino slumped in front of a dirty-book store to the strippers high-heeling to work as night catches up with day. They water a bit when the fumes from Polock Johnny's sausage emporium drift through the open windows of the gym.

"This is the class street of the world," Eli says from deep in the recesses of his black executive's chair. "If you want to find it, come to this street. You got the greatest people that walk God's earth and you got some of the biggest stinkers." He notices a friend crossing the street. "Hey," Eli bellows. "Hey, hey!" The friend looks up at last to see Eli in the window, clasping his hands and shaking them over each shoulder, back and forth, back and forth.

It is the wave of the champion that 52-year-old Eli Hanover, son of a Rumanian immigrant peddler, child of the tough East Baltimore streets, never was. He won 14 of 15 professional fights as a lightweight but in the process he had the truth about his ability stitched onto his eyebrows. "I wasn't no great fighter," he says. "I was just a preliminary boy." A steadier future waited for him at sea, where he spent 13 years sailing the world in the Merchant Marine. When he came ashore for good, waiting for him were his wife and the earliest of their nine children, an organizer's job with the seaman's union and the chance to get back in boxing.

He paid his dues training and managing a series of nondescript fighters before he began promoting in the mid-sixties. There are pessimists in town who say it was more curse than chance. Before Hanover could take whomever he was handling to Philadelphia or Washington or Richmond. Now he was stuck in Baltimore. Baltimore, where the only places he could put on a show were tiny Steelworkers Hall or the 12,000-seat Civic Center, which, a series of bad crowds has convinced Eli, is "a fat, greedy, white elephant." Rising land costs in the suburbs have kept him from building an arena with 3,000 seats that he insists he could fill any time he stepped off The Block.

Such confidence has deserted Hanover just once in his decade of promoting. When an attractive Civic Center card flopped in 1970, he went incommunicado for 18 months. He came back for another try, of course, declaring, "I felt like I just got outta jail."

Boxing was about to become a full-time job for him by then; he had retired from the seaman's union and was getting ready to unload the Jewel Box. It wasn't money that brought him back; although Eli says, "I ain't going broke," friends indicate that he isn't getting rich, either. The lure, most likely, was that he was needed. Needed, that is, as much as any city whose populace remembers TV's Friday night fights needs a boxing promoter. Replacements had come from Philadelphia as well as Baltimore, and they had failed. That does much for Eli's already substantial ego, particularly now that his business is picking up. "Let's face it," he says. "I'm Mr. Boxing in Baltimore. This self-praise stinks, but we're talking about actuality."

Baltimore's last successful promoters, Lou Fisher and Georgie Goldberg, struck it rich in the forties. They put on two or three fight shows a week, and they always had one on Monday. "Except when it was Yom Kippur," says Hanover. But time caught up with them. The ice rinks and ball parks that housed their fights fell to ruin, and when the promoters grew old, there was no one to take their place.

There still isn't, as far as gimmickry is concerned. Fisher and Goldberg once had a heavyweight named Curtis Sheppard who was putting opponents' lights out upon request. That wasn't enough for them. They bought a hatchet, painted it gold and gave it and the nickname Hatchetman to Sheppard. He carried the hatchet into the ring with him every fight after that. When he fought Jersey Joe Walcott, someone had to carry it out for him.

"The people that come to Steelworkers don't want no gimmicks," says Hanover. "They don't want no free T-shirts. They don't want no free boxing gloves. They want to see blood, that's what they want to see—blood. As long as it isn't theirs." The boxers who turn up regularly on Eli's cards seem eager to draw it or give it. "They are," he says, "ath-a-letes. You can't give the people what I call tomato cans. You know, no fluff-fluffs, no boo-boos, no ha-has. You do, you're out of business. You got to give the people ath-a-letes."

One of the fights Eli dreamed of would have matched Wes Unseld, the redwood-thighed center of the then Baltimore Bullets, with 6-foot-5, 280-pound Bobo Renfrow. This is the same Bobo Renfrow who, when asked to sing his school song during a tryout with the old Boston Patriots, warbled the Schaefer beer commercial. Bobo turned to boxing when football rejected him, and when boxing became too hard, he went underground. "He's working on the subway in Washington," Eli says. "I think he's holding up the street."

So Hanover must settle for fighters of lesser physical stature but equally strange reputation. Light heavyweight Josh Hall's performances at Steelworkers have led to rumors of a jaw made by Libbey-Owens-Ford. But he is 4 and 0 in the parking lot of The Frigate lounge in suburban Glen Burnie. It is surprising that welterweight Buddy Boggs has time for boxing at all. He claims to have wrestled alligators, driving a motorcycle off a bridge for the Annette Funicello classic, *How to Stuff a Wild Bikini,* and come up swinging after falling 20 floors in an elevator on a construction job. "Ronnie McGarvey, he's my Jesus freak," Hanover says. Once Eli paid McGarvey $650 for a main event at Steelworkers that the undefeated featherweight thought was worth more. "But I didn't argue the case with him," says McGarvey. "I just want to praise God."

Eli, meanwhile, is studiously watching the development of Leo Saenz, a 19-year-old middleweight whom Greyhound brought him last spring. Saenz is one of 14 children born to an itinerant Mexican-American fruit picker in Edinburg, Texas. When he was 14 and his family had journeyed to Kalamazoo, Michigan, Leo set out on his own. He survived a brush with the law over some stolen pants and began learning his way around the ring. "I was just practicing with those other dudes," he says. "They was using me. They thought I wasn't going nowhere. And one day, this old guy—his name is Johnny Gale—he sees me practicing for the Golden Gloves and he said, 'You got it, man,' and he sent me to Baltimore."

Gale's judgment has held up through Saenz's first 13 professional triumphs, eight by knockouts. Relentlessly aggressive, Leo is always hunting them. Trainer Terry Moore remembers Leo's reaction to one of the five decisions he has won: "Leo kept saying, 'I gotta knock him out, I gotta knock him out.' I said, 'Leo, you already done punched holes in the man.' He said, 'I know, but I gotta knock him out.'"

"This guy," Eli says of the kid, "is the best fighter I seen in the past 30 years potential-wise. If he don't become a champion, it's because he didn't try. He can be what you'd call your Rolls-Royce of boxing." Of course Eli says that, or something equally flattering, about every local product who appears on his shows and whose fists are worth taping. "If Buddy Boggs doesn't revive boxing in Baltimore," he once said, "then I'm getting out of the game." Bobo Renfrow was "the hottest, livest fighter in the country" and Ronnie McGarvey still "may be the best featherweight in the country." To every such pronouncement, regardless of its accuracy, Eli adds solemnly, "May this building fall on my head right now if that ain't the truth."

The carny barker's pitch is for the public, but the boxers aren't immune to Hanover's salesmanship, either. More than once one of Josh Hall's opponents has shown up over the weight limit. "My manager will be standing there," Josh says, "and I'll be trying to listen to him and Eli. Well, you know how Eli can talk. He'll look me right in the eye and say, 'You want to fight, don't you?' and the only thing I can say, is, 'Yeah.'"

Hanover begins to wonder if his magic is evaporating when he has fight nights at Steelworkers like the one just past. The regular clientele showed up—Jack Pollack, Baltimore's fading political boss, and Simon Avara, Governor Marvin Mandel's barber, and a gang of old pugs remembered only by each other—but they wouldn't fill the place. The thought of it grated Eli so badly that he made friends of his nonpaying customers buy tickets. "I'm sorry," Eli said, "but even the pay phone ain't workin.'"

Neither were the somnambulists in the first preliminary. "Hurry up and knock him out," a fan in the balcony yelled to lightweight Billy Bell, the local entry. "I got somewhere to go tonight." "Yeah, knock him out," cried a ringsider. "The man's got somewhere to go." Bell couldn't oblige them, but he remained upright and proved again that is the best way to ensure victory in Baltimore over an outsider.

The balcony dweller was helped toward the door by Donnie Branch, a paunchy heavyweight who delivered an unexpected first-round knockout, and Leo Saenz, who put away an alleged Nigerian prince in the second round of their fight. Each winner found himself with a shadow as happy as his victim was flat. Tagging along with Saenz was a rock 'n' roll guitarist who had strummed up $100 worth of action on his man. A cabbie named Doc had picked up Branch at Penn Station and decided to stick with him rather than head for Laurel Race Track and bet on Boone the Great, who wound up running last in the fifth race. "I'm driving my man home to Philadelphia," Doc announced after the fight from a perch on a well-padded wallet.

The happiness stopped outside the dressing room where Jesus (Pajarito) Nieves, Ronnie McGarvey's main-event opponent, was trying on gloves. "These are used," moaned Nieves' manager, Victor Cintron. "Any time you fight main event, you supposed to get new gloves. A big city like this and you get these gloves my little boy wouldn't wear." Nieves, who speaks little English, shrugged and walked into the ring to take 10 rounds of left-handed punishment from McGarvey. Knocked down once, staggered half a dozen times, Nieves endured with a stubborn nobility that earned him a standing ovation from the half-full house. It didn't change the unanimous decision against him, though. It didn't bring water from Steelworkers' dormant showers, either.

While Nieves toweled himself off for the drive back to New York City, where he would return to work in the garment district in the morning, Eli Hanover counted the night's receipts. Three thousand dollars. The break-even figure. Eli felt better than even the winners. He had proved again that he is where he is supposed to be. May the building fall on his head right now if that ain't the truth.

Tennis

CONNORS BURIES ROSEWALL AT WIMBLEDON

By Bud Collins

From The Boston Globe

Courtesy of The Boston Globe

The portrait of Dorian Gray Playing Tennis was slashed and showed its age. The bust of the hero was pushed off the pedestal and busted. It was the Sporting Symphony of Rosewall being drowned out by a hard rocker named Connors, a heartless vandal playing Variations on a Theme by Laver.

Seldom, if ever, has a young man in his first Wimbledon final been so devoid of nerves and hard of purpose against a great opponent as Jimmy Connors was yesterday in devastating Ken Rosewall, 6–1, 6–1, 6–4. The old master was had by the young butcher, a kid from Illinois described by his coach, Pancho Segura, as "a killer with the heart of a lion."

To the 14,000 in center court and millions of sentimentalists and nostalgiacs across the world, Connors seemed like a guy who would push wheelchair patients off into traffic. "Not everybody was for Rosewall," Connors smirked. "There were eight for me." An incredibly hard hitter, Connors was born two months after Rosewall appeared in his first Wimbledon, at 17 in 1952. The Connors claque included his mother (who went at her rosary so fervently during the 92-minute slaughter that she broke the cross), and his fiancée Chris Evert, who had set the championship example the day before in a final-round triumph over Olga Morozova.

Thus the lovebird double came through, paying 33-to-1 to the bettors who got aboard when the tournament began two weeks ago. "I think it put a lot more pressure on him with my winning," said Chrissie. "I really didn't think Jimmy would do it because I remember how nervous you can be the first time you're in the final—like I was a year ago when Billie Jean King murdered me."

If the teen-aged girls of England were shaken to despair by the earlier defeat of their poster child, Bjorn Borg, their parents mourned this beating of Rosewall. Wishful were the infrequent bursts of clapping whenever Rosewall slapped a winner or Connors bungled.

"Everything," Rosewall forced a grin, "that Jimmy touched turned to gold. He deserved to win, but I was disappointed by the score [the worst since 1967 when John Newcombe limited a German finalist, Willy Bungert, to five games] and disappointed by not being able to get into the match."

Jimmy wouldn't let him. "I've had people rooting against me before. I'm used to it," said Connors, well aware of the maverick status he has won from many of his colleagues in tennis by refusing to join the Players Union or play Davis and World Cups for the U.S., and through his lawsuits against the Union.

"I knew it would be worst here because Rosewall is so popular, and this would probably be his last chance after losing three other finals. I just wouldn't let myself think about that. Those problems are for them—I have to play for me.

"I was tired after playing nine sets Friday in singles and doubles, but I knew he would be too, after coming back to beat Stan Smith in five. And he's 39."

Connors analyzed his reactions to the situation well. "This was the final at Wimbledon—it made me quick and determined. . . . It's an occasion and I played unbelievably."

Yea, verily. It was remembrance of Rod Laver past—specifically as victor in the first opens at Wimbledon in 1968 and 1969. Connors muscled his left-handed ground strokes and returns of serve as crunchingly as he did a year ago in Boston while bringing down Arthur Ashe to win his first significant title, the U.S. Pro. He was more complete yesterday, crashing his volleys and serve, too, digging for extraordinary half-volleys and lobbing and smashing precisely. His serve had Rosewall groping and moping. The volleys and returns prevented Kenny from ever getting the magic started.

"I was always under pressure—I could never turn it on Connors," said Rosewall. The last 21-year-old to win at Wimbledon was Rosewall's sidekick, Lew Hoad, 18 years ago. "Connors is too strong for Kenny," Hoad accurately predicted.

"He kept the ball too low and he hit it so hard." Rosewall seemed shellshocked. Hard-harder-hardest is Connors' style. He knocked off 35 percent of his points on buzzing winners—bang, Bang, BANG right from the start. Rosewall struggled to hold serve in the opening game.

Connors won the next 10 games hitting all the lines, nearly blinding Rosewall with chalkdust. Connors wanted to keep the ball on Rosewall's forehand side as much as possible, and succeeded. Kenny gave him too many second serves to work on and Connors bashed them to the corners.

Even at the rare times Rosewall shoved him out of position, Connors invariably fought his way back into points and won them. Connors, having won in Australia, is the first American since Tony Trabert in 1955 to seize two of the Big Four titles in one year. (Trabert took France, Wimbledon, and the U.S.)

At the conclusion of a long day, before the last of the all-time record fortnight crowd of 305,627 (despite record rains) left Wimbledon, Billie Jean King salvaged some of her hopes by winning the mixed doubles with Owen Davidson, 6–3, 9–7, over Britons Lesley Charles and Mark Farrell. It was their fourth Wimbledon prize, and eighteenth altogether for Billie Jean, who said, "I'll be back trying to get that record"—19 won by Elizabeth Ryan.

The other No. 1 singles seed, John Newcombe, also had to settle for doubles achievement. He and Tony Roche won their fifth Wimbledon over Stan Smith and Bob Lutz.

The women's doubles went to Californian Peggy Michel and Aussie Evonne Goolagong, 2–6, 6–4, 6–3, over Aussies Helen Gourlay and Karen Krantzcke. Another Californian, 17-year-old Billy Martin of Palos Verdes, took the junior singles, 6–2, 6–1, over Indian Ashok Amritraj.

Despite the busting up given him by the brash kid, Rosewall's Wimbledon was nonetheless a masterpiece, containing sterling comeback victories over Amritraj, Roscoe Tanner, Newcombe, and that spectacular semi-final counterattack from two sets and match point down against Stan Smith. He's had glory and money beyond most athletes' expectations to console him. For Connors, who won $25,000, it's just the beginning.

"Maybe," Connors winked, "I'll be a sentimental favorite some day."

CONNORS BURIES ROSEWALL AT FOREST HILLS

By Dave Hirshey

From the New York Daily News

Copyright, ©, 1974, New York News Inc.

When the umpire shouted "Game, set, and match," it was more an act of mercy than of duty. The miracle had been long gone from 39-year-old Ken Rosewall. All that remained was the knowledge that it could hardly be worse.

At Wimbledon, Jimmy Connors had allowed Ken Rosewall to win six games and people said then that it was the worst championship debacle in recent memory. But yesterday, in the final of the U.S. Open, Jimmy Connors proved that embarrassment can yield to humiliation by making Rosewall look even older than he did at Wimbledon. The scores were 6–1, 6–0, 6–1. The awards presentation was more competitive.

It was plain and simple, the most one-sided final in the history of Forest Hills. Three times before, in 1881, 1882, and 1921, the title had been won at the loss of five games. But those were mere defeats. This was an execution. Swift and bloodless.

Rosewall served ten games and lost eight of them. He won only 20 points while serving. He won only 42 points all day. The official time will be recorded as 67 minutes, but it was over much earlier, really.

"The kid is vicious," said Pancho Gonzalez. "That's what makes him the player he is. He is a killer."

"The word," Connors demurred, "is eager."

Eager to prove he deserved his No. 1 seeding at Forest Hills. Eager to prove he would have won the Grand Slam had he not been banned from the French Open. Eager to prove simply that he is the best tennis player in captivity. In 67 minutes, he accomplished all that devastatingly. There was little time for pity.

"Pity?" Connors asked, with a bemused smile. "I've seen people pity Ken Rosewall and lose, 6–3, in the fifth. Even when I was up, 6–1, 6–0, 5–1, I still felt he would win. If I had let up just a little, he'd be all over me."

But Connors never let up. He doesn't know the meaning of the word. He plays every point as if it was his last, every opponent as if he were out to get him. And most of them are. His brash, swaggering style may have won him a lot of matches, but it has also won him few friends. Yesterday he not only played Ken Rosewall but 15,303 fans, including one gentleman who let the 22-year-old left hander know exactly what he thought of him. "Connors, you're a bum," the man yelled. Jimmy turned around, a puckish grin on his face, a Romanian peace sign on his hand, and replied, "You're right."

For most of the time, however, the crowd sat in shocked silence, waiting for a miracle that never came.

No one really expected Rosewall to win, but everyone fervently wanted him to. If emotion could win a Forest Hills final, Ken Rosewall, not Jimmy Connors, would have been the one receiving the check for $22,500, the silver trophy, the gold ball, the burnt umber car, the cherry push-button-light-up-at-night wristwatch, the cameo ring, the Pentax camera in the only award ceremony in history that threatened to eclipse the match itself.

But that's what could have been. What was, was that from the time the first bullet exploded from the rifle Connors disguises as a racket, Rosewall looked like a beaten man. It was 4–0 before he showed even the slightest sign of resistance. And when he finally held serve, Connors ran off 11 straight games. "That was the best tennis I played in my life," said Connors afterward. "I didn't miss a ball today. I thought when I beat Ken at Wimbledon, that was the best I could play. But today I had the feeling I wasn't running for the ball. I was gliding, strolling up to it and hitting winners. I started out so high I was afraid I would come down."

Instead, he soared higher and higher, his ripping two-fisted backhand repeatedly kicking up chalk down the lines, his volleys bold and precise, his serves pulverizing. The first set took 18 minutes, causing an elderly British journalist to utter, "Will someone please stop this senseless slaughter?" And indeed when the second set was over 21 minutes later, Rosewall, that familiar hangdog expression wreathing his face, looked up quizzically at the umpire, half expecting him to stop it.

"I never dreamt that I could have lost this match worse than I did at Wimbledon," Rosewall said. "I'm especially disappointed that I couldn't have made a better show of it since it'll probably be the last final of a major tournament I'll ever be in."

Rosewall, of course, has said that before, but this time, instead of titters, there was pathos. Even Connors was sufficiently moved to tell the crowd, "It's an honor for me to just be on the same court with Ken Rosewall."

It was a nice gesture, and the crowd responded with a warm ovation. Unfortunately, what Connors said was untrue. Ken Rosewall and Jimmy Connors were not on the same court yesterday.

ROSIE CASALS: WHY HASN'T SHE LIVED UP TO HER POTENTIAL?

By Catherine Bell

From Tennis

Copyright, ©, 1974, Tennis Magazine

It has been eight years since Rosemary Casals burst upon the international tennis scene at the 1966 Wimbledon tournament—a brilliant, exploding shower of West Coast talent careening through the staid All-England Lawn Tennis and Croquet Club like a small dark bullet, all burning temerity and chirpy assurance. She turned on a sixpence at the net, flicked volleys off her toenails, sped around the court as though she were an electric instrument plugged into an impossibly high voltage for so tiny a body.

Tennis played her; there was no other way of describing the impact of such fluid, charged, and uninhibited aggression. Such tennis was not the stuff women were supposed to know about. Rosie shrugged that idea off and went on talking of her manifest destiny, which was to be the best in the world.

Today, at 26, her game hasn't changed, but her public has. She hasn't won Wimbledon or Forest Hills, hasn't provided consistency, and attention has drifted away from her to other heroes. At home and abroad, she's become the Lost American—trailing behind Margaret Court and Billie Jean King, eclipsed by Chris Evert and Evonne Goolagong. Yet Rosie has class in tennis, true and immutable class, and it's hard to think of any player of our time who shares with her the capacity to turn sport, however briefly, into art. She has no predecessors, no followers. Like all innovators, she is impossible to copy.

But for all that, she has never won a major singles title. That failure is something she can't explain and won't excuse. She's too professional for excuses. She wants instead to be tough and truthful. She'll say: "Sometimes when you go on court, you have a feeling of being useless and you know everything is doomed."

Doom-laden Rosie this year went out of Wimbledon, the tournament she most wants to win, sometime after one o'clock on July 2 on court No. 3. Linky Boshoff ran and pushed, and Rosie did nothing. She played sluggishly, lethargically, she looked deathly tired. From the window of the women's dressing room, Billie Jean King watched her friend lose. She shouted encouragement and advice: come forward, come in, hit out. Rosie never noticed, never glanced up. The match was lost on a forgettable stroke and Billie Jean went away from the window.

The crowd sat patiently, attention suspended. You felt they were only there to see Rosie because the stands were there and she was somehow accidentally in front of them, reneging on her promise, acting out an annual ritual of defeat. There was no outward agony from Rosie, no histrionics, just an impassive acceptance that the fire was dead. The pattern of her game, drawn in ashes, blew away in the wind.

She returns every year to Wimbledon, though; there's a masochistic magnetism that drags her back, resignedly faithful to her ambition. Her name board on the court is yellow with age while those of her opponents now are mostly clean and white. It's probably the same one they painted for her in 1966, when everybody knew about her and everybody cared.

Now, almost nobody does. Stoically, she observes and accepts the parallel image: the fading name on the scoreboard and the fading memory. "They remember you," she says, "as you first came here. You're photographed like that forever. You only come once a year. They don't see you as a developing person, a continuity, like maybe they still see me in the States. At home I get a better public, a bit better press."

Rosie was born in San Francisco of Spanish parents who emigrated from El Salvador and came to California, as most Salvadorians do, looking for a better life. She says she's pure Spanish, that there's no mestizo blood in her. But it's hard to believe, looking at her high cheekbones and heavy lidded brown eyes and observing how she moves on court with absolutely unselfconscious ease, that there isn't some part of an older inheritance inside her, a vestigial Aztec soul. It's the same feeling Arthur Ashe and Miss Goolagong convey in their tennis—mobility and freedom uncramped by the arthritic stiffening of civilization.

Her family lived in a poorish black district now demolished to make way for the San Francisco Redevelopment Western Addition. "We were about the only white family on the block," she recalls. "All my friends were black when I was young." She found tennis in the Golden Gate Park, a place now fixed in history as the mythic center of Northern California creativity and spontaneous popular art.

In those days, before the tennis explosion, she was a solitary player, learning from her father and staying around older people. Her mother never took much interest in tennis and has seldom seen her play. "She's uncompetitive," says Rosie. Her father, though, still takes an interest and usually comes to watch her play when she appears in San Francisco.

The Golden Gate Park became the catalyst around which Rosie and tennis acted on each other and fused a magical chemical bond. Accident, or the lucky collision of events that people call fate or the religious are wont to term a divine plan, lured her to the park and put into her hand the agent of instinctive craft. She knew, she said, from the time she picked up a racquet and learned what to do with it that tennis was her talent and would be her life.

But it wasn't easy, any more than it was easy for Billie Jean in Long Beach, being a poor person in a game for the rich. There wasn't much money for Rosie—a little from her parents who were liberal and generous as far as they could afford to be, some from Herb Southerd, the then secretary of the Northern California Tennis Association (NCTA), and from friends and believers and members of the Golden Gate Park Tennis Club. Together, they collected enough to send her off to tournaments.

Rosie moved uncomfortably among rich people in the California tennis scene. As a group, they forced in her a bristling distrust that has stayed with her to this day. And Rosie, says a Californian who recalls her well, "turned pro at 11 years old." She laughs at this and nods her head "yes." She always disliked the atmosphere of junior tournaments, was always independent. The claustrophobia offended her wandering spirit, the dull little girlish pursuit of tin trophies impressed her not at all.

She hung around in San Francisco with a rough crowd and didn't always behave well at the genteel tournaments to which she was chaperoned. The legend of Rosie's childhood is characteristically filled out with incidents of singular adventure; once she turned up in the spin dryer of a local laundry and was sent home. There were other little disciplinary problems but these came to be accepted as part of Rosie, the dues of talent, and by 14 she was the tennis playing pride of Northern California.

She began traveling young, crossing the mountains to the East where the prestige tournaments were played. "I had to learn at this very early age," she says, "to cope with new scenes, courts, balls, players. There was red loam in Illinois and grass, where you had to worry about whether the ball even hit the strings."

All the same, coming from California and growing up precociously on fast cement had its advantages. The strong foundations of her game had been laid down on a surface that allowed her to develop securely an all-court technique. She always had good ground strokes, a good defense (she was national hard court singles 13, 14, 15, and 18 champion), although her nature was attacking. Other methods, the kind of tennis she found outside California, were grafted onto what she already had. Her talent was born and shaped on the sunlit side of the U.S. and it didn't bother her that she never won a national junior title in the East.

In any case, by the age of 16 Rosie had lost interest in the junior game; it had to be put aside, it didn't allow her to grow. Her inchoate conflict with the NCTA burst in weltering impatience. She found herself forced to play junior tournaments when she had beaten world-class players. She thought of herself then as firmly part of the international set. Looking back, she says flatly, with no arrogance, that "there aren't any young girls around now who are as good as I was at 17. Diane Fromholtz hasn't got it. Betsy Nagelsen's overrated. Martina Navratilova, maybe. The rest, no way."

Rosie was so good at 17 that Billie Jean chose her as a doubles partner and took her to Wimbledon in 1966. That meeting might have been accidental, too, but it probably wasn't. Billie Jean knows tennis and wasn't about to make a mistake regarding talent. She needed Rosie for doubles because Rosie was the best there was.

In singles, she allowed Rosie to go her own way more than is generally supposed. Billie Jean has always recognized Rosie's tennis as different from her own and she has never forced her own style upon it. There are critics, both of tennis and of human nature, who might say that Billie Jean tried to take San Francisco out of Rosie and substitute Long Beach instead.

That would be wrong. Billie Jean's tennis is a layered and laminated product of years of experimentation. Rosie's game has not changed in this way. It was cast at her, a glittering gem she caught and ran with, not looking backward. Technically, it's doubtful she learnt much from Mrs. King.

Psychologically, though, Billie Jean was her buffer against certain kinds of strain. "She cooled it for me, generally," says Rosie. Their friendship was unique in sport. But however much it meant to Rosie personally, it harmed her very much in the public's eye. As Billie Jean came to be less than popular, Rosie felt contaminated in the same way. Cruelly, it took her own independence and denied her individuality.

Rosie remembers her bitterest moment on the tennis court: "It was in 1968, or sometime, when we were playing in the doubles at Wimbledon and that was the first time I really felt the crowd against me. I hated them. We were out there breaking our asses, playing our game, and all they could do was feel like that. It really hurt. I've never forgotten."

That changed something for Rosie and precipitated within her an isolation from the crowd that has grown like an accretion of brittle scales. The public, she says, "doesn't own you. I don't owe anything to them. I'm not winning for anyone else. No, I don't feel any remorse or regret. Now, I play only for myself. The public are very insensitive and hypocritical. They hate winners. I've become tougher I suppose. I have my pride. I've been attacked, messed around, misinterpreted. Sometimes I feel threatened. So what? I'm doing what I want to do."

The press? Rosie's contempt for the press isn't resentment without a cause. She's been abused, now she's mostly ignored. "Yes, I suppose I was cocky at first," she says, "but the press are always looking for someone new. Once I was new, now I'm out. Hardly anyone writes well about tennis. They don't do their job like I do mine. They spend all their time in the bar." She seldom reads the things written about her.

It might seem no more than simple paranoia, this chip-on-the-shoulder feeling that the world for some unlooked for reason turned against her. But it's better distinguished as something deeply rooted in Rosie's notions about the reciprocal nature of human generosity. What really hurts is that it was the people who did not know her, or separate her identity from Billie Jean, who became so lost in their dismissal of her personality that they came to overlook her ability.

To know Rosie, says Julie Heldman, is to love her. "Everybody loves her." She means the players. Julie can recollect endless stories of Rosie's kindness stretching back to days when they would meet at junior tournaments playing in different age groups. She'll remember forever the time she lay suffering from some painful illness in a noisy dormitory far from home, and Rosie, 14 years old and about three feet high, hovered around being maternal and caring for her in an incongruous but typical reversal of roles. To those she trusts, and who in turn trust and accept her, Julie observes, Rosie is incapable of vindictiveness or ingratitude.

And if there is a flaw in her competitive mentality, inhibiting the possibility of even psyched-up hate, it might be this sympathy and the gentleness at her core.

She reads a lot, mostly best-sellers, to pass the time when she's not sleeping in airplanes over a shuffling jig-saw of U. S. cities. One of her favorite books is Myra Friedman's *Buried Alive*, a biography of Janis Joplin. It's Friedman's empathy with Janis that enraptures her. "It's a fantastic book," Rosie says. "I think Myra Friedman did a beautiful job in capturing what Joplin was all about. This volatile talented person, not knowing where she was going or where she belonged—that she suffered so much and meant more to people than she ever knew. . . . No, I never ever saw her. I've always regretted that."

It touches Rosie, the portrayal of Janis as the confused, lonely, and disordered person burning her life away, as it touches anyone who has the power to identify with another's pain. But she herself is disinclined to follow the identity further. She knows her own skill depends on physical equilibrium and there are no synthetic short cuts to that.

Coincidentally, Rosie lived next to Janis Joplin in the Golden Gate Park. Their paths never crossed, but in some subtle way they were closer than they knew. Janis' electric voice and Rosie's electric racket—both instruments finding new ways to explore what Myra Friedman called, in her analysis of San Francisco music, "the sensual center of life."

Janis would have approved of, if she had been interested, in Rosie's style of play—the selected, structured, and planned direction of energy. Rosie's very conscious of style. Her game, she remarks, is "aggressive, variegated, and flexible, it's naturally myself. I'm a gutsy type player, I know that. You gotta hang in there, right? I know how I'm playing, when my style's working—there's coherence. I don't like playing on grass, you can't control things, it's frustrating aesthetically. You can't take risks, not creatively."

Generally, Rosie's not articulate about her tennis. There are players who say that she doesn't possess much insight into her game, and that it is this quality, rather than temperamental lapses, which holds her back. C. M. Jones, the English coach, remembers speaking to her once, after watching her play a perfect tactical match against Virginia Wade. And what he remembers most is that, retrospectively, she could explain nothing about what she had been doing. Call it instinct, or whatever, it's not tennis to take lessons from.

That is the difference between Billie Jean and Rosie. About Billie Jean one remembers matches, with Rosie it's the strokes that linger. They might be marvels, have you jumping up and down, but they are pieces of mosaic rather than the pattern. Rosie will admit sometimes that she's confused by her own versatility. The rich variability of her style imposes on her the strain of choosing and defining her own limitations at any given point in a particular match.

Hers is a more complex problem than one facing Chris Evert. Chris knows her strengths and weaknesses and works within them; she's refined the possibility of error to a minimum and will go on playing in exactly the same way for the rest of her career. Rosie's tennis is stylistically polarized. So prodigious a talent can invite so many ways of wasting it.

And yet that's what is creative about her—the sense of possibility, of ultimate things unmuttered. For a small person who does not let the idea of absolutes overwhelm her, space and movement become playthings. Interminable surprise flows from the end of her racket.

Swimming star Shane Gould once said of her sport: "I have a love affair with the water." You feel Rosie has the same relationship with air and space and the ground underneath her. They are elements to be caressed and molded into frameworks for her most delicate drop volleys or to be sliced apart by startlingly savage overheads.

She's talked about that. There's no way, she says, of communicating the physical feeling she gets from the game. And the pleasure of her own play is not the same as the pleasure of the crowd. It's beautiful, but it's solitary. No other player conveys such a feeling of privateness in performance. On court, she never smiles, never changes expression. It's impossible to tell, passing by, whether she's winning or losing.

Of course, she has her idiosyncrasies. Between games, she'll retie her headband, pour water on her racket handle from a paper cup. Receiving service, she sways from side to side on muscled thighs that give her most of her power and all of her mobility. Coming into the net, her hair flies out behind her, mouth slightly open, eyes wary and apprehensive. There's a Spaulding advertisement that captures this moment. She floats starkly beautiful, in a stratosphere of sun and shadow, poised forever on the instant of commitment. It's a portrait of arrested force and impacted violence. Her world is action and the world stands still. She likes it. Yes, she says, that's me.

Artistically, it might be fine for Rosie to be going her own way, doing her own thing, caring not a rap for the mob. But it compounds the alienation she's achieved in a personal way by retreat into defensive self-sufficiency. A man in the crowd at Wimbledon, watching her, asked: "I wonder why no one wants to see this girl play?" It isn't only that the spectators have short memories and a preference for slap-bang, wallop tennis. It is more that, in the context of the game as a dramatic spectacle, Rosie expresses an insouciance that turns back on herself.

Emotionally, she gives the public nothing at all. She is not, in the obvious sense, an entertainer. Her matches are soliloquies. And as a woman, she presents herself in a way that provokes antagonism. She hides behind no fluttering, mendacious "femininity." It is as though she collects everything that women are not allowed to be or feel and throws it all uncompromisingly beyond every stereotype.

She came to an interview once, an act of generosity on her part, swaggered in and sat down. Just sat. No smile. Nothing. She as much as said: here I am, take me as this person, a woman who plays tennis, and if you can't then it's your fault.

Is it really all right, though? Or is the bland unconcern in her set speeches, rattled off in that flat, abrasive Californian accent, a discrete symptom of *belle indifférence?* She'll say that every time she goes onto the court she knows she is going to win, yet many times she will play as if she began with hope abandoned. The aggression that is so much a part of her game sometimes seems, both in her tennis and in her off-court behavior, to be somehow undirected; she does not really know what to do with it and does not trust herself enough to make it work for her.

They must catch up with her, too, the always attendant goblins of insecurity and uncertainty, and at these moments the lonely pursuit of glory can hardly be comfort enough for the never winning, the inexplicable failures, the "doomed days" she speaks of. Billie Jean has her bad days, her matches that get away, but she never makes you feel like crying, as Rosie does, at the disappointment of personal weakness and artistic betrayal.

In a profound sense, Rosie's losses are losses to us all because we are looking, consciously or not, for happiness and escape through play and, instead, find something like real life reflected back to us —with no coherence, no happy ending, and no solution.

THE PERPETUAL MOTION OF BILLIE JEAN KING

By Tony Kornheiser

From Newsday

Copyright, ©, 1974, Newsday, Inc.

Mother Freedom can't sit still. Her hands wave spirals in the air, her arms flap, setting the gold bracelet on her arms jangling. She appears to be orchestrating a symphony, motioning at right angles in a speeding compulsion. Her chair constantly swivels, her body rebelling against immobility.

In front of her, members of her tennis team—the Philadelphia Freedoms—are practicing. Fred Stolle works on one side of the tennis court against Brian Fairlie and Buster Mottram. On the adjoining court Tory Ann Fretz works against Julie Anthony. They are spread out in front of her like toy soldiers, occasionally looking upward for her approval.

But for a moment two weekend players on Court 2 have her attention. They are engaged in a spirited, although awkward, rally. And she loves it.

"Right on, right on," she says, half screaming, clapping both hands and rolling backward into her seat, almost falling over with joy. "Did you see that guy hit? Did you see that guy run? Do you see how much they love it? I love it. I love it."

Billie Jean King tends to repeat things. Not so much because she likes the sound of her own voice, but because she can't stop it in time. No thought is ever far from her lips. She talks in semi-squeals, words rushing from her mouth like bullets from a machine gun. It is sometimes hard for her to remember what she has said because she has said so much.

She says she still loves tennis, but she has so much more to do now. She might go to law school. She might go into politics. She has

already begun publishing a women's sports magazine and she wants
to create a women's all-sports tournament similar to the Superstars
concept that exists for men. She appears to be going in so many
different directions at once. Moving like a swarm of gnats, going
everywhere, going nowhere.

"Ooohhh," she says, momentarily slumping into her chair as if
needing a rest before making her self-analysis. "I'm so hyper. So
hyper. There's just so much that I want to do. I need three of me."

Since defeating Bobby Riggs ten months ago in one of the most
publicized sporting events in recent memory, Billie Jean King has
been riding a wave of fame, money, and publicity that has her
reeling. Her face has been on newspaper and magazine covers. Her
signature as player-coach of the Freedoms—the first woman coach
in male-oriented pro sports—was worth $500,000 to Dick Butera,
the Freedoms' owner. While claiming to turn down "99 percent of
the endorsement offers," she has still made commercials for tooth-
paste, deodorant, and suntan oil. Her visibility is staggering. Her
privacy has become just a fond memory.

"That's really the biggest price you pay," she says. "Time and
privacy are luxuries that money can't buy me now. In the back of my
mind I thought I could handle things becoming this big, but I didn't
really envision this whole trip. It's unbelievable."

Things that others take for granted are impossible in the post-
Riggs period. She can't walk more than a block from her Philadelphia home on Society Hill without signing autographs. She can't get
past her shrimp cocktail without being introduced to some guy's
sister who saw her play Riggs on television and can't believe that
yes, it's really her, right in this same restaurant.

"Americans bother you and Europeans stare at you," she says. "I
don't know which is worse."

She is public property now. She accepts that. She has to because
the thing she wants most in the world "is for everyone to love me."
But the accompanying paranoia has grabbed her. She believes that
everyone is prejudging her. "Pre-Riggs killed me," she says. "Everyone wanted an exclusive interview, and you can't give 350 of them
every day. I told them after it was all over I'd do them. I was wrong.
After Riggs it was worse.

"I'll see old friends, and they'll come up to me and say—I'll bet
you won't even talk to me now that you're so big. They won't even
give me a chance. Why is that? Why is that? Tell me why?

"I don't think people understand how much of your life is interrupted. You know what's the worst? The worst is when I cannot sign any more autographs and someone looks up and says—Hey, who do you think you are, Miss Hotshot?

"If they only knew. . . ."

But despite all the inconvenience, she doesn't plea bargain for sympathy. "I'm happier now than I've ever been," she says.

WTT has provided her with a new set of challenges to keep her interest up, right when she was losing it after going so many years through tournament tennis, methodically defeating all challenges.

In effect, she is WTT. Much like the signing of Rick Barry was supposed to give credibility to the American Basketball Association seven years ago, her role adds legitimacy to WTT. All around the 16 league cities she is outdrawing other tennis teams by as much as a 5–1 ratio. She drew 11,000 to Minnesota. Her upcoming appearance in the Nassau Coliseum on Friday is expected to draw 9,000 people—by far the biggest crowd of the season.

"You gotta get them into the seats. That's what a superstar does," she said, momentarily forgetting that earlier she was unable to define what a superstar is or does. "But I try to put that whole thing of carrying a league in the background. We're gonna have to sell the concept, and the concept will produce the stars. . . . What is bugging me is that the league doesn't share gate receipts. Now we are going out and selling tickets and the Philadelphia team isn't making any money from it. That's wrong."

Originally, King was supposed to sign with the Sets. That's what the league wanted from a media viewpoint and she recognized how much sense it made for her to play in New York. She turned down a $2,000,000 offer from Minnesota—"They were going to call the team the Kings," she said—and narrowed her choice between New York and Philadelphia. She picked Philadelphia because her friend, Butera, offered her a personal services contract. And because the man who owned the Sets at the time, Jerry Sapenstein, couldn't convince her that he was serious about staying in the league.

"I always thought I'd sign with New York," she said. "I love New York. But some guys seemed to get into the league quickly just to get out quickly. If I didn't know what the New York owner would be doing a year after the league started, that's pretty hairy. . . . I talked to Dick [Butera] about moving his franchise up there. But he wanted to stay in Philadelphia, so I went with him. I don't feel guilty about it. I gotta live, too.

"I signed in August. You know they could have had me well

before that for half the money, but they [WTT] wanted John New-combe first. Now look at it. Newcombe is with Houston and that city doesn't even know that tennis exists. You figure it out. It's the same old thing—no one wants to think that a woman can do it."

King is doing it, however. She is winning. She is packing the arenas. She is doing three and four interviews a day to promote the league, and she is coaching.

At first the coaching was hard. The men on her team weren't as responsive to her as she would have liked. Mottram and Fairlie virtually ignored Billie Jean and sought out Stolle's advice whenever they had a problem. But she persevered and now it appears she has won their confidence and respect.

"I knew there would be a problem," she said. "I knew it would be a real ego-crusher to take instructions from a woman. I made up my mind from the beginning that I would have to show them that I'd listen to them, that I wouldn't be on a power trip. I made them run a lot. Fred didn't like that especially. But he's in better shape now than he's been in for years. And gradually they came to under-stand that I knew the game. . . .

"I really take it seriously. Most nights I'm up till three in the morning worrying about how to coach, how to help a player. I've proved to them that I know what I'm talking about. We're close. We all go out and have ice cream together. . . . God, I love ice cream."

But she gave up ice cream for five months before Wimbledon, earlier this month. She wanted to win badly, to prove she could be a champion in tournament tennis despite the harrowing schedule she had allowed to grip her after the Riggs victory. She lost to the eventual runner-up, Olga Morozova. She didn't even make semis.

"That was the worst I've played in years there," she said. "Ooohhh, that . . . I was ready. I was eager. Dammit, I didn't want to lose."

She is 30 years old now, and for the first time she resents the nickname she gave herself—The Old Lady. She is feeling somewhat mortal about her tennis future now, admitting the possibility that it might have peaked and that the rest of her career will be less flam-boyant, less positive.

"I don't know," she said, "I think about it. Physically, I'm tired. I've had . . . operations, and the other girls are catching up to me. I don't know how I can go on. It may come to the point where the best I can do is make the semis in tournament.

"Most athletes don't know when to quit. I don't know if I'll know either. Maybe I'll be like Ken Rosewall, just happy to play the game. Maybe making the quarters—the semis will be enough for me. The next ten years could be the best ten years of life, but I don't think I can let myself become only wrapped up in tennis. I want to see the game grow, and I wanted to be part of that growth. Well, it's grown like crazy. It could get bigger. It will get bigger. But there comes a time when everyone has to get out."

Clearly she has branched out already. Financially she has no worries. She is already a millionaire, "at least close to it." Her opportunity to engage herself in other things have never been more appropriate. She talks of having children. "If I want them, I ought to get started," she said. But she doesn't think she would have enough time to give them just now.

Ultimately she sees herself as a leader of both men and women in some grand design toward equality in sports and society. She never talked in those terms before, mainly because she knew that other women on the tour didn't trust her. They thought she was on a power trip.

That has changed. The women have made her president of their tennis union and each time she wants to quit, they plead with her not to. Her coaching experience has proven to her that she can communicate well with men, even when she has the final say in their athletic activities. She is on the board of directors of a bank in her adopted home of Philadelphia. Her major duties there are in setting up a program to insure that women are not discriminated against in any phase of banking. She has seen exploitation close up and she is determined not to be part of it now that she can easily be tokenized for her face and her name.

But the future remains a question for her. "I could go one of two ways," she said. "I could get out of the limelight and maybe stay in coaching to remain in tennis and then work at publishing and banking and other things to help women. But I've been in the limelight so long, I'm not sure how I would cope with being out of it!

"Or I could stay there. Maybe get into politics. I don't know anything about politics. But I know I wouldn't screw the people. Wouldn't you say I'm in politics already?"

For the moment politics really intrigues her. Though she says she hates the cocktail parties and the glad-handing, she realizes their necessity. "I'd do it if I had to," she said. "I'd run for any office where I could do the most good. Sure a woman could get elected to something. That's like asking me whether or not I'd make a good

woman coach. I've been a woman all my life. Ask me about coaching. Don't ask me about being a woman politician. Ask me about
being a politician."

And then she thinks about it for a while, and a look crosses her
face—something very far away. As if she's trying on the podium for
size, feeling the crowd in front of her, sensing the way they respond
to her words. And she stays that way for maybe five seconds when
the Freedoms' trainer comes over and starts massaging her back,
waking her from the dream.

"Right on," she says, "right on."

THE BUSINESS OF WINNING

By Kim Foltz

From Gentlemen's Quarterly

Copyright, ©, 1974, Esquire Inc.

The red-white-and-blue new decor of room 2337 at the Boston Sheraton vaguely intimates someone is actually living in this cubicle of prefab plastic. A movie script in a red paper cover has been tossed onto the middle of a rumpled bed. An Agatha Christie thriller is spread-eagled face up on the floor amid a collection of the week's sports sections. The small table under a mirror near the door is covered with jumbo-size bottles of vitamins, golf books, and medicine. Metal tennis rackets are everywhere. Dirty jockstraps, shorts, T-shirts, Ace bandage boxes, 12 red-and-blue striped size-12 Adidas sneakers and an equal number of sweat-soaked socks are draped on the bureau, chairs, floor—the leavings of a man on the run, a tennis transient scrambling for a place on the big-money circuit.

Out of the window, looking inland, the landscape is dominated by the bandaged monolith of the John Hancock skyscraper. Plywood squares dot its wounded face, like a hundred eye patches, replacing the glass in windows which are cracking one by one under the strain of too much design and too little practicality.

Twenty-one floors below in the glass-walled, very pastel coffee shop meant to give the impression of being outside while actually being in, John Newcombe sits on a small, yellow-cushioned chair, his powerful body gingerly leaning against the delicate white-iron table as he carefully cuts his cheeseburger with a knife and fork. He avoids the cold french fries. He talks politely about his life as a rising sports star between bite-size portions of burger and double-straw sips from a vanilla shake. "There really isn't a number one tennis player as such. At any given time there's maybe five or six top players who are interchangeable in the top spot. I'm good, but not the unequivocal number one. Things change too fast to make that kind of judgment."

Newcombe had arrived at the Commercial Union Masters tennis tournament on a cold, gray winter day. It looked like rain in Boston, a cold, penetrating rain, a bone chiller that could dampen even the headiest spirits. But Newcombe paid slight attention, if that. He was insulated by his victories—the Davis Cup just a few days prior, and the U.S. Open in August. He was setting the tennis circuit on fire —the photographers' flashes, the blinding television studio lights, stadium lights, the warm sweaty handshakes of autograph seekers, the heated sessions with agents for product promotions and movie offers—everything was going in the right direction. He was gaining a following, generating media interest, becoming a hot prospect. Fame was within his grasp. At that moment, he was the undisputed number one tennis player.

Through the whirrr-click-whirrr of the papparazzi, he molds his body to staccato commands, conforming to their concepts of New-combe on magazine cover, on inside spreads, on newspaper sports pages. He smiles easily and often, even as he unwinds his legs from uncomfortable poses, never unriveting his bright blue eyes from the lenses, as the cameras snap. He tells of his success quickly, as if someone is going to snatch it from him before the tale is complete.

"I knew I was going to be a champ when I was 10. And sure enough, the next year I won the New South Wales State Tournament. After that I zeroed in on tennis alone—gave up all the other sports," the Australian says, spearing the last piece of hamburger with his fork.

Since he was 6 years old, Newcombe has been playing tennis and playing it well. He was a natural, taking on all comers and winning most of the time. He practiced hard—winning was important—but the game never became all consuming. Even though tennis was going to be his livelihood, he vowed it wasn't going to be his life. He allowed time for dances, girl friends, and horsing around with the guys, realizing, even as an adolescent, how lonely it was out on the court with all those people surrounding him, watching him, waiting, willing only to love the champ.

Newcombe's ascent into the big-money ranks didn't begin until he developed a psychological game plan in 1966 with the help of an Australian psychiatrist. During that 15-hour session, he began to see tennis as a mental contest where finely tuned concentration could defeat even the most highly developed physical machine. The two developed a strategy enabling Newcombe to "psych" himself into a winning frame of mind.

Before each important tournament he sits on the locker room bench, shutting out the noise of the showers and good-luck ass slapping, and takes 30 minutes to run through what's to come. He visualizes going out onto the court, the crowd, the newsmen, the flip, serves, volleys, faults, and his victory. Having studied films of all the top players in action—not to mention playing against them —he has their techniques, their idiosyncrasies, weak points and strengths down pat. "It's very important not to tense up once you're out on the court. The gangs of photographers, the TV cameras, the polite hush in the stadium, the millions of people watching and hoping you'll win or lose, all of this can put your nerves on edge— knock you off balance. But once I've gone through it in my mind, I know what to expect, so nothing surprises me, nothing catches me off guard."

Not until each game actually begins does Newcombe formulate his playing strategy. He watches his opponent carefully, sizing up his mental attitude, while at the same time he's chasing balls all over the court and smashing them back at his rival. Sometimes he teases his adversary with his technique, coaxing him into a trap. He'll use his forward backhand on the second serve time after time until he's convinced the other player that this pattern will be continually repeated. Then he'll switch, catching him off guard. The opponent usually never regains his footing.

When the going gets rough, as it did against Stan Smith at Wimbledon in 1971, Newcombe is apt to do almost anything to "psych out" his opponent. In the final match to determine the meet champion, Smith was winning 3 to 2 in the fourth set when Newcombe fell heavily near the net in a futile scramble for the ball. At first he didn't rise. Smith approached apprehensively. Silence. Newcombe struggled to his feet, dangling a contorted arm, as if it were broken. Having riveted everyone's attention to him, he flashed his sparkling eyes and grin. It had been a hoax. The crowd roared. Smith cursed. But a mood was set. Smith's intense concentration had been broken. He lost the next serve, fluffed easy volleys, all but self-destructed. Newcombe had charmed his way into capturing the audience, match, and title.

Just as important as his ability to size up opponents' weaknesses is Newcombe's intense concentration and the fierceness with which he plays. In the summer of 1972, Newcombe was playing at Forest Hills in the U.S. Open Tournament. It was early in the competition and he was facing a young player named Delaney. The match wasn't in the grandstand or stadium where "seeded" players battle in the hush of a removed audience. They were playing on one of the 20 field courts. Each is edged with a knee-high hedge, and people wander by, watch, talk, then wander on. Surrounded by this atmosphere of confusion, of "Hey, buddy, how are ya?" or "Mildred, hurry, Nastase just went that way," as he reached for the ball, Newcombe enveloped himself with a shell of intense concentration. Nothing existed except the ball flying back and forth and the guy across the net. Again and again he smashed the ball at Delaney. Even though he was hitting the hell out of the ball, Delaney could barely hold his own. And watching, all you could think was if Newcombe hit you four times the way he was hitting that ball, you'd be dead.

But his ferocious zeal and concentration on the courts have paid off handsomely. Since his first big wins in 1969—Wimbledon and Forest Hills—he's been steadily climbing in the standings and money. In 1973, Newcombe earned just over $150,000 playing tennis, placing first in five tournaments. And this year he plans to push his earnings even higher by carefully picking only the big-money tournaments and going all out to psych himself for them.

Off the courts, his easygoing manner, good looks, and boyish eagerness are making him money too. Partner in the T-Bar-M Ranch at New Braunfels, Texas (where he teaches summer tennis camps for both children and adults), Newcombe also endorses or promotes a myriad of products ranging from Rawlings tennis rackets, to Samsonite luggage, to Exxon gas. He's currently starring in an Australian-produced movie, *Game, Set, Murder,* in which he is poisoned by a woman. The movies, even if they work into a steady thing, are an exciting diversion for Newcombe; he doesn't plan to abandon tennis, not yet.

Continually running from one tournament to the next, one promotion to another, leaves Newcombe little time for himself. Last year he spent less than three months with his family—and that was in bits and pieces. Although his wife Angie sometimes travels with him, the three children usually stay at their home in Sydney, Australia. "I know I'm overextending myself," Newcombe says, slurping the last of his shake, "but I don't go looking for all these things, they just seem to find me. I keep telling myself I won't make any more commitments, but then my agent comes to me with some new proposition and I always end up doing more than I want to."

The minute he finished his shake, it was a quick grin, good-bye, and he was off again. He had less than an hour to pack and make it to the Boston airport for a Philadelphia-bound plane. It'll be a one-day, product-promotion stopover, then back to Sydney for the Australian Open. After that, it's back to America, to another city, it doesn't matter which one. They all begin to look alike—the tennis courts, the hotel rooms—when you hit more than 40 of them a year. But Newcombe doesn't mind so much; it's a living and he loves playing tennis. And in a profession where the money stops when the winning stops, Newcombe knows he has to scramble while he can.

Even for 29-year-old Newcombe, there aren't that many good years left—maybe 10 at the outside—before he just doesn't have the stamina to compete with the new, young crop of champs. So before the knee that's been giving him trouble on and off for the last few years finally gives out, or he just gets too old, he has to scramble for the money, for security. He has to scramble.

Golf

A MAGNIFICENT 9-IRON SHOT WINS THE MASTERS

By Art Spander

From the San Francisco Chronicle

© Chronicle Publishing Co., 1974

On a gray, clammy afternoon, during which hopes kept falling but putts rarely did, the pressure of the Masters golf tournament caught up to the egos and games of all the world's top golfers—with one exception.

It wasn't Jack Nicklaus, the man who was supposed to win, although for a while it seemed it would be. It wasn't Tom Weiskopf, the eternal runner-up, although until the fading moments it was a possibility. It wasn't even Dave Stockton, the bubbling optimist, even though he went into the final round with the lead.

Rather, it was Gary Player, the South African with the somber dress and solid game, who's made the globe his own little golf ball and, once again, Augusta National Golf Course his own little haven.

He fought off the tension and torment that had dashed the dreams of the other leaders yesterday and then, with one magnificent 9-iron shot to within millimeters of the 17th cup, he captured his second Masters championship—and his seventh major tournament victory.

Attired in his usual, and ironic, black clothes, ironic because of the apartheid racial policies of the white government of his home country, Gary shot a final round 2-under-par 70 for a 72-hole total of 10-under-par 278.

That put him two shots ahead of Stockton and Weiskopf, who tied for second with scores of 280, and three shots ahead of Nicklaus, Hale Irwin, and Jim Colbert, who tied for fourth with 281.

That also gave Player, 37, the first-place check, which this year was increased to $35,000, but the money is incidental.

What isn't incidental is his second Masters, and another step toward becoming only the second man in history to win all four of the major championships at least twice, a move he could complete by taking the U.S. Open in June in New York.

Gary, the only foreigner to win the Masters in its 38 years—in 1961 and yesterday—also has two British Opens, 1959 and '68, and two American PGA championships, 1962 and '72. His one U.S. Open triumph came in 1965.

Nicklaus, who has a record 14 major championships, double the number of Player, is the only golfer ever to win all of them at least twice, including four Masters' titles.

A lot of people were certain on the humid afternoon that Nicklaus would make it five. And, after eagling the par-5 13th hole to go 8 under par and create chaos at the top of the leader board, those people seemed to be right. But Jack lost his cool, which wasn't hard to do in the humidity, or maybe his direction. Whatever, he finished like a guy staggering home from an all-night party.

About the same thing happened to most of the contenders, as either the rolling acreage of 7,020-yard Augusta National or the ineffable pressure of attempting to win what some people consider the most important tournament of the year, picked them off one by one.

Stockton couldn't make a putt on the front nine, Weiskopf doused his hopes when he hit his tee shot into the pond on 16. Hale Irwin wasn't able to pull off the right shot at the right time. Jim Colbert made just enough bad shots to offset a spectacular one, an 8-iron he holed for an eagle 2 on the 18th. Hubert Green collapsed slowly, and Frank Beard did it quickly—going from 6 under par to 2 under par by hitting two balls in the water on the par-3 16th and taking a quadruple bogey seven.

For a while, it even seemed the moment was too great for Player. Gary, after taking the lead with a birdie on the 9th hole, to shoot a 2-under 34, made bogeys on 10 and 12.

But he birdied the par-5 13th and then, considering the circumstances, came up with the most memorable shot of the tournament.

"I had been hitting the ball well," said the little man (5-foot-6, 150 pounds) from Johannesburg, "better from tee to green than I had in any major championship. But I had been putting, except for Saturday, like a dub.

"I was 142 yards from the pin, and I told my caddy, 'Eddie, in all the years I've played here, I don't think I've hit that green six times.'

But I remember when I won the Masters in '61, I won it on the 17th hole. I went over the green, chipped to within 12 feet and made the putt for a par.

"I told Eddie, 'We're going to win it again on this hole.' I hit the ball right at the stick. I thought it would be in. Eddie said, 'It's in the hole.' I had been putting badly, so I said, 'We're not going to have to putt that one.' " He was wrong. He had to putt it. From six inches.

The birdie gave him a two-shot lead, and he and Eddie McCoy, his 32-year-old caddy, climbed the final obstacle, the hill to the 18th green, where Gary 2-putted for a par.

He walked over and gave Eddie, a black man like all caddies at Augusta, what is known as the Soul Shake, interlocking thumbs. And in a day or two, he'll give McCoy something even more substantial —a check "for at least $2,000, but probably much more."

Asked how he happens to know the Soul Shake, customary greeting of American blacks, Player said, "My best friend on my farm in South Africa, my foreman, is a black man, and that's the way they all shake hands down there."

Quick to pick up customs, Gary is also as quick to pick up dollars. The first-place check gave him more than $1 million in earnings on the American PGA tour. And, as he pointed out so effectively, being as confident in discussions as he is on the fairways, "I would have done it a lot sooner if I'd have spent all my time playing here, not staying home or playing around the world."

And he does play around the world. He's Henry Kissinger in spikes and doubleknits. Wednesday he'll tee off in the Spanish Open. The following week it will be in Japan. Then it's home to South Africa and in four weeks back to the U.S.

"You have to win everywhere to be a great player," said this Player, undoubtedly a great.

THE GREATEST GOLFER IN THE WORLD

By Nick Seitz

From Golf Digest

Copyright, ©, 1974, Golf Digest Inc.

Phil Ritson, his early teacher, remembers sharing a room with a 16-year-old Gary Player and waking in the morning to find Player staring into a mirror and declaring, "I'm going to be the greatest golfer in the world! I'm going to be the greatest golfer in the world!" He must have said it 50 times, Ritson remembers, and then he went out and practiced sand shots by the dawn's early light.

Twenty-two years later, Player is one of a very few golfers who could be ranked great, and he has lost none of his zealous determination. It is easy to imagine him today in front of a mirror repeating his vows or out slapping sand shots as the rest of us slumber heedlessly through the pre-breakfast hours.

Depending on the day you ask him, he speaks with iron resolve and eyes that burn with the intensity of automobile headlights of one towering goal or another. He wants to win more tournaments than anybody else ever, he wants to complete a second cycle in the four major championships, he wants to strike the ball as purely as Ben Hogan. And he continues to compete around the world week after week in his unwavering quest for immortality.

"Of all of us," observes David Graham, the bright young touring pro from Australia, "he most deserves his success. Sometimes he carries his positive thinking too far—he's the only guy I know who can shoot 80 and say he hit the ball super—but then he's a great self-promoter. He's a credit to the sport, and his record is better than people realize. The man won a major tournament 15 years ago and he won two more majors in 1974."

I buy Graham's assessment. We have had enough lightweight debates over Player's sincerity in matters of physical fitness, race relations, and international diplomacy. There is no denying that his enthusiasm can overflow the banks of thoughtfulness and spill out into ridiculous overstatement. For instance, he says with revival-tent fervor, "I know I've worked harder than any human being up to age 38, not just at golf but at developing my body, my public relations, my mind." A truly well-developed mind might not make a claim like that. A course on which Gary has just shot 67 always seems to be the toughest he has ever overcome. An almost compulsive competitor, Player has to have a test of character. If he doesn't have an obstacle to clear, he will erect one to keep up his interest, and at positive thinking he should give Norman Vincent Peale two a side.

But we should appreciate that Player is essentially a golfer and should be judged by us, as golf followers, essentially as a golfer. It is on the course, single-mindedly confronting—almost embracing—his next problem, that the real Gary Player reveals himself.

In 1974 Player was overshadowed by Johnny Miller, who almost forgot how to lose. Miller deserves the honors he got, including the PGA Player of the Year Award, but Player deserves more acclaim than he got. Certainly the PGA should re-evaluate its somewhat specious points system for determining a player of the year when Player finishes sixth.

Player in 1974 just might have come closer to winning the Grand Slam than anyone has. In 1953 Ben Hogan won three of the four major tournaments but didn't enter the fourth, the PGA Championship. Six others have won two majors in a season since the Masters began in 1934: Craig Wood, Sam Snead, Jack Burke, Arnold Palmer, Jack Nicklaus, and Lee Trevino. Did any of them come as close to the slam as Player? He won the Masters from behind and the British Open from in front (his seventh and eighth majors over-all), was tied for the lead in the U.S. Open after two rounds and was never more than five shots from the top in the PGA, matching the tournament record of 64 in the second round.

Player also won at Memphis in this country and took six titles abroad to go over 100 for his pro career. He capped the year by winning the Brazilian Open where he shot a shocking 59. "It was my best year," he says, "and maybe the best year anyone ever had." All this the year after major surgery, more serious than most of us realized, took him out of action and out of our field of attention.

As usual, Player came back from adversity with redoubled desire, in one case flying for two solid days and nights and disembarking from the plane to go straight to the course and win another tournament. He says he has traveled a total of four million miles to play golf, and that is one record that should outlive us all. Unlike the other superstars, he still practices as much as he plays, devising competitive games to make himself concentrate. He might hit chip shots, for example, until he sinks three dozen, come hell, high water, or darkness.

Where does he get his dedication? How does he sustain it?

To reply, Player flashes back to his boyhood. We are eating in a New York restaurant, Player with the meticulousness he applies to everything, cutting his steak into uniformly small bites, drinking warm water laced with lemon juice to aid his digestive processes. He talks of the death of his mother when he was 8 and the insistence then and thereafter of his father, a good golfer who worked in the South African gold mines, that affirmative thinking is the only response to a challenge. That was his first exposure to positive thinking.

An older brother, Ian, further influenced him at an early age to try harder than the rest, Player says in his new book *Gary Player: World Golfer*. Ian, who refused to be held back by a chronically bad knee, laid out a five-mile track where the two ran together. One day the young Gary wearied and went to his knees, wheezing that he couldn't finish.

He writes, "My lungs felt as if they would burst. Without any warning Ian yanked me to my feet and cuffed me on the side of the head. 'What do you mean you can't make it, man?' he exploded, his face flushed red with anger. 'You can do anything you want to. Remember that. There's no room for can't in this life.' I'll never know how I did it, but even though my feet felt like they were weighted down with lead and my leg muscles were knotted with pain, I ran the rest of that five miles without stopping for anything. Believe me, I was cured of ever threatening to quit in front of Ian again."

It was Ian, Gary says, who gave him his first golf club, which he had whittled from a stick.

Soon after Player devoted himself to golf he made Ben Hogan his hero. He still reveres him, although there has been friction between the two. Hogan's example convinced Player that a small man without great natural athletic ability could construct a winning golf game.

"I promise you Hogan knows more about striking a golf ball than any man who ever lived," Player says. "If I could just ask him five questions and get his answers I'd be a lot better player than I am."

You no doubt have heard the story about Player calling Hogan at his equipment plant from overseas for help with his swing. The conversation is supposed to have gone something like this:

"Mr. Hogan, this is Gary Player. I would like to ask you a question about the swing."

"Gary, who do you work for?"

"The Dunlop company."

"Well, call Mr. Dunlop." Click.

About the call, Player says, "I wasn't put out that he refused to give me advice. If you ask for something for nothing, you have to expect a tough answer. My feelings were hurt when he hung up on me. But when the two of us were inducted into the Hall of Fame in Pinehurst he was most charming to me and my wife."

Player believes Hogan, who has a photostatic memory, was rankled over a business misunderstanding when Player first came to this country in 1955. Player then had only $3,000 to his name, he says. The Hogan company offered him $2,800 to play its equipment. At the same time, First Flight offered him $9,000. Player at the time was being counseled by a man in England (he now is managed by Mark McCormack) and says he called the Englishman and asked what he should do.

"He told me, 'By all means, you must take the $9,000.' Then I asked him if he would arrange things for me with First Flight and explain to the Hogan company what I was going to do. He said he would but I later found out he never told the Hogan company anything. I was just 19 and had no business experience or I would have made sure it was handled properly. I think that caused the tension."

Many experts suspect Player has always fought a pull-hook shot pattern because he wants to swing shorter and flatter like Hogan. Player periodically proclaims victory over his roundhouse hook; after winning the '74 Masters he announced he had found The Secret. *Golf Digest* Instruction Editor Larry Dennis pried it out of him—Player said he was holding his head more upright so he wouldn't block his natural backswing turn—but going into the 1975 season Player was still hooking dramatically at times.

The fact is the tense-looking Player's game invariably is less imposing on the face of it than that of any other top player, what with his hooking and finishing his swing off-balance and using unorthodox strategy. He can shoot 68 and appear to be shooting 15 strokes higher. But he frequently brings off daredevil recovery shots. It doesn't hurt him to be off balance at the finish of his swing as long as he's in balance when he contacts the ball, and his strategy has a way of working out.

Hale Irwin, the U.S. Open champion, shakes his head summing up Player's game. "You can learn things from all these great players," he says, "but Gary could drive you crazy if you were paired with him often enough. I played with him the first two rounds of the British Open and he hit a lot of 3-woods and long irons off the tee that I couldn't understand. He left himself second shots that were harder than his first shots. But the name of the game is scoring, and he knows it. He has a great pair of hands, and I have to think he was born in the sand the way he comes out of it."

Says Phil Ritson, "Gary has the will power to completely blot a bad shot out of his mind. He forgets it immediately and begins planning the next one. Every shot is a separate little game with him."

Perhaps most crucially, Player gives every shot his utmost respect and concentration whether it's a trouble shot or a tap-in putt. "The thing I admire so much about him," says Byron Nelson, "is that he just never wastes a stroke, not once in a year. He plays each shot for everything it's worth."

There is a story about Player emptying a shagbag on the practice green and making one-foot putts for an hour. A fellow pro asked him what in the name of Harry Vardon he was doing. "I'm getting used to sinking putts," was Player's answer.

At 38, we see no indication that Player's awesome dedication is flagging. He reminds us when he and I compare all-time greats that a player really should not be evaluated until his career is done, and implies that his is far from ended.

Says Jimmy Demaret, a peer of Hogan's, "Player is self-disciplined and physically fit, and I think he can be a super player for five more years without exhausting himself. When he gets into his forties, his legs will get weak and then his nervous system will go. He won't be another Sam Snead, playing top golf at 62. He isn't big enough. But in my time Player and Hogan are the most dedicated golfers I've ever seen, and I've seen a few."

If the next five years are anything like 1974, Player might not have to play longer than five more years to satisfy even himself.

Horse Racing

CANNONADE CHARGES THROUGH

By Neil Milbert

From the Chicago Tribune

Reprinted, courtesy of the Chicago Tribune

Poised as Princess Margaret who lent a royal air to the occasion, a bay colt named Cannonade authoritatively won the 100th running of the Kentucky Derby this cool, clear afternoon.

The Princess was part of a record throng of 163,628 that participated in this centennial classic at Churchill Downs.

Not only was it a colossal crowd in terms of men, women, and children but in terms of 3-year-old thoroughbreds as well. The field of 23 was the largest in Kentucky Derby history.

As a result, it was as easy to get in trouble on the racetrack as it was in downtown Louisville last night.

Yet Cannonade resolutely stuck to the straight and narrow, avoiding the pitfalls that swallowed up his peers at virtually every turn.

Roughed up coming out of the starting gate, Cannonade remained cool, calm, and collected. He turned the other cheek and took his time, letting Jockey Angel Cordero play a part not unlike that of a parent leading his little boy across a crowded street.

After finding peace and quiet along the rail in the middle of the pack for the first half-mile, Cannonade swung outside and got down to the business of winning the horse race.

The field started to bunch nearing the far turn and Cordero found himself with a horse who wanted to run and opportunity beckoning.

Sir Tristram, who had shown nice early speed in pursuit of pacesetting Triple Crown and runner-up Hudson County, went into reverse.

Destroyer had moved up strongly, but he turned out to be only a pretender, not a serious contender.

A hole squeaked open between Triple Crown and Destroyer and Cannonade charged through. Hudson County was also equal to the challenge, but with a quarter-mile to go Cannonade was in command.

"This colt did everything I asked him," the jubilant Cordero said afterward.

"If the hole no open, I no be worried because I still got enough horse to go outside. He know what was happening and I say to him, 'You get me to the eighth pole, I get you the rest of the way.'"

The 32-year-old native of Puerto Rico kept his word. When Hudson County, four lengths behind at one point in the stretch, mounted a minor counterattack, Cordero took matters in his hands. About eight slaps sufficed, and Cannonade crossed the wire 2 1/4 lengths to the good.

His time for the mile and a quarter was 2:04, nowhere near Secretariat's record 1:59 set last year.

What Cannonade's performance lacked in speed it made up for in dollars and cents. This was the richest Derby in history with a gross purse of $326,500, and Cannonade's $274,000 share was an American record.

(The previous American record was the $250,000 won by Convenience for beating Typecast in the 1972 match race at Hollywood Park.)

Cannonade ran as an entry with Judger for trainer Woody Stephens and the entry returned $5, $3, and $2.40 at the betting windows. Runner-up Hudson County (lumped with nine others in the mutuel field) paid $4.40 and $2.60 and the show horse, Agitate, returned $2.80.

Agitate, according to Jockey Bill Shoemaker, was a victim of the circumstances that surrounded the 100th running of this most pompous of American races—namely the size of the field.

"It was some kind of an uproar out there," Shoemaker lamented. "I had to let him roll leaving the gate to get a position, and then I got pinched back. I wasn't as close as I wanted to be. Then, at the half-mile pole, something came off the rail and really knocked me.

"Considering all the trouble Agitate had, he ran a dynamite race."

Another who found himself constantly in jeopardy was Judger's jockey, Laffit Pincay. A formidable stretch-runner considered by many the better half of an entry that went off a 3–5 favorite, Judger finished eighth, never a factor.

Trainer Stephens said he had treated Judger with the pain-reliever Butazolidin (now legal in Kentucky), causing observers to suspect that the colt was not 100 percent.

Also disappointing were both halves of trainer Frank Martin's highly regarded entry—Rube the Great (who finished 10th) and Accipiter (18th).

Whereas both of Martin's horses are owned by the same man (Sigmund Sommer), Stephens' entry carried two sets of colors. John Olin owns Cannonade, while Judger is the property of Seth Hancock.

A native of Alton, Illinois, who's almost as old as the Derby, the 81-year-old Olin was not part of today's throng. Suffering from a heart ailment, he watched the race on TV at his St. Louis home.

Olin was also the breeder of Cannonade (by Bold Bidder—Queen Sucree, by Ribot). The head of Olin Mathieson Chemical Corp., he never previously owned or bred a Kentucky Derby starter.

The 60-year-old Stephens trained six previous Derby starters— Halt (fifth in 1949), Blue Man (third in 1952), Goyamo (fourth in 1954), Bourbon Prince (fifth in 1960), Never Bend (second in 1963), and Captain's Gig (10th in 1968).

Cannonade went into the Derby with a middle-income 1974 bankroll of $49,900. Lightly raced this year after a strenuous 18-race campaign last year, Cannonade scored his second triumph in five starts.

His first victory this year was in last Saturday's seven-furlong Stepping Stone here when he closed forcefully on the outside. As it turned out, that was the handwriting on the wall.

GENTLEMEN, START YOUR EXCUSES

By Phil Jackman

From The Baltimore Evening Sun

A good guess is 15 horses will run in the 99th Preakness next Saturday . . . which, translated, reads a winner and 14 alibis (minimum).

And some of the excuses will be wowsers, believe.

The losing jockey blames the owner, trainer, track, and horse while the trainer indicts the jock, owner, program seller, and stewards and the owner views the whole business as a Communist plot.

They put an "excuse board" up in the racing secretary's office at Pimlico a few years ago, but had to take it down when there wasn't enough room for all the entries and people started writing on the walls.

George Cusimano cited how one day, just as his mount broke from the gate, a pigeon flew by and crashed into the side of the horse's head.

Imagine the conversation back at the barn.

Owner: "What happened, George?"

Cusimano: "I ran into a pigeon."

Owner: "You been drinking?"

Then there's the ride Vince Bracciale took on a horse named Nez Percé a few weeks back.

Slow at the bell on a rainy day, Bracciale got hit square with a face full of mud and he couldn't see through his goggles.

He kept swinging out and passing what he thought were horses until he got the glasses cleaned off at about the half-mile mark. There wasn't a thing near him, meaning he had been zigzagging past horses that weren't there.

"I used to run jockey quotes," says Chick Lang, *Evening Sun* handicapper, "and the trainers used to school the Spanish-speaking jocks on what to say to the press after a race.

"One day, a guy won a big stakes race and afterward all he'd say was, 'I have no excuses.' "

But horse racing is no different from any other sport. How often have you heard a football team lost a game because of the barometric pressure, or that a baseball pitcher can't win unless the temperature is over 90 degrees?

Often, the alibis are valid, of course. Angel Cordero, who rode Cannonade to victory in the Kentucky Derby, could end up with a built-in excuse if London Company doesn't take the Dixie Handicap at Pimlico today.

London, it seems, loves company—in other words, he's studdish, or oversexed—and prior to a race in Delware last year he wore himself out chasing the pony which was taking him to the gate.

Horses often provide the reason why a race is lost. Many have been known to jump things on the track, like puddles, and break stride.

Near the end of a race over the turf course here, Manuel Ycaza lost a victory when his horse all but stopped to leap over a lighter shade of grass. The grass is lighter as the area is the former location of a water jump.

The reason the excuse is such a big part of sports is obvious. Confidence. A competitor has to feel he or she is best. To lose suggests otherwise and self-doubt is a tough thing to overcome.

Best excuse I ever heard of was provided by a guy hauled into court for making an obscene gesture at a passing limousine containing two judges.

"I did not intend to show disrespect to your lordships," he said. "I thought it was the mayor's car."

The judge accepted the explanation and released him.

So, get ready. Maybe the losers can come up with as many alibis as there have been Preaknesses. One thing is sure, they'll give it a run.

WHERE WINNING IS GOD

By Eddie Donnally

From Turf and Sport Digest

Copyright, ©, 1974, Turf and Sport Digest

It's a 12-horse field going five eighths on a star-filled November night. Breaking less than an eighth from the turn, six of you race head and head like a chariot team down the brilliantly lit racetrack. Suddenly the lights blow. All is black and panic among 12 horses and riders.

It's a full field again, only this time it's under the bright Florida sun. You break in front, going three quarters, then start to settle the giant chestnut between your legs with a long steady hold. The bit breaks and the whole bridle slides uselessly to the horse's neck.

Scenes from a movie? No, just everyday moments in a horse race; the kind that bring even the nonbettor to his feet and make good copy in the evening paper. Yet despite the excitement and its vivid press, little is known of the craft itself, and less of the men who practice it.

Every beer drinker from Boise to Buffalo knows what a blitz is. But how about a blind switch. Many of racing's own writers see only a blur during a race and a statistic after it, yet blunder through a description in sarcastic ignorance. It is little wonder Lester Piggott refused to make any comment at all after his second straight International win. Remember, it was racing's own writers who found it easier to pin Majestic Prince's Belmont defeat on Hartack not reading a slow early pace than on a prestigious millionaire owner's insistence on running a sore horse. If race riding is so thoroughly misunderstood by the experts, then it can hardly be understood by the fan. For it is a profession unlike any other, requiring a lifestyle larger than the dandy dwarfs who live it. The outcome of all the time, money, and effort spent by the breeder, trainer, groom, exercise, and pony rider will depend on the decisions he makes in the fleeting seconds required to run a race.

Riding is the sweet green smell of success. You're a kid on the corner one day and the bettor's hero the next. You're recognized in restaurants and plagued for hot tips by policemen, pimps, and politicians. You're managed by a mothering agent; hired by weight-conscious trainers and followed by a ready-made entourage of club-house slickies, high-styled sharks free to stalk the neon jungle for game worthy of their pygmy king.

Suddenly you're somebody, a name in the papers, a picture in the *Form*. Soon you believe the kind words of the sports writers and forget you earn your living with strong hands and a dirty face. You're not even old enough to stand up at a bar in some states and already make five times as much as your father, who had the same job for 20 years. It's so much, so fast, so easy and you think it can never end. But to ride even a magic roller coaster requires new tickets. One day your best friend, the apprentice allowance, walks out, never to return, leaving a 50-thousand-a-year ego with 5-thousand-a-year worth of air. But the sports writers aren't interested in that story. The trainers have new love affairs and the flunkies are still out partying. So there you sit, starry-eyed at the splendor but baffled at the breakdown. In the back of your skull rises an awareness of the almost total ignorance you've acquired about race riding.

Then you truly join this fraternity of Gidget-size gladiators and quickly learn that the real competition is for live mounts. Without them you only get dirt kicked in your face. You soon learn you can never be much better than the beast beneath you. Then you start to realize that being a jockey is like selling vacuum cleaners barn to barn. Only you are the only product.

At the average racetrack, if there be such a thing, there are usually between 50 and 100 or more licensed riders. On the average nine-race card there are between 70 to 90 possible mounts. So that means that for every rider that rides two, there will be one who rides none. Add this to the fact that the top 10 riders will average five or more mounts a day, and it's not hard to see why some riders spend a lot of time in the grandstand or at home. If you've been winning lately or have a yard-long reputation, you're in the running for a lot of open mounts. But otherwise, get out your exercise boots.

If things get really tough you can always try another circuit, one where there are fewer well-known or heavy-headed riders. But as the competition gets easier, the purses get smaller. Successful or not, you become a permanent transient and spend half your life packing and shipping. The motel rooms start to look the same. But that and a 10-year-old, 50-dollar-a-week trailer is all you can find. To get an apartment you have to sign a year's lease, and race meets just don't last that long.

But once you get there you still have to be light enough to make the weight. Probably 85 percent of all riders practice some form of weight control, stretching from the sublime to the ridiculous. Few people have ever had a pocket full of hundreds and eaten lettuce for dinner. The green Toledo scales is your own private snake in the grass. She greets you as you enter the Jocks' room and you step on her cautiously, exhaling and thinking light. For those who find it necessary to eat and drink, there is the hot box. Actually it is a series of two to four rooms, each with a slightly different temperature. The hottest and most unbearable is steam-heated and kept at between 140 and 180 scalding wet degrees. Here you "break out" or start sweating. Then there is a sauna room where the temperature is actually hotter, but the air is much dryer and thus more endurable. Finally there is a cooler room kept around 100 degrees. It is here that a rider spends the most time watching his good living melt into puddles on the tile floor. Any decent reducing rider can drop a pound every 20 to 30 minutes. But after three or four pounds your body begins to resemble a dishrag, and the most beautiful thing in the world becomes an ammonia ampule and a sip of ice water.

For those who can master the technique, there is a practice called heaving, flipping or regurgitating. This odd method is simply the practice of emptying the contents of your stomach into the most convenient toilet bowl. Once you have eaten to the point of bursting, it is simply a matter of inhaling air into the stomach behind the food, then bending over, contracting the diaphragm muscles, and forcing the undigested food through the throat. There is no nausea involved, and it is an exercise slightly more complicated than the push-up. But the more one eats the more one heaves, and the more one heaves the more one is hungry, thus the more one eats. It is a vicious circle that leads to gluttony, ulcers, and a pot belly. Still, for many reducing riders, it is the only possible means besides starving.

But in between all this grief you get enough mounts to begin to understand the nature of the craft itself. You've already learned some of the basics. You know that saving ground or staying on the inside is the shortest as well as the most crowded way to the wire. You know that the faster the first part of a race, the slower the finish. From that you understand why the smart rider who is in front is always trying to slow the pace and why the unwary rider who is too far off a slow early pace will have a much harder time catching his fresh horse the last quarter.

Gradually you learn to watch for certain patterns and move accordingly. Get to the inside of a horse you see trying to lug out and outside one trying to bear in. You learn that sometimes the promising space on the rail is actually a trap, and after you've had the door slammed in your face you learn when to close it yourself. If you're behind a wall of horses with your mount full of run and you can't or don't want to give up the ground by going outside, then you learn to wait patiently and watch for a split. Otherwise you try to get behind the one you think strong enough to make it through the crowd and then follow him until you see daylight. On a turn you learn how to keep a rival stuck three-quarters outside and behind you until the turn hooks into the stretch. There you have your horse change to his left or inside lead as you come down off the banked turn, leaving your rival "parked" farther outside and another length or two behind. You learn a dozen or so other tricks that add inches and sometimes feet to a horse's performance.

It doesn't surprise you that the line between good and dirty race riding is thin indeed. But it does seem a trifle crude that the stewards are not the only judges, and that anyone cutting it too close too often had better be prepared to physically defend his position from a fat lip.

But the naked violence that sometimes stems from the tempers of two already hot and dirty men is hardly as exciting as the controlled violence practiced in every race. If Baeza has a face of stone, it's because in a race he is as emotional as a rock. Imagine turning into the stretch, inches off both the rail and the heels of the leader directly to your front. You're forced to steady and at the same time decide whether or not that rider sees the other horse creeping up on his outside. Because you know that if he does then he will intentionally keep that horse wide, allowing you to sneak wisely through on the rail, avoiding the blind switch. But to think like that while squatting on your knees and peeking through a set of bouncing ears in a pack of 12 thoroughbreds charging almost 40 miles an hour around the last turn, when maybe $10,000 or at least next week's groceries are concerned, requires that kind of detachment. Riding a race is like riding a roller coaster blindfolded. The heart pumps and adrenalin bubbles, while a slow-motion mind searches by feel for the buttons to keep it on the tracks. No one is born with the desire to feel pain or to die. But after you've walked up close and held the bull by the horns there remains a buzz inside that makes you want to do it again.

It's a crazy game and not played like any other. In the whole country of more than 200 million there are less than 2,000 of you licensed to ride the parimutuel thoroughbred, on which the money wagered each day will weigh more than your entire lot. Every afternoon all of you that ride that day are segregated in that particular track's closed-off Jockey room. You're sent out in sets where all but one come back losers. You share the work, the thrill and the agony. You sit beside your opponent in the hot box and watch his sweat run like tiny rivers. You wait beside him in the starting gate and see him look shyly down the racetrack, knowing he wonders if the half-crippled, overraced animal under him will throw off his nerved ankle and drop like a trap door. You see him carried away in a wailing ambulance and visit him in the hospital. You all ride the same balloon and share the same life, but when the starting bell rings your brother becomes just another helmet and numbered saddle towel. You and the horse are the only team.

By now the talents you started without have by degrees developed, until after not so many years you have something George Allen might call "savvy." By performing the same act thousands of times your instincts have been grooved. Then one day you win a big one or maybe the big one. It's like they elected you king for a day. The grey-haired heavies look at you with respect and the beauties want a lock of your hair. But the day lasts only for a flash and Saturday's glory becomes Monday's fuzzy memory. But you did it once and you can do it again.

So you understand why the 45-year-old muscled midget struts through the Jock's room in his toupé and glances in the mirror at his rippling biceps. The green yearling has become the aging stud, well established in his territory, yet still a little jealous of the bold young bug rider.

You've seen a few dollars and a lot of dimes. You've dined with the rich and drunk with the poor. You've fought with the dragon of fear and won over more than him. You've beat a lot of good men and learned humility in the process. But most important, you've learned a lot from the beast who has carried you; of ability and attitude, of grace and grit and of spirit and style.

You might sit in the Jock's room toilet and laugh to yourself at

Shoemaker's size three boots dangling in the next stall. But hook him at the quarter pole and you realize he's every inch and ounce a warrior.

By now you ache in six different places before every rain. You've seen younger men disappear beneath a field of flying hooves. Every time you sit waiting in colors for the bell calling you to the paddock, you wonder if the next statistic will be you. Your insides tingle, yet you can't wait until that magic animal is between your knees, carrying you like a flying carpet into the whirlwind fury where control is king and winning is God. Out there, more than anywhere, you know what you're doing. A tight furious finish is a slow-motion symphony played in a vacuum.

That's why the 20-year veteran waits through six races on a cold Tuesday night to ride a 20-to-1 shot in the last race. For in the realm of race riding, reality is closer to a dream. A trip larger than life, sharper than the nine to five waking reality. It's you, and you are addicted to that one moment when you know you've won another one. It's your own natural high. Without it you're still on the ground, a foot shorter than the crowd.

THE MOST EXPENSIVE DAILY

By Frederick C. Klein

From The Wall Street Journal

Copyright, ©, 1974, The Wall Street Journal

What daily newspaper sells for $1 a copy, is about 80 percent statistical and comes with its pages stuck together in most places?

As any horseplayer knows, the answer is the *Daily Racing Form.* He pays the dollar and unsticks the pages, because he knows that aside from money, the *Daily Racing Form* is the most indispensable factor in his chances for success at the races.

"Come without my *Form?*" asks a patron at Arlington Park near Chicago on a sunny afternoon. "I'd rather come without my shoes."

And that is why, year in and year out, the *Racing Form* has maintained a special status in American journalism. Besides being the most expensive U.S. daily, it is also one of the oldest (a predecessor paper dates back 141 years) and is the only one devoted almost exclusively to a single sport: thoroughbred racing.

What's more, the *Form* is the closest thing to a monopoly in the publishing field. That's because it—not the racetracks or any industry trade group—owns the performance statistics on every racehorse, jockey, trainer, owner, and breeder doing business in the United States. Its figures also are recognized as official in Ontario, Mexico, and Puerto Rico. The information, which the *Form* zealously protects, is the basis of most racetrack betting; no track could operate profitably without the newspaper for any length of time.

By virtue of this franchise, whose roots lie deep in racing history, the *Form* enjoys a subsidiary benefit that other publishers might well envy: a virtual immunity from public criticism from the industry it serves.

Racing officials are quick to express their gratitude for the way the

Form helps promote their sport, and they believe that, by and large, the paper does a generally good job of coverage. Nonetheless, they have chafed of late as the paper's distribution problems have forced the elimination of some material that horsemen deem essential. And they say that as racing has grown, the accuracy and completeness of the *Form's* statistics haven't kept pace.

For the record, though, everything is peachy. "I don't think the paper is nearly as good as it was, but don't quote me on that," the head of one large Eastern track says. "We've got to live with them, and they can do more to us than we can to them."

Michael Sandler, a handsome man of 62 years who rose from the *Form's* circulation ranks to become its publisher last February, agrees that the threat of any major competition in the turf publishing field is remote, but he disputes claims that his paper is going downhill. "Sure we have problems—changes in traffic and transportation patterns have made it harder for us to get out in time—and we've had to make adjustments," he says. "But when you consider how much more racing there is these days, I think the wonder isn't that we make mistakes but that we make so few."

Indeed, the *Racing Form* is an impressive enterprise. It publishes daily editions year-round from plants in Hightstown, New Jersey, Chicago, and Los Angeles, and it publishes regional editions in Seattle, Toronto, and Vancouver during the racing seasons in those areas. All are linked by an extensive communications network. (The *Racing Form* comes with its pages stuck together at the top in its tabloid Chicago and Los Angeles editions. The paper says it does this to discourage newsstand browsers. There's a quick way to separate the pages. Open the paper in the middle and tear a small piece from the upper left-hand and right-hand corners. Then open each side in the middle and pull.)

It has some 950 employees, including 180 in its track-and-field division. This category includes writers, chart callers, chart takers, workout clockers, and teletype operators. It has at least two staffers on hand at every racing meeting in this country and staffs the major tracks with as many as six people. Besides thoroughbred racing, it covers harness and quarter-horse events in some areas.

The paper's daily circulation averages about 160,000 during the May through September period when racing is most active, and about 120,000 at other times. On Kentucky Derby day, the first Saturday in May, it turns out more than 300,000 papers.

On some summer Saturdays, the *Form's* various editions carry complete past-performance listings on horses running at as many as 40 tracks—some 3,500 horses in all. Some editions must be revised up to seven times during their press runs, to accommodate all that information.

In addition to the newspaper, the *Form* publishes the *American Racing Manual,* an annual volume that runs to 1,500 pages and includes the records for the year of every participant in the thoroughbred sport, human and equine. Its Chart Books, published monthly, contain a complete record of every race run in the U.S.

Although it carries very little advertising, the *Form* has been consistently profitable over the years. It won't disclose sales or earnings, but Mr. Sandler, the publisher, notes that he has been with the paper for 30 years and can't recall it ever finishing out of the money.

The *Form* is part of Triangle Publications Inc., of Radnor, Pa., one of the nation's largest closely held companies; 1973 revenues are estimated at $215 million. Triangle also publishes *TV Guide,* whose circulation of 18.7 million makes it the largest-selling U.S. weekly, and *Seventeen,* a magazine for teen-age girls. It has cable-television outlets in Philadelphia and upstate New York.

Triangle used to own *The Philadelphia Inquirer* and *Philadelphia Daily News* but sold them in 1969 for $55 million. In 1971, it disposed of its extensive television and radio-broadcasting holdings for $110 million.

Triangle is controlled by the redoubtable Walter H. Annenberg, who has been U.S. ambassador to England since 1969; he, members of his family, and several foundations and nonprofit corporations that they support own all the company's stock.

Although reports to the contrary are numerous, Triangle officials say that Mr. Annenberg hasn't been involved in day-to-day company affairs since he became an ambassador. But Triangle's presidency has gone unfilled since his departure, apparently awaiting his return.

The *Racing Form* owes its domination of its field to Mr. Annenberg's father, Moses L., a peddler's son who came to this country as a boy and, through a variety of endeavors, eventually became one of its richest citizens. The elder Mr. Annenberg, nicknamed "Moe," was reputed to be a keen, ruthless businessman who made a point of trying to control anything he got into.

In 1922, along with two partners, he purchased the *Form* for $400,000 from Frank Brunell, who had founded it 28 years earlier in Chicago. He then went about buying up its main rivals, including the New York-based *Morning Telegraph,* which dated its origins to 1833, and the *American Racing Record,* which covered Kentucky racing out of Cincinnati.

Those in hand, he offered to buy out his partners in the *Form.* They balked, so he cut the price of the *Telegraph,* which he owned outright, sending *Form* circulation plunging. According to a biographer of the Annenbergs, this maneuver proved persuasive.

Ownership of racing newspapers propelled Mr. Annenberg into the business of providing a racing wire service for illegal bookmakers, a field he came to dominate nationally in the 1930s. The venture proved lucrative but legally troublesome; in 1939, the federal government closed the racing wires and indicted him for income-tax evasion. He pleaded guilty the following year and received a three-year prison term. He died in June, 1942, days after being released from prison because of ill health.

Moe Annenberg's problems with the law have made both his son and Triangle unusually publicity-shy about the past, a characteristic the *Form* shares. In 1969, on its 75th birthday, the paper carried a lengthy story on its founding and history but omitted any reference to the Annenberg family or Triangle.

Among *Form* oldtimers, of whom there are many, Moe Annenberg is still referred to as the "Old Man." They regarded him with a mixture of fear and admiration. "He'd cut off your legs if you crossed him, but if he liked you, he could be generous as hell," one says.

Of the racing papers in the Triangle stable, only the *Form* survives; the *American Racing Record* is long gone, and the *Morning Telegraph,* which covered East Coast tracks, folded after a 1972 printers' strike.

The *Telegraph's* operations—but not all its skilled employees— were transferred to the computerized Hightstown edition of the *Form.* People inside and outside the paper say that continuing difficulties with the changeover have contributed to an increased number of mistakes in that edition.

Many in journalism bemoaned the *Telegraph's* passing for other reasons; in the days when it covered show business and other sports as well as racing, its roster of writers included such luminaries as Ring Lardner, Ben Hecht, Louella Parsons, Walter Winchell, and Heywood Broun.

In recent years, the *Form* has continued to cut back on nonracing news. It still carries a general sports column by the highly regarded

Barney Nagler and one-paragraph summaries of the day's major national and international news events from the Reuters wire, but that's about it. The latest casualties were its movie and Broadway theater reviews. They ceased after movie reviewer Whitney Bolton died and theater writer Leo Mishkin retired.

Other *Form* writers are well thought of by their sports-writing colleagues; among them are Charles Hatton, a 44-year veteran of the paper who covers New York tracks, and Joe Hirsch, who, at age 46, has put in 26 years.

"Joe Hirsch is a very able, hard-working guy. I don't think anyone covers Kentucky Derby news as thoroughly as he does," says Walter "Red" Smith, the nationally syndicated sports columnist of *The New York Times*. "Charley Hatton is one of the last of the oldtime, graceful sports writers. I love it when he writes that a horse won a race *con brio* [with vitality]."

Cartoonist Pierre Bellocq, who draws under the name of "PEB," regularly enlivens the paper with drawings that burlesque the racing scene.

Otherwise, however, the *Form* gets lower grades journalistically. This stems in part from the coverage limitations imposed by the paper's drive for earlier deadlines; even the most important races rarely get more than a paragraph in the next day's paper, with only slightly less concise recapitulations following a day later. The non-statistical content of the paper has been reduced mostly to advance stories on races to be run that day, columns devoted to racetrack history and chit-chat, and esoteric features on breeding.

As a matter of policy, the paper refrains from launching investigations of its own into racing scandals. Thus, it has been "scooped" on a number of important stories in its own backyard. Last year, for instance, reporters Jim Bolus and Billy Reed of the *Louisville Courier-Journal* and *Times* won national prizes for stories that disclosed financial conflicts of interest, hidden ownership of horses and the prevalence of illegal bookmaking at Kentucky tracks. Following its usual practice, the *Form* limited its coverage of those matters to reporting the doings of official bodies.

Aside from occasional comments by its columnists, the *Form* rarely editorializes. When it does, it invariably supports racing-industry views on issues. "We don't have the expertise to criticize track managements," Mr. Sandler contends. "We stick to running a newspaper and let them run the tracks."

On the other hand, the paper has fairly strict standards of personal conduct for reporters and others who represent it at the tracks. Betting is allowed ("Everyone in racing bets sometimes," Mr. Sandler says), but heavy betting is frowned upon, and employees have been fired for this vice.

Perhaps remarkably in a sport that depends on gambling for its livelihood, substantiated instances of *Form* employees being involved in dubious or illegal betting schemes have been very rare. The only such case that present staff members can recall occurred some 15 years ago. It involved a teletypist who was paid by a New York numbers racket operator to falsify a betting figure that had little interest for horseplayers but that determined the day's numbers payoff. He was fired.

The heart of the *Form* is its statistical services, however, and it is to this that it devotes most of its resources. In terms of sheer volume, this task is immense. The paper's computers in its plant at Hightstown, which opened in 1968, contain past-performance records on some 90,000 horses and about 1.2 billion bits of data all told. Typesetting there is directly tied to the computers, but at Chicago, Los Angeles, and the small regional editions, such work still is done mechanically. At the latter places, blocks of type spelling out the up-to-date record of each horse active in the area are labeled and stored in cryptlike shelves, ready to be used when the horse runs again.

The *Form*'s record gathering starts at the track with the chart caller, whose job is to pinpoint the position of each horse in a race —and its distance behind its nearest rival—at from four to six locations, depending on the length of the event. This is no mean feat when a dozen or so horses are in a field, and people who can "call" a race accurately are hard to find.

The caller barks his rapid-fire description of the proceedings to a call taker, who scribbles as fast as he can to keep up. After the race has been run, the caller sits down to write a one-paragraph description of its progress, done in inimitable *Racing Form* style ("LONETREE broke alertly to draw clear at once, continued slightly removed from the inner railing and was fully extended to prevail. MR. PROSPECTOR went evenly along the inside. . . .").

It all goes to a teletypist, who transmits it to the *Form*'s local office for publication. There, editors and clerks also get the data into the form used in the paper's past-performance records on each horse that ran; each line in such records contains more than 20 pieces of information.

Besides its race charts and past-performance listings, the *Form* keeps tabs on the morning workouts of horses at big tracks; this information, too, is considered vital to the betting public. Racing commissions in some states provide workout clockings, but in most places, this is left to the *Form*.

No part of the *Form*'s content is as frequently criticized within racing as its workout clockings. Like chart calling, clocking is an exacting trade, made more so by the fact that at most tracks, trainers aren't required to announce their horse's presence for morning exercise nor disclose the distance they are to "work." This leaves it up to the clockers to identify the horses by their appearance and divine the trainers' intentions.

Allegations abound that some workouts aren't reported in order to promote various shadowy betting interests. Mr. Avery Brown, director of track and field services, defends his men. "It's tough to get good clockers these days," he says. "Our guys have to be out at the track and sharp at 4 or 5 A.M. in some of the worst weather imaginable. People aren't willing to put up with that anymore. Even so, our guys do their best. I'd say 98 percent of their mistakes are honest ones."

But in keeping with racing tradition, a story must be told here. It comes from Pat Lynch, chief publicist for the New York tracks. "One of the great clockers in the old days was a guy named Harry Mann, who was nicknamed the Owl," he says. "Nobody could handle a watch like he could. When World War II came, he was working the Maryland tracks, and the government came to see him. They were testing some shells at the Aberdeen Proving Grounds down there, and they wanted a racetrack guy to time them. The Owl told them to forget it. 'You guys don't want racetrack clockers,' he said. 'They'll hold out all the fast ones.' "

Long Distance Running

THE COURAGE OF A LONG DISTANCE RUNNER

By Ira Berkow

From Newspaper Enterprise Association

Copyright, ©, 1974, Newspaper Enterprise Assn., Inc.

The sun's morning rays were already growing warm as they spilled in an orange stream across the East River, and then onto the concrete promenade where Kathy Switzer ran. A boat horn sounded; birds were in the trees. She felt easy and light. It was a beautiful morning. And when she heard the footsteps behind her she turned and looked, more out of instinctive curiosity than alarm.

A hundred or so yards behind, she saw a man in sweatshirt and sweat pants in a leisurely trot—obviously a fellow jogger. Subconsciously she felt relieved about that.

Kathy has had some uncomfortable experiences while jogging alone. Now, she always clips a pencil-thin aerosol can of "dog spray" to the drawstring of her sweat pants, to ward off some dogs and some people.

One afternoon several months ago, while she was jogging through Central Park, five tough-looking youths jumped out of the bushes. As Kathy came up hill in her 18th mile, the boys made lip-smacking sounds, and said how they liked her long legs and supple body. She recalls now that she was too tired even to be scared, paid them no heed, jogged around them and continued down the hill. They were too stunned by her insouciance to follow.

When she runs on the promenade, she runs along the iron barrier beside the river, as opposed to running close to the park area. It is similar to the precaution of the gunfighter who always sits in a saloon with his back to the wall.

The footsteps were coming closer behind her. She did not turn around this time. Just another case of fragile male ego, she said to herself. Men often pass her, she believes, because they don't like the feeling of running behind a woman.

Anyway, she did not want to think further about those footsteps. Kathy was in training for an important race for her, the Olympic Airways–sponsored New York City marathon run of 26 miles, 385 yards. In the last year she has made tremendous progress in her times. She says she has cut 20 minutes off her time. With blue eyes smiling, she adds that she has lost 20 pounds, too.

This marathon event is important because she hopes to run it in less than three hours, a feat she equates to a miler breaking the four-minute barrier. And the satisfaction of such improvement over the year has been euphoric, she says. "The feeling—that you are doing all you can to be the best you can—is incredible," she has said.

Kathy received national attention when she became the first female to run in the Boston Marathon, in 1967, when she was a 19-year-old college student at Syracuse University. She had signed the application form "K. V. Switzer," and wore a hooded sweatshirt on this rainy day. She was finally discovered when the day brightened and she removed her excess clothing while running. The Marathon's co-director, Jock Semple, a white-haired Scotsman, believing she was desecrating the event, gave her hell with his brogue and tried to rip the number off her back. Fellow runners came to her aid, and she remained in the race to the finish.

Later, the Amateur Athletic Union barred her and other women from competing with men (she had run distance on her college team, too). She successfully fought that ruling, with the help of others. In 1972 she was running in the Boston Marathon again, but this time legally.

Kathy Switzer has been striving since the Boston Marathon of 1967 to earn a place for herself and other women athletes in the male-dominated sports world. She feels women, even in athletic events, are always looked at as women first and athletes last, by officials, some participants, and many spectators. She recalls in her first Boston Marathon when, after some 20 miles, she was so fatigued she could hardly keep her eyes open. Strangely, she heard clapping. She opened an eye and saw an elderly couple alongside the road, and the lady was applauding.

Kathy figured the lady was cheering her perseverance. As Kathy jogged by, she held her head high, and overheard the lady say, "Look, dearie, isn't that cute—it's a girl and she's wearing earrings!"

Now the slapping steps behind her got closer, louder. A sudden wash of panic came over Kathy. The man shot his arm around her neck. He stuck a steak knife under her ear. Kathy couldn't scream; the sound was caught in the pit of her stomach.

"Gimme your money," he said. "I'm gonna cut you."

He was about 5-foot-8, an inch or so taller than she. He weighed about 160 pounds, some 35 pounds more than Kathy. His arm around her neck was viselike.

She heard her voice, coming from some distant place, saying, so absurdly rational in this monstrous moment, "But you can plainly see I have no money."

"Come with me," he said. He began pulling her toward the cluster of trees and bushes. "I'm gonna cut you."

Sights and sounds and thoughts swirled for Kathy. The trees, the sun, the concrete, the smell of the man, the pressure of his muscles, the squashing of her neck, the sparkle of the river, the knife point jabbing the flesh behind her ear. Thoughts of rape, of no help nearby, of being slashed and—how crazy it seemed later in the telling—the rage at how unfair that all her vigorous training for the marathon should be washed away in a pool of her own blood.

She knew she had to get her hand on that aerosol can clipped to her sweatpants, and hidden under her warm-up jacket.

The man wasn't aware of Kathy's attempt to get the can. She knew even under this great pressure that she could not make a mistake, had to be precise, couldn't drop the can, had to get the hole pointed in the exact direction.

She touched the can. And now everything went fantastically slow, like in a dream sequence. She brought the can up, spraying all the way. She remembers seeing the stream of spray—the sun filtering through it—rising from the man's waist to his chest to his neck to his chin and into his eyes.

The man clutched his eyes and ran blindly off. Kathy dashed in the opposite direction. She got to a phone and called her friend Phillip at their apartment. He called the police.

Kathy, shaken, soon pulled herself together and a couple of hours later was in her office, working at her public-relations job at AMF, a sports equipment company.

And after work, before dark, she jogged her regular evening route of ten miles. Kathy Switzer still had a marathon to run.

Yachting

THE RACE TO MACKINAC

By Don Olesen

From Insight

Saturday, 8:25 A.M.: *Weatherly* sleeps. Her decks are sticky with last night's spilled drinks, fractured Fritos, and abandoned popcorn. Nothing stirs. I stick my head down the hatch. "Hello, anybody aboard?" No answer; just a volley of snores. Loud and rolling, soft and crooning, sharp and staccato.

I tiptoe below deck on the big 67-footer. Eight berths are filled with slumbering humanity. At least three more bodies are visible in the sail locker forward, draped over soft sail bags. There are empty plastic glasses and overflowing butt cans everywhere. A sour smell of stale booze hangs in the air.

One sleeper opens a bleary eye, which regards me coldly. "What's the weather?" Meaning, is there any wind out there. "Flat," I say. He mutters an obscenity and closes the eye.

Weatherly, a converted 12-meter sloop out of Menominee, Michigan, successful defender of the 1962 America's Cup, snoozes in the middle of bedlam. The Chicago Yacht Club docks are jammed with fine sailing yachts, crammed into every inch of floating space, rafted side by side. Their spars make an aluminum forest. They are scrubbed, glistening. They radiate richness.

Narrow piers are a traffic jam of jostling sailors and rubbernecking sightseers. The sailors are staggering under burdens of sails, food, and sea bags. They are cursing the sightseers, who are underfoot.

8:40 A.M.

On *Weatherly*'s afterdeck, a hatch swings upward revealing a sleepy head. It introduces itself as Joe McGauran, 27, associate county planner. He has spent the night in the lazarette, a little storage area.

"Must have been a helluva party," I say. It was, Joe acknowledges. The crew of *Omega*, a Milwaukee yacht rafted alongside, hijacked a four-man marimba band last night and set it up on *Omega*'s foredeck. High hilarity aboard *Weatherly-Omega* continued until an unconscionable hour.

It has been said that the Chicago–Mackinac race is a lousy time surrounded by two great parties, and so this 66th running is off to a thumping good start. In a couple of hours this rich armada— more than 200 yachts, perhaps $10 million worth of beautiful playthings—will set off in relays, smaller boats first, bigger boats last. And they will race 333 miles up Lake Michigan to that storied isle of horses, horse manure, fudge, tourists, and ripoff saloons known as Mackinac Island, up where Lake Michigan turns the corner into Lake Huron. It is, they say, the longest fresh-water race in the world.

9:05 A.M.

Joe and I start picking up the shambles on deck and below. One by one the snoozers stumble out. We douse buckets of water over the deck and mop down the sticky debris. Owner-skipper Doug Jones is up now. He wears white cotton slacks, a blue shirt, and moth-eaten Topsiders, or deck shoes. He doesn't say much. Doug looks a bit like actor Warner Oland playing Charlie Chan.

And now a kind of miracle takes place. Out of her sticky sloth, *Weatherly* assembles herself and becomes clean, gleaming, even moderately well organized. It seems to happen spontaneously.

Noon

Scott Fruechtl, 18, is swayed up to the masthead in the bo'sun's chair and dangles up there more than 85 feet in the air, checking out gear aloft. Scott is a paid hand on *Weatherly*, a pretty good summer job for a young fellow. Now he rejoins us earthlings. "Wait'll we get out," he tells me. "Then you'll really see me work." True. He's a one-man whirl.

12:45 P.M.

A shore party solicits $50 in cash from the skipper and heads ashore to buy last-minute groceries, cigarettes and sundries at extravagant prices at an apartment complex grocery.

Franklin (Frank) Wedge, Memphis, Tennessee, looking immaculate and rested (he slept in a hotel last night) comes aboard and starts checking out the weather reports on *Weatherly*'s radio. They aren't too hot. Frank, who used to live in Marinette, is our navigator. He came all the way from Tennessee for this race. In the next 60 hours or so he may sleep occasionally, but nobody will catch him at it. He is tall, sandy haired, almost courtly of manner.

1:55 P.M.

Weatherly's 92-horsepower diesel grumbles into life, lines are taken aboard and out we head, yacht and 14 crew members, out through the breakwater gap, out where Lake Michigan is green and clean.

Chicago's lakefront is a blizzard of white sails, as though somebody had popped a godlike pillow and scattered the feathers to the breezes. The smallest boats already have started. Our section of big yachts will start last of all, at 2:45 P.M. We head into the light southwest wind and hoist our mainsail, 1,300 square feet of superbly crafted dacron. I'm handling a stainless steel wire backstay; run my hand along it and get stabbed by the "meathooks"—little barbs of projecting wire. First blood.

2:33 P.M.

The breeze freshens just a bit, pulls north-northwest. We hoist the genoa jib: 1,100 square feet. By now we have enough sail flying to cover a doubles tennis court.

2:38 P.M.

"Seven minutes," Joe McGauran calls. He's timing the start with an $18 wristwatch with sweep second hand. No stopwatch. Heresy.

"Five minutes." We tack, or come about, heading up toward the starting line. Skipper Jones has the helm. When we come about, up to seven men on the foredeck go insane, wrestling the great brute of a genoa physically around from one side to the other; two others work the handles of the big coffee-grinder winches, strapping the mighty sail in tight; one man "tails," taking up the slack of the sheet (the line that hauls in the sail); and two of us handle the backstays that help brace the 90-foot mast.

Skipper Jones is cool at the helm, deadpan, seldom raising his voice. He is a human computer with a mental inventory of every block, pin, sail, line, stay, winch, tool, and instrument aboard—where it is and how to use it. Skipper and afterguard discuss which end of the line to hit at the start. We tack again: thunder of feet on foredeck, screaming of winches, flailing of sturdy arms. Jones cons this great, tender, bulky brute of a boat through the fleet with calm precision, as though steering a shopping cart through a supermarket aisle.

2:45 P.M.

Bang! a flawless start, right on top of the fleet, to windward of everybody, right next to the committee boat. A triumph for helmsman and Joe's $18 wristwatch. Angry words from the adjacent boat: "You're barging!" (in effect, trying to muscle into the starting line). Jones keeps his cool. Under the rules, he's right.

Why do seconds matter at the start, when you have 333 miles and scores of hours to go? But they do. Long races are won and lost by seconds. Since no two boats in this race are precisely alike, each yacht has a "rating," or handicap. *Weatherly* has the highest rating in the fleet, making her theoretically the fastest boat. She has to "give" time to everybody else. Even if she gets to Mackinac Island first, other boats could beat the blue paint off her on corrected time.

"It's going to blow like hell this afternoon," McGauran announces. "You've got to think positive." The Blue Canoe—the crew nickname for *Weatherly*—loves a blow. In lighter airs her magnificently built wooden hull is far too heavy to beat today's crop of lighter fiberglas boats studded with fancy sails.

3:00 P.M.

It's not blowing like hell, just light and fluky. We're doused by a brief rain squall. Hazy sun, deep green water.

3:20 P.M.

We hoist a brand new, untested "flanker"—a flat spinnaker, or pulling sail. Frantic flurry on the foredeck. Not pulling right. Up spinnaker staysail with flanker. No improvement. Down flanker. The sail changing is nervous and incessant. It will continue throughout the race.

4:40 P.M.

Wind up. Joe McGauran: "Now we're truckin'!" Speed on the log, or speedometer: 7.5 knots, better than 8.5 miles an hour.

Signs posted below deck, next to the galley or kitchen: "We've got SPIRIT" and "LOVE" and "Sailors have more fun" and "Ice-boating is cool."

So it goes in the first two hours.

Living

What is it like to live in a long, skinny house that tilts, rocks, rolls and occasionally tries to stand on its head? Well, it's different.

In anything but a flat clam, a sailboat "heels" or leans to one side or the other under its press of sail. *Weatherly* may heel at an angle of 35 degrees or more. You cannot sleep comfortably at 35 degrees. In fact, you cannot sleep at all. And so *Weatherly* has eight berths that are hell to climb into but deliciously comfortable once you are in.

Each berth can be tilted to one side or the other, depending on which way the boat heels. You pull and haul on a pair of little block-and-tackle rigs until your berth is level with the world, if not with *Weatherly*. This is beautiful until the watch on deck tacks 15 minutes later and *Weatherly* flops the other way, threatening to pitch you four feet to the cabin floor.

Walking is a sometimes thing. It is hard enough to walk below deck when your world leans. But when nature throws in a violent pitch and roll, you progress by creeping, crawling and slithering from handhold to handhold.

The astronauts surely have less trouble than sailors in conquering weightlessness. When the Blue Canoe pitches up, you're weightless at the top. When she bottoms, your chin burrows into your collarbone.

Weatherly's cabin is Spartan, functional, cluttered, and purely male. After 24 hours or so it wears the odor of old sweatsock. With 14 men occupying such limited space, storage room is a lost dream. Everybody's sea bags, shoes, cameras, books, foul weather gear, and toilet kits gradually ooze into one great avalanche pile near the companionway. If you left something in the avalanche, forget it; it's lost.

In a racing yacht, even calls of nature are different. Minor summonses are handled quite simply; on deck, over the lee rail, with one hand clutching a shroud or lifeline and ecology be damned. More serious calls involve the "head," or toilet, which is jammed into a cramped little room. This handy unit can be tilted at one of three different angles to compensate for the boat's lean. A jolly undertaking, this, particularly when *Weatherly* is bucking. It once took me three minutes to tuck in my shirt tails.

Eating is different. Somehow, Joe Zeratsky, 24, got drafted as chef, possibly at gunpoint. Joe is big, genial, redheaded, a biochemistry student at the University of Wisconsin—Madison. One supper, assisted by Dave Verwolf, 28, who runs his own graphic design business in Chicago, the chef whipped up a modest little spread of two dozen scrambled eggs and three pounds of bacon. This was served in relays to the crew, on plastic plates, and eaten with plastic "silverware."

When I volunteered to "wash" the dishes afterward, the supply of hot water was quite limited. "The silver?" Joe said. "Oh, just wipe them with paper towels and stick 'em in this plastic bag. That way they'll think they're dining at the Holiday Inn." So much for hygiene.

Another time we had chop suey prepared and frozen by the mother of Gary (Gutsy) Schahczenski, 22. The boat has a refrigerator-freezer, so the stuff was in fine shape. Joe thawed it and served it with instant rice, only there wasn't enough rice. But this does not stop a creative galley chef. Joe ripped open some packages of Hamburger Helper, pirated the noodles therefrom and cooked them up to supplement the rice. Delicious, too.

Personal hygiene is different, too. After a day or so, most of us stank like billygoats, which didn't matter since the smell was mutual. Gutsy liked to take Marine showers, dousing himself with cologne. This prompted the skipper to remark, "Gutsy, you smell like toilet bowl cleaner." The remark was unwarranted. He smelled more like Air Wick.

Little messages are posted everywhere. One reads: "To whom it may concern: If you are sleeping forward, carefully move any spinnakers, they are all packed and they explode like TNT. . . ."

Another reads: "Keep this galley clean. If you mess it up, clean it up." Nobody is assigned to the dirty work—washing pots, plates, and "silver," scrubbing the head. But it gets done, quietly; somebody always volunteers.

We accumulate trash in enormous plastic bags. The first day or so, somebody took them aft and dumped them into Lake Michigan. This produced a mutter of mutiny from a few of us. Next time around, one of our environmental militants took the bag aft and stowed it in the lazarette, to be taken ashore on Mackinac Island.

Gives you an almost holy feeling.

Calm

And when the breeze dies, torment sets in. "Move, you bitch!" somebody mutters. The skipper broods, orders one sail change after another. That first night out of Chicago we sat in almost glassy calm at sunset and this enormous fleet was scattered over perhaps 20 miles, suspended on glass. And you could hear things far across the water—odd snatches of song, whistling, voices, laughter, a burst of radio music. On deck our crew was talking Watergate and cursing the calm.

Or . . . Noon, Monday; all but dead in the water off North Manitou Island. To the east is Traverse City, Michigan. And tempers begin to fray for lack of sleep. The heat on deck is intense. Now, occasionally, a crew member snaps at a mate. I am off watch, sitting on the afterdeck, feet over the rail, reading Kurt Vonnegut, Jr. The gang on the foredeck is discussing the ill-spent youth of Joe Zeratsky. Flat, flat. We fool with the great baggy spinnaker; it remains limp. The skipper is sacked off below with a copy of *Modern Metal Market* on his chest. A pre-race telegram posted near the galley reads: "Best wishes *Weatherly* for fair wind, a pleasant passage, a great race." Somebody curses.

Breeze

The crash of falling cooking pots jars me awake at 6:30 Sunday morning. It's a new world. Last night was calm. Sometime during the night a breeze came up and the damn boat is bucketing along, leaning over on one ear. All eight berths, mine included, are crazily canted to keep them horizontal. I hear the boom of a wave and the patter of spray on deck. I'm off watch until 9, but I go on deck to watch the show.

It's beautiful up there; not really rough, just fine lively sailing. Sunshine. Ranks of whitecaps charge us. We're 25 miles east of Milwaukee. All you can see of Beertown on the horizon is the square top of the First Wisconsin Center. Nothing else. Neil Van Dyke, 22, a civil engineer, has the helm; actually it is a big, stainless steel wheel the size of a hula hoop. This is great sailing and Neil wears a

Cheshire cat grin. His watchmates, clad in yellow oilskins against the spray, are huddled along the windward rail like a flock of brightly colored birds.

Above us, wind orchestrates a deep throbbing hum in the rigging and thousands of square feet of sail belly and strain. The sheets—dacron lines that strap in the sails—are as hard as steel rods. You could bang one with a hammer and nothing would budge, just nothing.

This mass of bellying power is raised, lowered, strapped in and eased by manpower, working through the enormous mechanical advantage of winches. And I think: If one little pin on a crucial block lets go, the flying block would pulp a man's skull. Or a winch handle could go amok and remove his teeth. Or a shackle could fail and drop the powerful spinnaker pole on somebody's skull. Or . . . Or . . . Under awesome tension, little things have a potential for havoc if they fail.

When this big bucket hits a wave crest and drops, it's as though God had suddenly kicked the props out from under her. And after about three hours of this I am suddenly, very quietly, very neatly seasick off the afterdeck. It happens every time, even after a lifetime in little boats. Embarrassing. From now on I'll be fine.

Now it's noon. I'm wearing a windbreaker jacket, heavy ski sweater, long flannel shirt. I'm sitting in bright sunlight, at noon, on July 15, in the middle of Lake Michigan and I'm cold.

Night

Sleep aboard a racing yacht is a sometimes thing. The coffee-grinder winch is located 15 inches above my berth. So is the deck. When the watch above elects to make a sail change, which is every ten minutes or so, it sounds like a buffalo stampede augmented by small boys running slats along a picket fence.

In between stampedes, the skipper decides to start the big rumbly diesel engine. Not to move the boat; that, of course, is against race rules. But he must charge the boat's batteries and work the compressor of the refrigerator-freezer. So that the frozen chop suey from Gutsy's mother won't thaw and spoil.

On deck, the night watch is eerie. The digital depth sounder in the cockpit flicks red numerals at the helmsman—56 fathoms, 57 fathoms (336 and 342 feet deep). The three compasses glow red, the battery of other instruments green.

The skipper volunteers several pungent, carefully selected words about a nighttime goof in sail handling by the foredeck crew. These outbursts are rather rare and there is nothing particularly personal about them.

But most of the time on night watch, we just sit; and sometimes all we hear is the gurgle of the cockpit scuppers, and the snores of the watch below. And Dave Verwolf brews coffee below, and you pour a steaming cup by the dim light of the navigator's gooseneck light. And it tastes marvelous; it's cold up there!

The cold communion of the night tends to make warm friends of watchmates, men who may have been total strangers yesterday, or the day before. The watch below climbs into sleeping bags; our watch on deck talks about women, but not for long. Pretty soon the talk turns, as it usually does, to other boats, other crews, other skippers and their foibles. And to other races long gone and well remembered—of blows, broken gear, two days of wet berths, cold chow and seasickness. Otherwise sane men throw over jobs, wives, and their sacred honor for the privilege of sharing such delights between Chicago and Mackinac.

And, when the other watch trickles up four hours later, one by one, each man momentarily is a stranger to our group until, within minutes, he becomes a part of it again.

We are on watch one night. It is 3:20 A.M. Cold. Our watch is silent. Suddenly a yell from below. Frank Wedge and I converge in the cabin, he from his navigator's booth, I from the cockpit. Gutsy has had a bad dream; he awoke to find his mates gone, the boat deserted. He sees us, smiles foolishly. Peace again.

Out on deck, the full moon is dead astern. It gleams on the great curved wingsweep of the genoa, which glows like silk.

And then a miracle: dawn. Fantastic. The moon sets dead astern in Lake Michigan, a red sun pops out of South Manitou Island dead ahead. And there is the sweet fresh scent of soil, grass, evergreens. Beautiful air! It's morning.

Weatherly

Everything about the converted 12-meter yacht *Weatherly* is a bit on the heroic side—her size, her construction, and her past. She was built in 1958 by Yankee craftsmen to a design by a widely known naval architect, Philip Rhodes. Four years later she stood off a brisk challenge by the Australian 12-meter, *Gretel,* and retained the America's Cup for the United States in a series of races sailed off Newport, Rhode Island.

This is the world's most prestigious sailing series and the competition is white hot. A 12-meter seldom returns for another go at the rococo old mug. Older boats are outdesigned and put on the shelf —or, in the case of *Weatherly*, converted into yachts. Douglas E. Jones of Menominee, Michigan, bought *Weatherly* and turned her into a Lake Michigan yacht with cruising accommodations.

In her America's Cup days, *Weatherly* had no bunks, no galley, no engine, no navigator's niche. She was pure sailing machine. Jones made her livable. He also installed a sophisticated battery of instruments, a radio-telephone, refrigerator-freezer and a 92-horsepower diesel auxiliary engine. There is a $2,500 Loran unit for ocean navigation (Jones has raced her in Florida waters). He even installed a stereo tape player never used while racing; it runs the batteries down.

Weatherly is 67 feet long. She has a maximum beam, or width, of 11 feet. She weighs 64,000 pounds, has a draft of nine and a half feet, meaning that her keel reaches that distance below the water surface. Her inventory of sails is awe-inspiring—sails for every conceivable kind of wind condition and point of sailing. Her mainsail is 1,300 square feet; her biggest genoa 1,100; her biggest spinnaker more than 2,000. A plaque below deck reads: "Like a woman, the rigging costs more than the hull." There are chauvinists afloat, too.

Weatherly was built by master shipwrights, and no expense was spared. Her hull is of double planked mahogany. Frames are made of both solid and laminated oak, set closely together. There are massive bronze reinforcing members throughout the boat to give the hull extra strength. In this plastic age, construction of such quality is a vanishing art.

And boats like *Weatherly* are a vanishing breed.

Finish

All Monday we've been plagued by calms—flat, fluky, shifty calms. Everybody is feeling growly and owly. All day we have ghosted along within sight of a smaller yacht, *Namis* of Chicago, as though linked by an invisible cable. We cannot lose her. We curse *Namis*, the calm, the hot sun, the boat, ourselves.

At dusk we get a little more woe via radio. *Sassy* of Detroit rounded Grays Reef Light two and a half hours ago. We are still miles from the light. We're out of it.

And then with night comes a sweet fresh breeze. It freshens. Our great pregnant spinnaker bellies out and we bowl down in darkness on Grays Reef Light, in a dead heat with *Namis.* She bears down and rounds just ahead. We pass the light, dim and mysterious in the gloom, then get ready to head up toward the Straits of Mackinac and the finish.

Down comes the spinnaker, up goes the big genoa. There is a traffic jam on the foredeck; at one point I could count 11 bodies up there, thrashing around in the dark, thumping and cussing. But it gets done. And the Blue Canoe tucks her ear down and really trucks, because this is her wind, and going to windward is her very best point of sailing.

Now the moon is up, the night is warm, the sailing superb, and 12 of us are lined up along the windward rail, whooping it up. Joe McGauran has the helm. The old girl is driving; in the dark it feels like 50 miles an hour. Boat for boat, we can lick anything on the lakes. Foot by foot we gain on *Namis* and then drive by her lee, and somebody sets up the chant, "Bye, Bye, *Namis,*" to the tune of "Bye, Bye, Blackbird," and everybody roars out the refrain. Not a sound from *Namis;* just the glow of her red port running light retreating astern.

The mighty Mackinac Bridge is a string of pearls, getting bigger by the minute. At 1:30 A.M. Tuesday we're under it and, dammit, I think our 90-foot spar will scrape the roadway which, of course, it doesn't. We bear off for the finish line, raise the spinnaker and boil down on Mackinac Island.

The island and its old fort loom above us; the race committee cannon bangs ashore. Race is over. On with the diesel, up into the wind, down with headsails. And finally, down comes the huge mainsail, fisted in by all hands and neatly furled. It has been flying for 59 hours, 37 minutes, and 30 seconds—nearly two and a half days.

We motor in, clearing and storing the spaghetti tangle of lines on deck. We're tired, fuddled, muddled, physically exhausted and emotionally let down.

No welcoming committee at dockside, just a couple of girl friends up from Marinette-Menominee to welcome the sailors. Out of 200 starters, *Weatherly* is the fourth boat to finish the race, which sounds brave. On corrected time she is 14th out of 21 boats in Section 1, which is lousy.

There isn't much of a celebration aboard *Weatherly* that late night.

What's to celebrate? As dawn comes up hot and clear, I snatch two hours of uneasy sleep on the sail bags forward and wake up with the sun in my face. I pull my duffle out of the avalanche, pack up, and head for home. Leaving *Weatherly* and her crew is like leaving 15 old, tested friends. Was it only 60 hours?

Outdoors

DEATH STALKED THE RIVER

By Walt Walbert

From Outdoor Life

Copyright, ©, 1974, Times Mirror Magazines, Inc.

The aircraft came over just above the treetops. We heard it coming, and I grabbed up the red windbreaker that we had swung as a forlorn signal every time we heard a plane. I ran out onto the fallen tree that extended halfway across the river and waved frantically.

It was a light plane, carrying only the pilot. He went over no more than 25 feet above the trees, so close that I could see his earphones and make out his features. It was hard to believe that he could fail to spot me. Just after he passed us, he turned in an almost vertical bank and came around in a tight circle.

I think I danced a jig on that half-submerged tree trunk.

"We're found!" I yelled to my partner. "He's seen us. Thank God!"

But then the plane leveled and straightened, resumed its original course, and droned swiftly out of sight.

To this day we don't know whether it was a search plane whose pilot momentarily thought he saw some trace of us or an ordinary plane whose pilot circled for no special reason and then went his way.

That pilot gave Ron Stricker and me a heartbreaking minute. To have believed that rescue was finally at hand, only to have the hope snatched away and go back to the interminable waiting, was almost too much to bear.

The date was July 4, 1973. Ron and I had been marooned since June 23 on the Steel River in roadless Ontario bush north of Lake Superior. Our boat was jammed among half-submerged treetops where we could not free it, and almost all our gear and supplies had been lost. In those 11 days we'd had nothing that resembled a meal.

The two of us grew up in Saginaw, Michigan. We have been friends since we were 12 years old and have always shared an intense interest in fishing, boats, and the outdoors. I'm 23 now, with a wife and little daughter. We live in Lansing, and I work for an engineering firm. Ron is still in college, single, and lives with his parents in Saginaw.

We had made a number of relatively easy float trips on Michigan rivers, including several on the Rifle and parts of the Grand. We had dreamed for years of a trip on a wilderness river, and early in 1973 we agreed we wouldn't wait any longer. We began to lay our plans while the February snow was still a foot deep on the lawn. From then until the day we started, we were as excited as kids on Christmas Eve. We talked, ate, and slept white water, lonely campfires, and our outfit list.

The first thing was to decide on the river. I wrote to the Ontario Surveys and Mapping Branch at Toronto for more than 20 topographical maps, and we settled down to select a route best suited for what we wanted to do.

Out choice narrowed finally to an interesting-looking chain of lakes and rivers between Terrace Bay, on the north shore of Lake Superior 70 miles east of Nipigon, and the town of Longlac 75 airline miles to the north. Longlac is on Ontario Highway 11 east of Geraldton. Everything in that watershed drains south to Lake Superior.

We could drive to our starting point at Terrace Bay on Highway 17, the beautiful road around the north shore of Superior. From what the maps showed, we believed we could make a circular trip by water. We'd go north from Terrace Bay into Long Lake, go the length of that lake, and then go south through a chain of lakes to the Steel River and down the Steel to Santoy Lake and Highway 17 a few miles east of Terrace Bay. The Steel River was listed officially as a canoe route with marked portages.

The next step was to buy a suitable boat. I agreed to take care of that. I wanted a boat that would serve me for years to come on almost any water. That meant, first of all, that it had to be portable. I had no garage at my apartment in Lansing and no space in which to store any kind of boat, not even a canoe. I gave the thing a lot of thought and finally settled on a kayak.

Most boatmen experienced in wilderness river travel might question the wisdom of that choice, but it was no ordinary kayak. It was a 17-foot, two-man model that had been tested under the toughest conditions in just about every part of the world.

The boat was made in West Germany. It had good seats and a strong floor, laminated ribs, and a rigid collapsible frame of seasoned ash and metal. The covering above the waterline was waterproof canvas. Below, the skin was hemp-and-rubber as strong as a heavy-duty conveyor belt. Air-inflated sponsons along the gunwales made the boat unsinkable so long as they weren't punctured, and they provided great stability. The boat could carry as much as 1,000 pounds, but the entire boat folded and packed into three compact bags that could be carried in a car trunk.

In 1956 a German adventurer had sailed across the Atlantic alone in one of these kayaks. Amundsen had taken one on his expedition to the North Pole, and Admiral Byrd had used one in the Antarctic. If the boat had passed such severe tests, I reasoned it would do all I required.

All I can say is that what happened to us was in no way the fault of the kayak. If I were starting the same trip over again, I would ask for no better boat.

I left home early on the evening of June 14, drove to Saginaw, and left my wife Jona and our 3-year-old Stacy with Jona's parents. Next I picked up Ron, and we headed north with my small sports car crammed with boat, bulging gear bags, and tent.

We crossed into Canada at Sault Ste. Marie at 3 A.M. The Canadian customs officers were astonished when we told them what we intended to do and that we were carrying our boat in the little car.

We had left home on Thursday evening. We ate breakfast in Wawa Friday morning and at 10:30 that morning we were in Terrace Bay.

A canal and the Agusabon River come down from Long Lake to Superior there, and we expected to paddle up that waterway on the first leg of the trip. But we were forced to change plans. The canal was full of pulpwood.

We swallowed our disappointment and cast around for an alternate route. We talked to a number of local people and finally concluded that our best bet would be to go to Longlac by bus, put the kayak in the water at the nearest suitable place, and complete the second half of the trip, mostly along the Steel River. We were told that it was a first-rate route and that we would find excellent fishing in the lakes along the way.

The trip to Longlac took most of Saturday. We drove to Schreiber to board the bus and went by way of Nipigon. I arranged with the Ontario Provincial Police to leave my car at their Schreiber post, and that proved to be a fortunate decision.

We got to Longlac a little after midnight. Jim Boyd, the bus driver, offered to let us sleep on the bus, and we took him up on it. Longlac was the end of the run.

On Sunday morning Boyd borrowed a car and drove us to a nearby fishing camp and outfitting place run by Norm Skinner. Skinner suggested that we put in at McLeod Lake, 22 miles south of town.

We arranged for him to drive us there in his pickup truck. It was a rough trip over an old logging road, but by midafternoon our camp was set up on the shore of McLeod. Our big adventure was finally to begin. Ahead lay about 100 miles of wilderness lakes and river in roadless country.

We left camp right after daybreak on Monday in a cold rain, but by early afternoon blue sky was overhead. The kayak was loaded with about 150 pounds of gear and supplies in addition to the two of us. Except for two or three packets of dehydrated food, our foodstuff was all in ordinary cans or packages. The boat rode high in the water, handled well, and was very stable. We were off to a good start.

The first two days were peaceful. We had allowed two weeks, and since we were doing only half of what we had planned, we could take our time. We made two portages. They were short and easy, although a bit hard to find. We were catching plenty of walleyes and northern pike for our meals. We had bought jigs and salted minnows from Norm Skinner.

We made our third and longest portage on the third afternoon. Half a mile of walking brought us to the head of Kawabatongog Lake and the most beautiful spot we had seen.

The lake is a long widening of the south-flowing waterways that feed Steel Lake and the Steel River. At the end of the portage is a beach of clean sand strewn with bleached driftwood, and to the south the shores stretch away, cloaked with pine and other trees.

Ron and I agreed to lay over there for a day to fish, swim, and loaf. The fishing was disappointing at first. Two hours in the kayak failed to yield a single strike, but after supper I cast from the beach and landed two eating-size walleyes in half an hour.

Cold rain the next day put a damper on our layover. We left that campsite on Friday morning. We had been away from home a week, our time was half gone, and we had to move along.

We camped that night on Eaglecrest Lake, only a short distance from the head of the Steel River. We had caught a good-size pike just before leaving Kawabatongog, and we saved it for our evening meal.

We had a good supper that night—fried pike, rice, corn, biscuits, and coffee. We were tired from a long day of travel, part of it on a narrow stream choked with logs, and we ate with great relish. We had no reason to expect what we would soon be facing.

We had a light breakfast Saturday morning, broke camp, and started down the lake. The weather had been bad much of the time, but now the sun came out and the day turned fine.

That morning we met the first people we had seen since leaving McLeod Lake on Monday—two men fishing from a canoe. One of them turned out to be Andy Lamothe of the Ontario Provincial Police. That brief meeting proved to be very fortunate for us.

We portaged out of Eaglecrest into a lake not named on our map, and the Steel lay directly ahead. We didn't stop for lunch, and shortly after noon we felt the quickening of the current under the kayak. The Steel was wide and slow at first, but it soon narrowed and deepened between rock cliffs, and the water started to run like a millrace. The river was fast, and it was awesomely powerful.

There were no dangerous rapids, but the river was only 20 to 30 yards wide, and trees had fallen in on both sides, obstructing much of the channel and forming dangerous log jams that were hard to avoid.

We got into trouble quickly. In many places the current seemed to flow from one side to the other to spend itself against sheer walls of rock. The water pulled us with it, and in spite of all we could do, one of those sudden shifts of direction drove us into a tangle of drowned treetops.

We lodged fairly solidly. The water was shallow enough for Ron to get out of his place in the bow and pull us free. He worked the boat clear, but then the river tore it from his grasp, and I shot downstream alone, leaving him standing there in waist-deep water.

It was no emergency. I thought it would be easy to go ashore as soon as I came to a slower stretch and wait for him. But a quarter-mile downstream there was another sharp bend. As I neared it I saw another tangle of drowned trees on the outside of the bend.

The river was boiling under that jam with murderous force, and one man paddling was not enough to keep the kayak clear. I was swept beneath the branches of a big tree, and the current began to pull the boat under. I grabbed a branch and hung on frantically. The kayak swamped under me, overturned, and was tugged from beneath me. I was left dangling there while the boat went downstream, bottom up.

I struggled ashore and took after it, running through brush, climbing over and crawling under fallen trees. I saw the kayak roll upright, and our gear was still in it, but then it overturned again, and our food bag broke free and floated away. We never saw that bag again.

One thing made it possible to keep the boat in sight for the half-mile I chased it—it hung up again and again in the same kind of jams that had caused the accident.

The river made another bend, and on the far bank a 200-foot cliff fell sheer to the water. I could see a tangle of trees there. The kayak smashed into that tangle and stopped, bottom up.

The water was over my head and too fast for swimming and there was no shore at the foot of the rock wall. The boat had lodged on the opposite side of the river, and I could find no way to get to it. I walked back upstream and joined Ron.

My matches were soaked and worthless, but luckily Ron had three-quarters of a pack of dry ones. Our ax was either in the kayak or in the river, but we broke off dry cedar and got a fire going. The evening was chilly. I was wearing only blue jeans and an undershirt, and I was wet from head to foot. Ron wore long johns, a wool shirt, and a windbreaker, so he was in much better shape than I for the cheerless hours of darkness.

We gathered wood as long as we could see and dried our clothing beside a brisk fire. Our insect repellent was gone, and black flies and mosquitoes attacked us savagely until the cool of evening came on. We curled up by the fire, huddled close together for warmth. We slept fitfully, warm on one side, freezing cold on the other, awakening every little while to put more wood on the fire. It was the worst night I can remember.

At daybreak we started downstream on the bank, hoping to retrieve the kayak. We didn't have to think about breakfast, because we had no food.

Salvaging the kayak was out of the question, because of the depth and swiftness of the current and the rock cliff that made it difficult to get down to the water. As a result of an attack of polio when he was young, Ron has difficulty in climbing. He could not get down that cliff, and by myself I lacked the strength to work the boat free.

Of the equipment that was still wedged in the bow of the kayak, I pulled out what I could reach—one tote bag that held the tent but no poles, my gear bag, Ron's sleeping bag, and two air mattresses. Packing the things back to where we had camped was hard work. At one point we had to float everything across a muddy slough on one of the air mattresses. We finally completed the job, sorted things out, and took inventory.

The tent could hang by its ropes from trees. The sleeping bag would have to serve the two of us. Our ax was gone, and so were our fishing tackle and all our pots and pans. For cooking—assuming we found anything to cook—we had an aluminum drinking cup that held half a pint. We both had pocketknives, and there was one spool of fishing line.

Almost all our food was gone. We didn't even have a candy bar, but there were three packets of dry milk in my gear. Each of them would make the equivalent of a quart of regular milk.

Our mishap was the kind of thing that every boat party on a wilderness river dreads. We were stranded about halfway between Longlac and Lake Superior, some 50 miles from our starting point and about the same distance from our destination.

We agreed on one thing from the start. We would wait where we were for rescue. We could not possibly walk out, and to wander away from the river would only make it more likely that we would never be found.

Hunger wasn't much of a problem the first day. We didn't seem to miss food, maybe because we were too worried to think about it. We hung the tent that afternoon, and that night was better than the first one, partly because I had plenty of insect dope in my gear bag and also because we were worn out and slept soundly.

We had lost the kayak on Saturday afternoon, June 23. By Monday we were really hungry. All we could think about was food. We lost strength fast, and we could see each other getting thinner and thinner as time passed.

The second day I surprised Ron by walking into camp and asking, "Do you feel like eating?" I had killed a small toad among the rocks on the river bank.

We put the toad's front and hind legs in my drinking cup, boiling them to make a broth. We shared it and then ate the shreds of meat. It was our first food since breakfast on Saturday morning.

Toad hunting became a major occupation. The toads were scarce, and none was big. They were hard to catch among the rocks. We gave up trying to grab them with our hands. Instead we broke off light poles of dry cedar, sharpened them to a point, and used them as spears. We also cut a notch in them for each day that passed, and so managed to keep track of the days. Our best catch was five toads in one day. Some days there were none. The average was two a day.

We have since been asked a number of times whether toad legs taste like frog legs. We don't know. To begin with, we had no salt or other seasoning. In the second place, the toad legs yielded so little meat that we really couldn't taste much. Yet it was astonishing how a few sips of the hot broth and a shred or two of meat lifted our spirits and dispelled the gloom for a while.

We rationed the dry milk very carefully, allowing ourselves only a scanty cupful each evening, heated over the fire. It warmed and cheered us, and I suppose drinking it warm helped us to sleep.

I can't say that time dragged. Much of the daylight hours were spent hunting toads and gathering wood. Without an ax, it was hard to get enough wood, and we worked slowly, taking care not to injure ourselves.

Our camp was among the trees, where a search pilot or observer would have difficulty spotting us. There was an open ridge behind the camp, and we collected wood, evergreen branches, and moss there so that we would be able to send up a smoke signal as soon as we heard a plane. We did make smoke several times, but it never did any good.

We also stretched a length of fish line across the river and hung a red bandanna in the middle of it. Just upstream from our camp the river was shallow, and I waded across there and tied the line to a tree on the other bank.

Being lost or marooned in a remote wilderness is a strange emotional experience. Ron and I felt more concern for our families back home than we did for ourselves. As Ron remarked one evening: "At least we know we're alive. They don't." The mental strain was harder to endure than the physical discomfort. Our hopes for rescue stayed high, but underneath there was always a nagging doubt that we would be found in time.

We knew one thing was in our favor—our families would realize that we were in some kind of trouble. We were due back home on June 30. I had a date to attend my sister's wedding in Saginaw that day, and Ron was scheduled to leave the next morning on a trip to western Canada. When we failed to return, search machinery was sure to be put into gear. Ron thought we might be found rather quickly then. My hopes were not so high. I expected that it would take a week or more.

Our hopes were borne out in one way. Starting on July 1 we heard aircraft each day and felt sure the search was on. But for three days the weather was so bad that we saw none of the planes, and we knew that the pilots would not see us.

On July 4, the day the light plane circled us and then flew on, we decided we had waited as long as we dared. We were slowly starving to death. The next morning, we agreed, we would try once more to work our boat out of the log jam and go down the Steel.

It was the wrong decision—one born of starvation and depression. That afternoon we took a short walk downriver to test our strength. We had waited too long. We could hardly walk. There was no hope of pulling the boat free.

Back home, our families were living through a nightmare, but they did their best to end it quickly. Jona's father is a police officer in the Saginaw County sheriff's department. He and Ron's father knew what to do. They phoned the Ontario Provincial Police in Schreiber and kept in daily contact with the police there. The first thing the police did was to locate my car at the Schreiber post. Then they knew we were either dead or stranded somewhere in the bush, not driving home in the car. The air search got under way, handicapped by the worst kind of weather.

One other thing proved to be in our favor. Andy Lamothe, the officer we had met on Eaglecrest Lake, reported that chance encounter promptly, and that narrowed the search area to the Steel River. Lamothe made one mistake, however. He told the searchers our kayak was blue. The deck was, but the bottom was gray, and the boat was lodged bottom up in the river. Not that it mattered. The searchers didn't see the boat.

The morning of July 5 broke clear and bright after days of cloud and rain. Our strength was about gone, and the task of breaking off enough wood for our fire was becoming almost too much for us. We both felt that unless rescue came very soon, it would come too late.

About 10:30 that morning we heard an aircraft following the Steel from the south. I grabbed the red windbreaker, staggered out onto the fallen tree, and started to signal.

The plane roared over, low enough so that I could see the pilot and the observer. Almost overhead, it tipped up on one wing and whipped around. For the second time in two days I yelled to Ron that we had been found. That time, it was true.

The searchers had spotted the red bandanna before they saw me. They did not sight Ron at all, and for several hours it was feared that one of us was dead.

The aircraft made four or five circles to make sure we knew we were found. Then it headed back to Terrace Bay to pick up a canoe. It was after 5 P.M. before we heard the plane coming back, and they were seven long and uneasy hours.

The two-man rescue crew, an Ontario police officer and a man from the Ontario Department of Lands and Forests, landed on Eaglecrest Lake and canoed down to our camp. That took two more hours, but they finally reached us. Never in our lives have we been so glad to see human faces.

They brought two small bottles of glucose, one for each of us. They would not let us pack up our tent or lift or carry anything. We must have looked at least as far gone as we felt.

We were in the hospital at Terrace Bay at 8 P.M. The doctors who checked us marveled because we were not in worse condition. But even so, Ron had lost 20 pounds, and I had lost 15. It was the toads, everybody agreed, that had kept us from worse consequences.

We thanked the fates for them at the time, but almost starving to death on a toad a day for 12 days is anything but pleasant—especially if the hunger is coupled with endless waiting for a rescue that you know may never come. Weeks later Andy Lamothe went in with a party and extricated the kayak. It was undamaged, and I have it at home now.

General

WHERE HAVE ALL OUR HEROES GONE?

By Roger Kahn

From Esquire

Copyright, ©, 1974, Roger Kahn

We stood waiting outside the old ball park, Jerry, Lefty, and I, tense and chattering in expectancy. The wooden hot dog stand beside the parking alley had closed and the September dusk was dying and we would all be late for dinner. Still, beside the alley outside the old ball park we had to wait.

"I know they park their cars here," Lefty said. Like the young Dylan Thomas, Lefty was scrawny, curly, dirty.

"You sure now?" Jerry said. At 12, Jerry had grown a Rotary chairman's jowls.

"My sister knows this cop," Lefty said. "The cop told her."

"What are those guys doing in there this long?" Jerry said.

"Playing cards," I said. "My dad told me after games, the ball players play cards. Especially when they lose, like today."

"Let's go home," Jerry said.

"Look," Lefty said. "You want to see a ball player? A big-league ball player? Or do you want to go back to the house?"

"I'm hungry," Jerry said. "I wish the hot dog stand was open."

"I want to see a big-leaguer," I said. "I've never seen a big-leaguer on a street."

Like all important memories, the day returns in patches of gold. Peanut bags littered the sidewalk and the time could not have been good. 1940. A country riding from Depression into war. A world of Stalin, the Greater Asia Co-Prosperity Sphere, Dachau. But Lefty's sister had found out where the Dodgers parked their cars, and in that troubled September, twilight glowed.

"Who do you want to see most?" Lefty said.

"Durocher," I said. Leo Durocher. Playing manager. The bald-headed shortstop. An artist at getting rid of the ball quickly. A genius at hustling pool. Fought with Babe Ruth. Didn't matter. Great manager. Leo The Lip.

"I'm for Reiser," Lefty said. Pete Reiser. The kid with all the tomorrows. Hallroom boy. Bats left or right. Throws left or right. Maybe he'll hit .400. Pistol Pete.

"Medwick," Jerry said. Joe Medwick. The big stick. Former batting champion. Then a fast ball crashed into his head. Fighting back now, fighting that fear. Ducky Medwick.

We gabbled in aimless excitement until at length four ball players appeared at a narrow gate. They looked about, considering the children. Twenty of us were milling near the cars. The ball players broke into quickstep, heads down. They said nothing. They had lost.

Durocher wasn't there, nor Pistol Pete, but with rising shock I recognized Ducky Medwick. The old batting champion was a short, heavy-set man, who scowled and sucked a great cigar. He rolled the cigar over his teeth as he walked.

"Mr. Medwick."

No response.

"Mr. Medwick."

He kept walking. The four ball players reached the alley and slipped into a large black car with such briskness that they might have been bank robbers.

"Can I have an autograph, Mr. Medwick?" I called through an opening window.

"Get away from the car, kid, before we run ya the fuck down." Mr. Medwick had concluded my first colloquy with a major-league ball-player.

At supper, talk wheeled about significant matters and men. Spitfires and Wendell Willkie and a sermon by John Donne, borne into vogue by Ernest Hemingway. My parents ruled the conversation sternly. What are you reading in school? *Macbeth?* Ah, yes, *Macbeth.* Have you noticed the consistent rat imagery in that play?

"Nope."

"Well, it's there nonetheless," my father said.

"Something terrific happened today," I said. "I went to the ball park."

"I thought we were discussing *Macbeth,*" my mother said.

"I hung around after the game," I said. "I met Ducky Medwick and he talked to me."

"Ducky Medwick?" my father said, almost shouting. "He talked to you?"

"I thought we were discussing *Macbeth,*" my mother said.

Durocher has become Sinatra's oldest groupie. Pete Reiser never hit .400. One day in 1942 he dove for what Red Barber called "a long, high drive." The wall embraced Reiser's body, which was never the same. Joe Medwick sells insurance in St. Louis and still scowls. Yet when I meet them, a knot explodes in my stomach. Leo The Lip. Pistol Pete. Ducky Medwick. Major-leaguers, and they are talking to me.

My wisest child, who is seventeen, regards this response as an aspect of lunacy. "What did they do," he says, "except play ball?"

"What they did was this. They were heroes."

"Heroes," Gordon says, his smooth face wrinkling in confusion. "From baseball?"

"Well, that was my game, my father's game, my grandfather's game. It was baseball."

"But why would your heroes come from there? Why wasn't your hero a writer or a musician or President Roosevelt?"

I have been dumb to answer. My son looks on my baseball reveries with interest, amusement, disdain.

Let me now describe, for you, for Gordon Kahn, for all the people who have never heard of Ducky Medwick, a time, a climate, realities of the past. With years a man comes to distrust memory. The mind is a dreadful sentimentalizer, forgetting old hangovers and ancient catastrophes. We truly like the past because we know how it comes out. The wars are done. The loves are told.

But as one glances back, amid the clink of convivial glasses, things tend to blur into a faintly purple haze. Then we find ourselves announcing, "Well, those were gentler, simpler times." Once that is done, we fall prey to simplistic misty explanations. Why did we look upon fine athletes as creatures slightly higher than the angels? Those were the times, my friend, the simple, gentle times, when everyman was either hero or hero-worshiper. Pour me another three fingers, pal, and I'll tell you about a catch I saw in the Polo Grounds in the summer of 1939. Absolutely the damnedest catch that ever was.

Without sentimentality, in murky morning, one cannot argue sensibly that we came to worship athletes in times any simpler or gentler than today. During the 1920's, America's first great hatching of sports heroes broke through. The names were Tilden and Ruth; Dempsey and Rockne; Gehrig and Grange. It was also during the 1920's that Capone raged, Jay Gatsby died, and stock-market profits fell like suicides. The 1930's gave us Joe DiMaggio and Joe Louis. They also inflicted Depression on the country. The 1940's provided an arrow of dark fire, Jackie Robinson. The forties also writhed with Pearl Harbor, the murder of two million Jewish children, Hiroshima, Nagasaki, the Cold War.

Come back then to that alley, near the demolished ball park, and consider sport as it was in a complex, darkening, angry world. The athletes, all of them, were Depression men, they had known unemployment, felt hunger, seen breadlines. They had been raised on farms, or in bleak clapboard houses, and the options before them were sparse. One could play ball—it was not play, of course, but labor—or failing that, one could look for work. Except there wasn't any work to find.

Cookie Lavagetto, the old third baseman, has talked about what it meant for him to make the major leagues. "My people lived in Oakland," Lavagetto said, "and nobody was working. We couldn't get jobs. The first time I came up in spring training I hit a single and when I got to first base I was so happy, I burst out laughing. Next time I came up the pitcher threw four fast balls at my head. He thought I'd been laughing at him. I couldn't have kept myself from laughing. With that hit, I was taking the whole family off relief."

This hunger to win, born deep within a man, almost insatiable, possessed the athletes of 1940, and communicated itself from field to grandstand in a profound and not quite definable way. Watching a pitcher throw beanballs, observing the runner try to spike the catcher, you recognized the desperation with which these major-leaguers fought for jobs. Baseball was quicker then, more violent, and therefore more dramatic. Drama is essential stuff for heroes.

Few made much money. After Pete Reiser won a batting championship in his second season, the Dodgers celebrated by paying him $8,000 next year. You not only had to be good, but you had to stay good year after year, if you wanted to crack the $10,000 barrier. It is one small truth of capitalism that a lean and hungry athlete plays like hell.

In 1940, it was easy to focus on hungry athletes and what we thought we knew of them, because sport itself was clearly focused. Last spring, while dial-spinning on a Sunday, I watched basketball (CBS); hockey (NBC); golf (ABC); two baseball games and a tennis match (local channels). All this in one minute of kaleidoscopic chaos. What season was it? The commercial season, primarily.

But in 1940, the sports fell tidily into place. Football presided in autumn. The college games began in late September, ran until Thanksgiving and then, as everyone burrowed in for winter, football receded in the consciousness. The pro game, which ran longer, had a narrow following. As one sports editor put it, fiercely, "The pros are potbellies. A bunch of beer swizzlers playing lazy football. And the only thing worse is the bunch of beer swizzlers watching." Winter brought what were then minor sports: basketball, indoor track, and hockey. You grew excited about a miler or perhaps a great outside shooter, but only in a limited way.

Boxing dominated certain weeks. Old newspapermen say that a good heavyweight fight was the best of all prescriptions for ailing circulation. Still, even in Joe Louis' prime, good heavyweight fights came rarely. Usually it was Louis against an opponent, who soon lay prone. Subsequently everyone smiled at the latest member of what sports writers called The Bum-of-the-Month Club.

Baseball was the sport for all the seasons. You followed it through the winter, spurred by newspaper accounts of debates about salary. Would Camilli hold out? (He never did.) Would he get what he was asking? (He never did.) The papers played each man's signing like an adventure, let the stories build from winter day to winter day. Then, finally, nirvana came, proclaimed in 24-point type. CAMILLI INKS PACT: GETS RAISE.

In mid-February the ball players made their way south and you envied them imagined joys in Florida. You studied each dispatch from spring training. Ernie White throwing well. Uh-oh; the Cardinals have another good one. The actual season ran from April to October the way it does today, but in those times baseball results completely dominated sports pages. If you lived in New York, you followed the Dodgers, the Giants, and the Yankees and you followed their farm teams as well, rooting for unknown athletes in Montreal and Newark and Jersey City. If you lived in Johnstown, Pennsylvania, you rooted for the Johnstown Johnnies, a Class D club that played in a small ball park near a river. Everywhere towns that were too small for even the smallest minor league fielded muscular bands of semiprofessionals, who played baseball once or twice a week at two dollars a game. Towns smaller than that ran amateur games, the married men struggling against the bachelors, with the women and children watching and waiting to cheer.

Baseball's dominance had grown across generations until it became, in Donald Hall's phrase, the game of all the fathers and all the sons. Mystically in the major-league parks identification sprang between fan and player. The men in white, the home team, hungrily playing this game, were enacting a fantasy that bridged generations. To play this game. To play it well. To play it like a major-leaguer, there on the green and brown and white geometry of the ball field.

Watch Pistol Pete run for a long fly ball, double to right, steal home. Damn, but that was a glorious thing. "When I grow up I'd like to be able to do that," I told my father once.

"I'd like to have done it myself," he said solemnly.

We were father and son, set apart by tribal rivalries half as old as time, but at the ball park, we were held in common thrall. We both would like to have been Pistol Pete Reiser.

"You know," a retired ball player has told me, "when I think of all the people I influenced, the fathers and sons who never met me, I get scared as hell. I was pretty much like any other guy, struggling to keep my job, and the life we lived wasn't much. Mostly I remember Pullman cars and soot. It was only later, looking back, that I thought, 'Son of a bitch, I was a hero.' That's what scares me. I got drunk, chased puss, and down around home I had to carry out the garbage. I wasn't a very heroic guy."

How could one know? That question cuts to the heart of the riddle. One could not know, for athletes, like movie stars and princes, stood as remote from middle-class life as Mount Olympus. We never saw them plain.

You couldn't tell what ball players were like by reading newspapers. The best writers composed with wit but the stories, even the finest, lacked proximity. They were researched from where they were written: the press box.

No one poked about locker rooms. A journalist of that era says with misplaced pride, "I limited my stories to the games. I was never a jockstrap sniffer like the young guys." What happened on a Pullman or on a team bus went unreported. You never found out about Durocher's belligerent vulgarity or Babe Ruth's roistering ways.

Long afterward, a reporter from *The New York Times* amazed me by insisting that Lou Gehrig had been a tightwad and somewhat hostile. "We were sitting in a soda place," he said, "and Gehrig told the waitress that he wanted *his* check. I think the bill for both of us was 30 cents. Gehrig was earning $40,000 that year."

"Why didn't you write that?" I said.

"Couldn't," said the reporter. "It would violate a confidence."

Couldn't or wouldn't, the reporting was always limited and sometimes rotten. The most serious of the radio announcers, Red Barber, described every ball player as a gentleman. To this day Barber insists that he has not heard obscenities on a ball field. The most famous radio man, Bill Stern, went somewhat further. He invented two or three sports stories every week.

According to Stern, Abraham Lincoln did not die in silence. From his deathbed, Lincoln summoned a nearby general and said, "Keep baseball going. The country needs it." The general's name, Stern cried exuberantly, was Abner Doubleday.

Stern pictured a dejected Frank Frisch walking off the Fordham campus, ready to quit on school, on life. A kindly priest saw him and encouraged Frisch to graduate, then give his life "to the great game of baseball. And that priest's name," Stern shouted, "was Eugenio Pacelli. Yes, the same Eugenio Pacelli who is famous the world over today as Pope Pius."

We listened in wonder. We believed. Sport was terribly important to presidents, to popes, to us. From the baseless fabric of imagination, we endowed the players with superhuman magic. Then, having converted jocks into gods, we set about worshipping our own creation.

We have voyaged a long way from the alley beside the old ball park, and none of the young people here is named Lefty or Jerry. They sit about a room, seven of them, high school freshmen to seniors and they will talk about sports and anti-heroes. They are children of the middle class, attending Scarborough Day School in Briarcliff Manor, 40 miles north of New York City. In another time, most would have been urban children, subway riders. Now they live in rolling suburbs, mow lawns of brilliant, competitive green, drive cars.

"I don't have any real athletic heroes," Stephan Zades says. He is a dark-haired senior with a fine build. "I admire the money they make. I want to make it myself, but that's something else, isn't it?"

"Baseball," I say. "The game itself was everything to us."

"Baseball?" Stephan says. "It's kind of dull. It's slow-paced. It's boring. I follow basketball and hockey. John Havlicek and Bobby Orr. I like them and I like their salaries. I guess I like track the best. I go down to Madison Square Garden whenever there's a good meet. But I don't exactly stand in line to meet track stars." Stephan grins. "I wouldn't hassle myself to do that," he says.

April Cattell is fair and trim, a sophomore. "I watch the interaction between players," she says, "but I never get excited. I don't like the competitive aspect of sports. I'm not very competitive myself. I don't think it's necessary to prove yourself through sports."

"We used to play team games," I say, "and if you lost today, hell, you'd win tomorrow. Baseball till it got cold, then football. Sometimes girls played street games with us. Variations on baseball, a game called slap ball."

"I'm frustrated working on a team," April says. "I like gymnastics, individuality."

Peter Dolgenos is one of the junior class intellectuals. He wears eyeglasses, speaks slowly, has small hands.

"I'm not good at sports," Peter says, "I don't have the coordination. I love to watch sports on television. I watch a lot. But being great at sports is a narrow accomplishment. To me, sports is a distraction that we need, but only that. A distraction. Politics is more important."

"Do you have a hero in sport?"

Peter's pale face screws up in concentration. "I like baseball," he says, "and I guess Tom Seaver is more a hero to me than Nixon. But Seaver is a hero by default."

Bob Zarakas, a freshman, has a young athletic build. He likes to play, he says, but he's turned off by watching.

"We'd watch," I say, "and dream we'd be there."

"I like to swim," Bob says, "but I sure wouldn't want to handle myself like Mark Spitz."

David Potel, a well-built senior, enjoys football and basketball. "But the way they do it on TV turns me off."

"Oh, I don't know," says Steve Zades. "TV is better than a seat in the back row, which is all you can get."

Judy Bernz says that sport is performance and if she had an idol there, it would come from ballet.

Gordon Kahn nods. Because of my own work, he has met ballplayers all his life. "Some are fantastically nice," he says, "but they aren't heroes."

"Who's a hero that we've met?"

"The pianist," Gordon says. "Claudio Arrau."

They describe television with contempt. No one will use an underarm deodorant because of an athlete's endorsement. They laugh at commercials, they insist. "I like some of the sports movies," Stephan Zades says. "It's good to see things where they treat athletes as people."

"The old movies," I say, "used to treat athletes as heroic people."

"We've seen them," someone says, "on late television. *The Babe Ruth Story.*"

"It's pretty bad," David Potel says. "Bad corn."

"But now," I say, "Hollywood people claim they are trying to treat athletes honestly as people. Has anyone here seen *Brian's Song*?"

"*Brian's Song,*" says Gordon Kahn, "is *The Babe Ruth Story* gone sophisticated."

"Dying isn't the issue," someone says. "Babe Ruth dying or Brian Piccolo."

"Sports is diversion," Peter Dolgenos says.

"We like certain sports," Gordon says, "but we're more interested in more important things."

"We aren't jocks," someone says.

"Besides," Peter says, returning to his theme, "how can anyone have a hero when the President of the United States is Richard Nixon?"

While I was considering my notes later, Gordon called and spoke apologetically. "So now you know," he said. "We don't take athletes for heroes. I suppose if you want, I can round up a few jocks, but they might be pretty dumb."

"No. I don't want that. We weren't jocks ourselves."

Indeed we were not. Like Stephan and April, we worked at studies. We put out school newspapers, discussed independence for India, and secretly rooted for Cataline to destroy the stuffy Cicero. Sport lay beyond, a kind of idyll, remote as Camelot and just as glorious.

Today's young people grow up with sports in the living room. The games are specially adapted to the quick pace and bloodlust television demands. Basketball has abandoned its pattern of deliberate play. Professional teams must shoot every 24 seconds. Football discreetly boasts of its showy violence—"He really got his bell rung, folks"—and runs a play every 30 seconds. Baseball, which has not made real adaptations, suffers, and Steve Zades finds it slow and boring. There was a magic to going to a ball park once, leaving the house, the trip to the field, being there. The magic of television is electronic. The tube is always nearby, available as last season's woman. David Potel responds by turning away.

Wherever an athlete starts today, he reaches the offices of a lawyer or an agent, if he is good enough. The lawyer or agent, if he is good enough, says something like this: "We can make beautiful money together. A hundred thousand, maybe two hundred thousand a year. Now here are the rules. Be nice to the press. Newspapermen can help you. Watch your image. Don't get drunk where anyone can see you and for Christ's sake be careful with the broads. Play hard, but don't get hurt. You've got too much going to be injured. This above all: when you do television interviews, smile and don't use the word shit."

Ball players wouldn't talk to us when we were young. Today they talk at us ceaselessly. Catch my good friend, Willie Twoshoes, after he wins an NBC game of the week with a 420-foot home run to center.

"Hi there, folks. It's Tony Cleancut here, just thrilled to be bringing you an interview with today's superstar, Willie Twoshoes. Hey, Will, what happened out there?"

"Well, Tony, he got the pitch up and I give—er, gave—it a ride."

"You really hit it, Will. Now is there something that can help the young people watching the show? You know. The youngsters, I mean."

"Yeah. When the pitch is up, give it a ride."

"Hot darn. That's something, Will. Did you hear that, kids? 'Give it a ride.' "

"Allus happy to help the youngsters, Tony."

"Great, Will. And say, you look pretty clean shaven even after nine tough innings. What kind of razor did you use today?"

"The No-Gash, Four-Track, Tony. If there's one thing I like more than helping kids, it's shaving with my Four-Track, No-Gash razor."

"Kids. Ladies and gentlemen. You heard it first-hand. From the mouth of the great Willie Twoshoes."

You turn away. I turn away. The youngsters turn away. Together we retch slightly and grow beards.

Newspaper and magazine sports journalism have come about since 1940. Some old idolatry persists, but it is modified by a new muckraking. Editors want athletes quoted almost as they speak, portrayed almost as they are. Reading sports pages and articles, one has little sense of strolling through a pantheon. Like the newly hirsute women of the girlie journals, athletes are becoming practically real.

The sports industry itself has bloomed into diffusity. Football and basketball and hockey sell themselves with skill, but from their competition comes uncertainty. There is no sport like old baseball, no single national game, no one sure seedbed for universal heroes.

What can the hockey rooter say to the basketball fan? "My man can skate your feller's legs off."

"How's his jump shot?"

"Say, you like tennis?"

"Golf."

"Who do you have in the fifth?"

"Harness racing or flats?"

Diffusion. Confusion. Disinterest.

Once leagues were compact and stable. Rivalries built. Next year the Boston Celtics will find themselves facing something called the New Orleans Jazz, which is neither music nor an X movie, but a basketball team. Each year we are assaulted by new franchises, new leagues, which feeds a certain sense that we are being hustled. What is this—sport, or General Motors grinding out new models and new mileage figures to lay claim to our dollars? The bright young people feel this. They resist.

Sports flourish as a marvelous subdivision of show business, infinitely more real than police stories and series about kindly physicians. Athletes, seizing the boom, earn more and more. Ad-men, seizing the athletes, seek to sell us. But we have been contemplating heroes, rather than hustlers.

Take everything, diffusion, tougher journalism and the rest, and go beyond, to know why the athlete, whom we idolized from great distance, is a callow hero to Stephan, David, and April. With his warts and shaky syntax, he is overwhelmingly available, playing too many sports for too many hours on too many television sets.

Worshipped is the word that goes with hero. Had someone stationed a TV camera on top of Olympus, would anyone have worshipped Zeus?

"Hello, Hellenists. Howard Cosell here, bringing you an exclusive interview with the big feller. Say, Big Z., is it true, as reported, that you once made out by pretending to be a swan?"

"I'm glad you asked that, Howard. I appreciate this chance to set the record straight and so does my agent. The story is nonsense. Actually, I'd disguised myself as a chicken."

Let us pray.

EBBETS FIELD REVISITED

By Jeff Prugh

From the Los Angeles Times

Copyright, ©, 1974, Los Angeles Times

> "All I knew about Brooklyn was that it was some strange, outer world. . . . When they told me I'd been traded to Brooklyn, I didn't know what on God's great earth to expect."
> —Dixie Walker, the People's Cherce

The borough of Brooklyn is just another ugly face now—blemished and toughened by unflattering changes time has wrought.

Police sirens wail. Ramshackle storefronts are boarded up. Buildings are plastered with the same grotesque graffiti that adorns subway trains. Color the old neighborhood rough, predominantly black, with hardly anything the way it was.

Where have you gone, Jackie Robinson? And Leo The Lip and Pistol Pete? And Campy and Pee Wee and The Dook? Who's on third, anyway?

Whatever happened to Hilda Chester and her clanging cowbell? And Shorty's Band, alias the Brooklyn Sym-Phony? And everybody else from the days of "Dem Bums"?

All that's left are memories now.

Gone, but not forgotten, is the love affair with the boys of umpteen summers ago. Gone are the cheers that rocked ratty old Ebbets Field. Gone, some 3,000 miles, is a baseball team called the Dodgers.

It has been 17 years since they left for Los Angeles in quest of riches that owner Walter O'Malley said he was denied in this borough of 2.5 million persons across the East River from Manhattan.

Today, the feelings—and nonfeelings—for the Dodgers of old and new are mixed. Mostly there is bitterness, nostalgic affection, aching hearts over the team that got away—and a lukewarm indifference toward the now-generation L.A. Dodgers.

Just about anybody over 30 fondly remembers how it used to be. And the kids and post-teens? Well, the old Dodgers are about as exciting as a stodgy history book. The New York Mets are where it's at.

Emerge from a subway tunnel at Flatbush Avenue, and the mind's eye cannot even fantasize where the old ball park was, out there amid the soot-blackened apartments and auto-body shops and noisy streets where some say you shouldn't walk at night.

Standing there on a hot afternoon thick with August humidity, a stranger knows only that a high-rise apartment complex stands on what used to be Ebbets Field.

But where?

"Can you tell me," a reporter asked a woman in a market, "where the ball park was?"

The woman, fiftyish, plump, and carrying a sackful of groceries as heavy as her Brooklyn accent, said:

"Aw, honey, you don't wanta go over there! Why, that park hasn't been there for years. There's nothin' you'd wanta see there now!"

Prodded into offering directions, she said:

"You go down this street here, about two blocks, and you'll see the Ebbets Field Apartments, right across the street from what used to be Intermediate School No. 320. Now it's Jackie Robinson School."

A few minutes later, the monstrous apartment structure looms, 25 stories of faded, yellow-brown brick.

You locate Bedford Avenue, which borders what used to be the right-field screen and where Duke Snider must have smashed a million home runs.

Youngsters, mostly black, play in the apartment courtyards. Teen-agers cruise the streets in low-slung, shiny cars, like a scene out of *American Graffiti*. Men and women stroll the sidewalks.

You ask an apartment security guard to point out a plaque commemorating the ball park, and he motions toward a dark cement cornerstone near the manager's office. Obscured by shrubbery are the words: "THIS IS THE FORMER HOME OF EBBETS FIELD."

Hand-painted signs, posted throughout the courtyards voice the ultimate irony: "PLEASE . . . NO BALLPLAYING . . ."

Welcome to Brooklyn, 1974.

The old neighborhood is a fascinating mixture of faces, places, voices—and feelings.

Across Bedford Avenue is the Dodgers Service Station, where Robinson, Snider, Campanella, Reese, Hodges, and other players parked during games.

It is symbolic of ethnic changes since the Dodgers helped make Brooklyn a household word. The owner in the 1950's was a Caucasian nicknamed Whitey. He sold to an employee, Johnny Brock, who is black. He operates the station with his younger brother, Buddy.

"The Dodgers? Yeah, they're still my team," said Buddy, munching a salami sandwich on his lunch break. "Naw, I'm not mad at 'em for leavin'. . . . O'Malley did the same thing others would do, I guess."

He wore a dark blue uniform embroidered with his name and the misspelled word, "Dogers." Reminiscing about his boyhood, when home-run balls crashed through the station's floor-to-ceiling windows, he said: "As soon as we heard the crack of the bat, everybody ran!"

Names flashed through his head. "Junior Gilliam was always my man," he said. "Snider . . . Robinson too. Today I like Cey, Garvey, Wynn, Russell. They got some good baseball brains runnin' that team now."

And what about his baseball-watching nowadays?

"I'm glad the New York Mets are here," said Brock. "That means I can watch the Dodgers on TV. . . . When they left for the West Coast, I felt a part of me was gone."

A green-and-white ice cream truck drove up and parked at the pumps. It, too, bore a misspelling: "BILLY BOY ICE CREAM—The Dary [*sic*] Bar on Wheels."

The driver, Jim Romsey, 32, said he's a Met fan now, but remembers watching the Dodgers as a boy. "We saved 10 lids from Borden's ice cream," he said, "and they let us into the bleachers free."

A friend in his twenties, Raymond Cuevas, poked his head through a window in the rear of the truck.

"Hey, do you know where I can try out for the Dodgers?" he asked. "I wish they could talk to my coach. I play shortstop. He says I can make it."

Down the street, there were more reminiscences at a corner bar, the Hide-A-Way Lounge.

A juke box belted out soul music by singer Barry White as a handful of black patrons sipped beer around a bar that bore a baseball-schedule calendar reading: "FOLLOW THE METS on WHN Radio."

When a visitor informed the customers he was writing a story about the Dodgers, they mostly looked back to yesteryear.

A portly man who resembled the old rock 'n' roll singer, Fats Domino, was asked about the Mets's calendar.

"Naw, I don't pay no attention to the Mets," he said, staring glassy-eyed at the beer in front of him. "There was nothin' like the Dodgers. . . . Pee Wee Reese, Cookie Lavagetto, Dixie Walker, man, they were all fighters! Always arguin'! . . . When they went away, it was the worst thing that could happen."

The bartender, a young woman named Barbara Pew, said she doesn't follow baseball but her seventh-floor apartment across the street "is right over where second base used to be."

She said new tenants of Ebbets Field Apartments—recently rechristened Jackie Robinson Apartments at Ebbets Field—are shown a floor plan which pinpoints the erstwhile location of home plate, first, second, and third bases and so on.

Her husband, Clarence, 34, a slender man with a neat goatee, reflected the sentiments of many Brooklynites. His heart was with the old Dodgers. . . . "Hodges, Snider, Campanella, Junior Gilliam, Robinson . . . all them cats."

He told of attending Jackie Robinson's funeral almost two years ago and how Bedford Avenue was jammed with crowds watching the motorcade honoring the man who broke baseball's color barrier in 1947.

"Gilliam [now a Dodger coach] would make a good manager," he said. "My man is Hank Aaron, and they didn't want him to manage. Today, it's always later for the colored."

Pew said it bitterly, with the same feeling he expressed about the Dodgers' move to California.

"Everybody likes the Mets 'cause they screw up so bad," he said. "Nobody over here likes watchin' the Yanks. As far as the Dodgers are concerned, nobody talks much about 'em today."

Then he asked about the 1974 Dodgers.

"Tell me," he said, straight-faced, "is Maury Wills still playin' with 'em?"

The answer was "no," and he shook his head.

"It's not the same for me anymore," he said. "I swear to God—I don't even know who's playin' first base for the Dodgers now."

"There'll never be another Brooklyn. . . ." Brooklynites say it affectionately when they recall their romance with a bygone baseball era.

The Brooklyn Dodgers meant many things to millions. There was the rollicking humor of Casey Stengel and Babe Herman and three guys converging on third base. There were the underdog Dodgers, scrambling to win headlines from the elite Yankees and Giants across the river. There was the sociological breakthrough when the late Branch Rickey signed Robinson, Roy Campanella, Don Newcombe, and other blacks.

Their success unified the ethnic conglomerate that was—and still is—Brooklyn. It is a melting pot of Poles, Jews, Irish, Germans, Italians, blacks, and others who live in villages called Park Slope and Bay Ridge and Flatbush and Canarsie, among others.

So-called WASPs reside there, too, although long-time residents say they are a minority. "I'm one of them," said Tommy Holmes, once a sports writer for the defunct *Brooklyn Eagle,* "and sometimes I feel like an endangered species."

Brooklyn was a city until 1896 when it was annexed as one of New York's five boroughs. Had it remained a separate municipality, its population of 2.5 million would make it one of America's largest.

Until Leo Durocher and Larry MacPhail helped turn the Dodgers into a respected team shortly before World War II, Brooklyn was to the rest of the nation something to laugh at on radio quiz shows, the home of the Brooklyn Naval Yard and the Brooklyn Academy of Music.

Baseball and rickety Ebbets Fields (capacity: 34,000) soon became bigger than Brooklyn itself.

The crowds were boisterous, knowledgeable, colorful. They hero-worshipped the home club and shrieked at visiting teams in a dialect all their own.

They said "moider" for "murder," "earl" for "oil," and nicknamed batting star Dixie Walker the "People's Cherce."

"There was a feeling in that ball park that probably will never be recaptured again," said Walker, now a Dodger coach. "I'll always be fond of my years in Brooklyn, even though I didn't know what I was getting into when I went there. The people loved the Dodgers as if they were a part of them."

And Los Angeles fans?

"They're a different class," said Walker. "They're more subdued —orderly. They seem to have more to relate to in California than just baseball."

Others say Ebbets Field offered fans plain-folks intimacy that is a million light-years from the antiseptic, palm-studded grandeur of Chavez Ravine.

"You were so close to the field, sitting anywhere in that old park, that you could hear the players talking to each other," said Red Patterson, a Dodger vice-president who used to write for New York newspapers.

And there are others who remember. . . .

A man in his seventies named Bill Boylan used to pitch batting practice for the Dodgers—between deliveries along his milk route in a horse-drawn wagon.

"The fans argued about baseball—it was their life," said Boylan, now press-room supervisor at Shea Stadium. "I never thought the Dodgers would leave Brooklyn. None of us had an inkling it would happen until the last week of the season in '57. All I know is what the ex-players and fans tell me today. There'll never be another Brooklyn."

Jimmy Ohanian weighs 300 pounds and is proprietor of Elgin Tire Center, where the old Dodgers bought automobile tires.

He remembers the day in 1960 when a giant wrecking ball smashed Ebbets Field to the ground.

"Every time that ball swung," he said, "it not only tore up the ball park but it broke my heart. I felt like running over and yelling, 'Stop it, will ya!' "

His younger brothers, Eddie and Richard, looked back at baseball in those days.

"The players were different," said Eddie. "We'd wait for guys like Hodges and Furillo and Robinson and Snider out by the gate, and they'd talk to us, put their arms around us, as if they were our fathers."

He shook his head.

"Ball players are more afraid of the fans today. Also, they're more educated. I remember Hodges and Reese weren't shy about talking on our level. Today, so many ball players are up there so high they can't look down anymore."

Eddie Ohanian drew contrasts. There was the barbershop down the street, where Gil Hodges and Duke Snider good-naturedly talked with the kids. "We could ask 'em anything," he said, "like, 'How come you're not hitting?' and they wouldn't bite our heads off."

And today?

"Well, the Mets have picture day," he said. "From 12:30 to 12:45, a kid can take pictures of certain players. What a crock of crap! Big deal! Today it's so bad you've gotta make an appointment!"

Outside the tire shop, more sirens wailed. Dogs barked next door at the K-9 Universal Security Dog Center, where a man with tattooed forearms was training a German shepherd on the sidewalk, shouting, "Down now! . . . Down! . . . Get down!"

And there was the market not far away where the fiftyish woman with the sackful of groceries had told a stranger where Ebbets Field no longer was.

"If anybody says this place is a ghetto, don't believe 'em," said the woman, Mrs. Anna Boyarsky. "We've got everything within a few blocks here. Good schools. A museum. Botanical gardens. The library and historical center."

She smiled proudly.

"See? We've got everything," she said. "There's really nothing missing here!"

Except, of course, the Brooklyn Dodgers.

HOW TO PLAY SECOND BASE

By Laurence Sheehan

From The Atlantic Monthly

Copyright, ©, 1974, by The Atlantic Monthly Company, Boston, Mass.

Reprinted with permission

Second base is the most important position in baseball. Nobody realizes. A lot of coaches don't even bother to tell their second basemen the first thing about the job. They don't think second base is worth the effort.

The unfortunate name of second base is partly to blame. It just sounds like a hand-me-down. I think the ill-fated manager Joe McCarthy of the Boston Red Sox also once said something like second base is neither first nor third. That was the situation when I was playing for Centerville School, and I doubt if it's improved much since then, not at Centerville or in the majors.

Why is second base so important? Because when an easy grounder or a high pop-up is hit to that position, and you kick it away, or misjudge it and let it bounce on your head, the whole team gets demoralized. The shortstop comes over and says, "Too bad the school bus didn't clip you this morning." The first baseman slaps his leg and laughs. The pitcher gives you the finger in front of everybody. Of course there may not be that many people at the game, so the public humiliation won't count for much. Centerville hardly ever drew a crowd because it was always in last place in its division, thanks in part to slight miscalculations by the second baseman.

I got my little sister Evie to come a lot when games were played at Legion Field in our neighborhood. But she didn't understand baseball. She would see me strike out on three consecutive pitches or get run through by a steaming grounder. But she wouldn't find such happenings interesting enough to report to our parents. I'd have to tell them myself at supper.

You might say that for Evie my baseball failings went in one eye and out the other. She was a lousy fan. I sometimes wondered why I had her come to the games at all, which I did starting when I made the team in sixth grade and got my uniform. I don't think she even knew what number I wore (9—The Thumper's own!). Anyway, if it weren't for the bubble gum my black pal Herman kept giving her, she probably would have stopped coming long before she finally did. Herman played third. She would chew gum or eat an apple or orange from home, and watch out that no one stole our gloves when we were at bat, but basically Evie paid no attention to what was going on. She usually sat on the opposing team's bench, to my great embarrassment. It was closer to the water fountain.

Back to second base now. There are tips that can make anybody play this position better and I'd like to pass them along.

By the way, I didn't mean to imply I minded my teammates groaning and hooting at my errors. I mean I minded, but I understood. And basically we had a close-knit infield. It wasn't any dream infield, such as the Bosox built around the great Bobby Doerr and Johnny Pesky in the same years I was at Centerville, but we had a pretty good team feeling. Erwin, our regular pitcher, would put up with four or five errors in one inning before going to the finger. Lover Boy, the first baseman, would laugh at errors and kid a lot, but actually he didn't care where the ball went or even who won. His mind was always on his girl friends who were waiting for him up in the nearly empty stands. Bert, our team captain at short, would come over after I'd let one go through my legs, and say, "All right, let's get back in this game now." And of course Herman, who never made an error himself over at third, would not get upset by anything I did. Or anybody did. He was the coolest cucumber on the squad.

Not even State Street's Butch Mendoza, the division's Home Run King and number-one razzer, could get through to Herman. We had no regular coaches on the bases. Older players on each team did the job. Mendoza liked to do it for State Street. He'd coach first base and rib Lover Boy about his shaggy hair and his white cleats, and Lover Boy would nod and smile, probably not even hearing Butch's taunts, too busy dreaming about those girls of his up in the stands and about his plans for them all after the game. When Butch coached third he liked to rib Herman about his color. "Hey, boy, where's your watermelon today?" he'd say, or "How come you're not picking cotton this week?" At that time blacks were few and far between in our town, no matter what grammar school you went to, and Butch probably thought of Herman as a foreigner. The important thing is, Herman paid no attention to Butch and never did make an error before his eyes.

I'll spare the outfielders on Centerville. Like most outfielders they were hotshots, and I suppose because they managed to get more hits and runs than anyone else, they had a right to parade around out there and editorialize on every move the infielders made.

Now, then, the hardest play to handle is the infield fly. I say anytime a ball goes higher than it goes farther, it is going to be a son of a gun to catch. In my playing days, half the time I wouldn't even know when one of those high pops was entering my territory. I'd need to hear Lover Boy call over, "Hey, little man, here comes trouble!"

Anyway, you've got to get set. A good thing is to get your feet in motion. And bend your neck back far enough so your eyes see more than the brim of the baseball cap. Everything about school uniforms is fine except the brims on the caps. They are made for adult heads, and if you stand 4-foot-3 and weigh 75 pounds, the hat will be like an awning on your forehead. The only thing you'll be able to see without any strain is your feet, which as I said should be in motion anyway—as you commence dancing into position to make a stab at the catch.

Of course, once you get your head tilted back far enough so you can see past the brim of your cap, you risk being temporarily blinded by the sun. Even on cloudy days it is possible for the sun to come out just at the crucial instant and make you lose sight of the damn ball, assuming you ever saw it in the first place.

Another bad thing about the high fly is that it gives you too much time to think. Like the drowning man, a ten-year-old tends to experience all the important moments in his life while waiting for a baseball to drop. Moments such as when you saw your name on the Centerville School baseball roster for the first time.

To tell the truth, the reason I got to play second base for Centerville for three years in a row is that my growth was stunted at the time, and provided I didn't swing at the ball when I was up to bat, opposing pitchers tended to walk me. My strike zone was about the size of a civics workbook. If I waited out the pitchers, I could count on getting on base almost every time.

Not that I wouldn't go for the hit once in a while. I would pretend to miss the signal telling me to wait for the walk that would invariably come from the third-base coach when I was up. The signal was always the same: doff cap, scratch left knee, blow nose in hanky, in that order. By the end of the season every team in the division knew all our coaching signals, but it was too confusing to try to change them.

Anyway, sometimes I would just ignore the signal and go for the hit. Each time I missed the ball, of course, the third-base coach would slam his cap on the ground or throw his hanky down, mad as can be. The opposing team's catcher would grin and hold the ball up in front of my eyes for my inspection before tossing it back to the mound. I would ignore all this and just dig in deeper with my cleats and take a couple of fierce practice swings. Digging in was itself a problem because the batter's box was furrowed over from other stances. Following the example of The Thumper and Vern Stephens and other Beantown sluggers, the boys in our division liked to get a really firm hold on the planet when at bat. They would dig and kick with their cleats like dogs tearing up the ground after peeing, and the result would be a set of gullies in the batter's box among which I was supposed to find a place to stand. I had the narrow stance that comes with a 4-foot-3 frame, and sometimes I had one foot on a hillside and the other in a gully. No wonder my average was low.

That's really part of the story of how Herman and I got to be friends—we were built the same. We were the only two to make the team in sixth grade. Herman made it on his talent in spite of his size and I made it on my size in spite of my talent. In a way we came up together from the minors. Also we tended to sit right near each other in classrooms because our last names started with the same initial and in those days everything was done alphabetically, from choking on cod-liver-oil pills to taking cover in the lavatory during practice A-bomb attacks.

Now about the high fly. Your own thoughts are not the only distractions when you're looking for a ball somewhere up there in the blinding blue infinity of outer space. People are chattering all around you. Once I heard my sister call to me, "Hey, I'm going to play on the swings now, OK?" Another time, when we were playing State Street, Butch Mendoza hit a real rainmaker somewhere in my neighborhood. Running down the line to first, Butch had plenty of time on his hands, so he hollered, "Hey, kid, you're gonna miss it, you're gonna miss it!" Of course I was; nobody had to broadcast it.

State Street always won the division and usually went on to win the town title by beating the leader of the other division. They were tough boys at State Street. If they didn't beat you in the game, they'd beat you up afterward. A lot of the State Street players had stayed back in grades a couple of times, which gave them the edge of experience over the boys at Centerville. I don't know how old Butch was, I did hear once that when he finally graduated from State Street he was eligible for the draft. That may have been an exaggeration, but no question, he was big. He would pole tremendous flies that our outfielders wouldn't even bother running for. There was no proper fence at Legion Field such as they have at Fenway Park, and after a certain point, say 250 feet out, the field slanted sharply into an old cemetery and it was the devil finding the ball if it got that far.

Butch and one other boy in our division were the only ones who could reach the cemetery, so it really wasn't a problem. The other boy played for Mount Carmel but I don't remember his name. He missed a lot of games, anyway, because he often had to work on his family's farm after school. Mount Carmel was in the town's last rural section and boasted a number of hayseeds on its squad, boys with eyebrows that grew together and hard bones.

The only other good team in our division was Spring Glen. It always amazed me how the rich families who lived in the Spring Glen section of town could produce so many ball players. As far as I could tell, Ted Williams, Dom DiMaggio, Walt Dropo, Birdie Tebbetts, Billy Goodman, and the rest all came from humble backgrounds. On that basis I used to think there was some connection between rough childhoods and good batting averages, which is why I sometimes wished my own house would burn down, to give me an edge.

My final advice on high pops is to play them on the first bounce. Just let the ball drop and say you thought the infield fly rule was in effect. Of course the infield fly rule is in effect only when two or more players are on base, and then the batter is automatically out. Actually, though, high infield flies are never hit to the second baseman when the rule happens to apply. That is one of the unfair parts a second baseman learns to live with.

I could go into what kind of glove to buy and how to keep it oiled and such, but you probably know all that. Anyway the glove doesn't make the ball player. When I was named to the team in sixth grade, I talked my folks into buying me a nice new glove with a big web and all, in honor of the miracle. But the only thing I ever caught in it was a cold—that's what Lover Boy always said. In comparison, Herman's glove looked like it had come off the world's last buffalo. It had no padding and hardly any webbing and one of the fingers was always coming unstitched. But Herman nabbed everything that came anywhere near third base.

I guess Evie knew Herman's glove was magical even though she hardly watched the action, because she would hold it in her lap for him between innings. Mine she just kept handy. Herman would pay her off in bubble gum for the service.

Now for grounders. I used to practice fielding grounders all winter by flinging a ball against the concrete wall in our basement. It drove my parents batty and scarred the patio furniture in storage and worst of all it taught me how to catch only one kind of grounder —the grounder that comes directly at you and bounces into your glove at knee level. In three years of play in our division, this particular type of ground ball was·never once hit to my position.

The key thought at second is not to catch the grounder, anyway, but to stop it. That keeps the right fielder off your back and if you manage to find the ball after it's bounced off your knee or chest, you still might be able to get it to first in time for the out. A danger here is to get so excited about actually getting the ball in your bare hand that you send it sailing over the first baseman's head and over by the swings. So concentrate on the throw to first during infield warm-up at the start of every inning. This is when the first baseman throws a few grounders to the other infielders to loosen them up. Lover Boy was always careful to give me a grounder underhanded, so I would be more likely to catch it and not have to trot out into shallow center to get the ball back again.

Maybe even more important than handling pops and stopping ground balls with your chin if necessary is the second baseman's role in boosting team spirit. A lot of boosting comes in the form of infield chatter in support of the pitcher. "Come on you kid, come on you babe," is a proven morale-booster. So are "No hitter no hitter up there" and "Chuck it in there, baby."

I was practically the psychological cornerstone of the Centerville infield because Erwin, our regular pitcher, was left-handed. In the course of winding up, especially when there were men on base—as there usually were—Erwin would always pause briefly and be forced to look in my direction, as a southpaw, before collecting his energies for the assault on the strike zone. Sometimes he had a faintly disgusted look which seemed to say, "Well, I suppose you're getting ready to make another error." But I knew the importance of giving him confidence and I would stare right back and say, "Come on you kid, come on you babe, no hitter no hitter."

Erwin sucked on Life Savers during a game, which I don't approve of for a second baseman. If the second baseman gets knocked down by a runner, or happens to trip of his own accord, with a Life Saver in his mouth, it is quite possible he will get the candy jammed in his throat. I chewed gum and recommend the same. Chewing gum keeps your mouth from getting dry as a resin bag on those hot, dusty days when baseball was meant to be played, and it relaxes your jaw muscles, which are the first to freeze up under tension.

Covering the bag properly is another important duty. I never had much practice taking throws from the catcher, to put out base stealers, because in such cases the Centerville catchers either threw the ball way into the outfield or hit poor Erwin with it as he tried to get out of the way. I did handle throws from the outfield a lot. Naturally our outfielders had to show off their powerful throwing arms so, on an attempted double, say, I would face two means of extinction: (1) breaking my hand on the hard throw from the field, or (2) getting run over from behind by the base runner.

Actually I never got spiked or knocked down by runners, but there were many close calls. By far the most dangerous man on base in the division was Butch Mendoza, as you might have guessed by what I've mentioned about him already. Once Butch knocked Herman on his ass coming into third. Right away we had to bring in a young kid at Herman's position who was almost as bad as I was out there. I remember Lover Boy saying, "My, my, we are now fielding a hole at second and a sieve at third!"

Herman was nowhere near the base and Butch should have been called out for running outside his normal course. He deliberately picked Herman off because of Herman's color and maybe even more because of Herman's indifference to Butch's many taunts. He should have been called out, but even the umpires were afraid of Butch Mendoza in those days. He was three times Herman's height and twice his weight, I'd guess. So Herman got carted off by Bert and Erwin and me, wind knocked out of him, and as it turned out, one arm busted.

In the meantime, I remember, Evie got up from the State Street bench, where she was sitting, naturally, and hit Butch with what was left of the apple she'd been chomping on. Got him in the face with her apple core after he'd crossed home plate. She turned and ran toward home and Butch was too surprised and out of breath anyway to do much about it. He just looked confused. I felt like catching up with Evie and buying her a Popsicle for trying to avenge Herman as she had done. I guess I knew, even as I helped cart off Herman, who was chewing his bubble gum like crazy at the time, to keep from crying probably—I guess I knew Butch had done something he would be ashamed of in later years, provided he ever stopped to think about it. And little Evie had done something she'd never stop to think about, because she was at that age when you can deal with villains cleanly.

In any case I couldn't have walked out on Centerville even though we were losing by about 12 to 3 at the time. We got Herman settled down and took the field again and finished the last two or three innings. I think State Street got a couple more runs off us, to rub it in. We never got on base again, but that didn't make any difference—we stuck it out. That's really about the last thing I wanted to pass along about the job of playing second base, whether you're winning or losing, or making five errors per game, or seeing one of your teammates get a bad break, or losing your only fan. Stick it out. That's what second base is all about.

TRIBULATIONS OF THE FATHER

By Gerald Eskenazi

From The New York Times

Copyright, ©, 1974, The New York Times Company

Reprinted by permission

The alarm clock scrambles my head as if a puck has struck me. I look at the time—6:30 A.M. My mouth tastes as if brown paper bags had been wedged in it overnight. But I will persevere. After all, there are 75,000 others like me across the United States. We are going to take our boys to their first hockey clinic.

"Mark," I say, gently at first, then shaking his 45-pound sleeping form. He rubs his eyes and says, "Is it time, Daddy?" I look at the edge of the bed. There, laid out for my benefit is his incredible array of gear. They are:

Skates.
Elbow guards.
Inner jock.
Outer jock.
Padded pants.
Knee guards.
Socks.
Shirt.
Helmet.
Stick.
Garter belt.

I had heard often, during many trips to Canada, the slogan, "Don't send your boy to the rink—take him." Togetherness. I stared at the equipment, and my confidence began to desert me. The night before, I had gone through a dry run and got the dressing down to 32 minutes.

But it took me two minutes to explain the straps on the inner jock this morning. Finally, it's on. The garter belt gets strapped. Elbow pads, shin guards, the socks, the pants with suspenders, the shirt. Finally, the skates. Tight on the bottom, loose on top, I remember. The skate key becomes an unwieldy weapon. I perspire. Perhaps I don't really want to send my 5-year-old out there, perhaps I am empathizing. Perhaps I am frightened for him.

I slip the scabbards over his blades and he trundles off toward the car, insisting on carrying the equipment bag. His mother finally peeks out of the bedroom. She had virtually hid during the getting-dressed ceremony—a rite of manhood to be shared only by father and son. He was going into the jungle alone for the first time chasing the lion.

The rink, Skateland in New Hyde Park, Long Island, is cold. In front of me, their tiny legs dangling over benches, are the gladiators. Some are dressed spectacularly—matching uniforms, even shoulder pads. One boy has the name "Dondi" stenciled across the back of his shirt. Another wears a Joe Namath No. 12 jersey. Another a football lineman's shirt with No. 86. A few other fathers are there, and we acknowledge one another with nervous, self-conscious smiles. Most of the boys have been brought by their mothers.

It is 7:45 and the boys stand in line next to the rink, getting their names checked off. My boy takes the ice—and falls. Up again—and down. Then all the boys are on the ice, and it becomes a ballet choreographed by an alcoholic with the D.T.'s. They flop over themselves, over other's feet, over sounds.

Suddenly, The Coach blows a whistle. "Over here!" he barks, and Mark and the others move to center ice. Someone, I swear, has tied my son's skates together.

"Didn't you hear me? Over here," he shouts this time. "When I say here, I mean here. When I say stop, I mean stop. When I say go, I mean go."

Dr. Spock, what should I do?

I listen. The group of 50 boys is broken into smaller groups. They follow their leaders around the ice. Mark follows on his stomach, making more headway after falling and sliding than by standing and skating.

The fathers huddle together, a guerrilla band plotting an overthrow. We talk and laugh about what is happening to our young boys, and should we just watch? Our laughter is overheard.

"Parents, keep your voices down," screams The Coach. For the first time I notice his mustache. Thin, covering the middle of his lip. Just like the Austrian house painter's.

And then the fathers and mothers are yelling at their children. "Get up. Don't sit there. On your feet. Listen to The Coach." A boy comes over to the boards looking for his mother. Tears drip over his mouth guard. "Mommy, my feet hurt," he complains.

My son sees me and waddles across the rink. He has to go to the bathroom. Buttons snap and suspenders tug, but I manage with him. I take him back to the rink. His skates are bad, a fellow father, Dave Napell, tells me. I take my son off the ice and Dave tightens the laces.

Later, they become loose again. "Can I take my son off to tie his skates?" I ask The Coach. "No, he'll have to suffer," I'm told.

Mercifully, after two hours, I'm told he's going into a group for beginners—6 o'clock Saturday nights. Now I can sleep Fridays. I'll have all day Saturday to get him ready.

At night, I'm more relaxed. I have stopped worrying about The Coach turning him into a fiend. Mark doesn't have to leave in the middle of the drill for the bathroom anymore, and I think it's because he has found another use for his outer jock, which is cup-shaped.

He still tells me he doesn't like it when The Coach yells. But all day Saturday he asks me, "Is it time yet, Daddy?" He is in ecstasy on the ice when he touches the puck. He doesn't even have to come off now when his glasses get fogged.

THE DRAMA OF HAWKING

By Jack Murphy

From The San Diego Union

Copyright, ©, 1974, The San Diego Union

I hadn't thought of hunting as a spectator sport until Mike Connolly invited me to go hawking.

Mike is a master falconer, owner of two sleek peregrines, and the willing captive of a sport which has enchanted mankind for 6,000 years. Men were practicing falconry before they learned to write.

It was agreed my wife and I could witness a duck hunt.

"Choose a day that suits you," said Mike, "hawking is my life. I exist mainly to serve these birds."

That's largely true. Mike constructs his work (he's a carpenter, a framer of houses), his family life, and his social activities around the hunting schedule of his two peregrines, Witch and Ruby.

"It's not very good for the ego," he noted with a wry grin, "but the falconer is subservient to his hawks. It's my function to see that they have an opportunity to kill something to eat every day. That's about the extent of our tie.

"If I fail them for as much as two or three days, I'm on thin ice."

I began to understand the appeal and the excitement of hawking on a recent morning when we met in the vicinity of Del Mar where, it was hoped, the falcons would have duck for breakfast. Mike arrived in a pickup truck with camper; his companions included two hooded peregrines and a spotted German pointer, Molly.

Molly is useful in getting birds off the water. When a falcon is in the sky, ducks are possessed of fear and caution. The ducks are safe on the water because the peregrine kills by swooping on flying prey. Usually, the duck is doomed. A duck might fly at 60 miles per hour, but the peregrine is three times faster.

On this occasion the falconer had observed canvasback ducks swimming and feeding on a small pond at the edge of a golf course. The conditions were right for hawking; lots of open terrain where Connolly could keep his eye on the peregrine and be seen in return.

Mike lifted his prize peregrine, Witch, from the camper, removed her hood, and the falcon perched on his gloved fist. She seemed a noble creature, regal of manner and fierce of disposition.

But the female peregrine, with her long scimitar-shaped sideburn markings, has a disconcerting resemblance to Mike Marshall, the Los Angeles Dodgers' cranky relief pitcher. I kept a discreet distance from the falcon.

The falcon rested on Connolly's fist for a moment, then she was airborne (flying low with quick wingbeats) then gaining altitude. At that instant, I grasped the drama of hawking.

The bird was free of all restraint, wheeling high in the clear winter sky. If it chose, it could fly forever, over the horizon, to the ends of the earth. Mike Connolly had invested six years of training and care in this falcon but the link between man and bird was terribly fragile.

My heart leapt as Witch, distracted by a flight of pigeons, flew beyond the range of my binoculars. Mike stood in the middle of a brown field, calling the peregrine and swinging a lure (a leather strap fitted with duck feathers) to attract the falcon's attention.

Suddenly, she came into view again, at first a speck in the sky, then growing larger, flying very fast. Mike ran to the pond nearby and hurled rocks he had stashed in his pockets to startle the indolent canvasbacks.

When the ducks took flight they found themselves in awful peril. The falcon dropped on one of the canvasbacks but just nicked it and flew on. Then another duck flew madly with the peregrine in furious pursuit. It was a mismatch, but again the duck survived. The falcon missed.

"Maybe she wasn't hungry, maybe she didn't care enough," shrugged Connolly after the bird returned to his fist and allowed herself to be tied around the legs with straps known as jesses. "They're not perfect; they don't perform the same every day. But I've met my responsibility, I got a duck into the sky for her."

Mike Connolly brings devotion to falconry that even critics of the sport would admire. His commitment to the birds is total. I believe I understand the attraction. Every time he goes hawking he experiences suspense and excitement basic to man's nature. A man who has hunted with a falcon most likely would sell his shotguns.

We left the pond where the frightened canvasbacks had sought shelter and drove to a nearby field. It was time for the other peregrine, Ruby, to get her daily exercise. She flew from Mike's fist and soon there was a fresh crisis. When Ruby gained altitude, she glimpsed a coyote running in the field, a coyote with a ground squirrel in its mouth.

Ruby stooped on the coyote, demanding that the animal surrender the ground squirrel. Laughing, Connolly whirled his lure to attract the falcon's attention. When she responded, he released a pigeon from a leather bag.

The peregrine stooped with flashing wings and soon she was feasting on squab. It happens every day in nature, a matchless drama. I shall not soon forget.

THE SHOT WAS A FIZZLE

By Furman Bisher

From The Sporting News

Copyright, ©, 1974, The Sporting News

Well, I guess you noticed that America has been played for a sucker again. And went along with it goggle-eyed and willing. And paid anywhere from 10 to 26 million dollars, which is a helluva point spread if you're a banker, for the privilege, depending on whose guess you choose to buy.

Didn't just swallow the lure, but the whole line down the rod to the reel. But what else could you expect from a clientele that'll buy tickets to see a hole in the ground because a man died in it? Floyd Collins was 50 years ahead of his time, but his act was 50 years behind. See, you're not supposed to be careless enough to get killed.

Robert Craig Knievel and the Snake River Canyon steamshot and the con job has been lingering in my mind because I can't get Bob Pleso out of it. You see, little Bob Pleso was the only one to call the shot.

He said he'd be taking a bigger chance at Phenix City, Alabama, than Knievel would at Snake River. He was right—and has a tombstone to prove it. Knievel is still alive and waiting for the audit, sitting back there on his Butte in Montana. That $6-million check he flashed around the country was bogus. The act was pure carnival, with Knievel his own barker. And the shot was a fizzle.

Knievel, the tense, gallant, valiant, daring rocket-cyclist, pledged himself to be shot across the gorge at Twin Falls, Idaho. He flashed about the country in a suit designed for men who get shot out of cannons, with a diamond-studded swagger stick and a limp. He not only didn't keep his pledge. He never even made the water.

He stands there now, firmly imprinted on the memory of the U.S., in his red, white, blue, and starry suit looking about as heroic as Richard Nixon. Remember, this was the relatively loathsome egotist who visited 39 cities to say good-bye.

Remember that line? "If I miss, I'll just get to where we're all going a little earlier than you and wait for you."

What hokum! What rot! Especially from a dude who came quivering out of the canyon thanking God he was still alive. People had paid money to develop knots in their knots. He was loaded in that rocket that looked like something you see at an amusement park. Then the steam blew and the net result was something like one of those pistols you buy at a party supply store. A flag pops out of the barrel instead of a bullet and printed on the flag is the word "Bang!"

America has spent its first 200 years biting on the fraud and the flim-flam. We seem to covet our right to make fools of ourselves. We thrive on flirtations with disaster—as long as it's somebody else's. This bunch laid out their money to see somebody get killed and got exactly what they deserved. P. T. Barnum would have approved of it all the way. The world should have been tipped off when Bobby Riggs muscled in on the show.

It was Barnum who first detected our highly developed culture of suckerism, and guys like Knievel and Riggs who've encouraged it and capitalized on it. We're still showing up early and standing in line to push and shove to be first to be taken by the fast-check author, the old shell game, the bogus stock deal, the loan shark, dry holes, roller derbies, pigeon drop, and rigged wrestling.

Anybody knows if Evel Knievel had wanted to get from one side of the Snake River gorge to the other, the sensible way was to rent a plane or build a bridge.

I guess you thought I'd never get around to Bob Pleso. Or, if so, why.

Who is—or was—Bob Pleso? And how did he earn his six-foot plot in some cemetery?

He was a little guy, no more than 150 pounds. Had a wistful face and a waist no bigger than Tommy Nobis' thigh. As I recall, he also had a very calm manner for a fellow plotting his own self-destruction.

He sought fame and fortune. He was campaigning, not 39 cities in a private jet, but in an eight-cylinder automobile driven by some press agent.

"This is Bob Pleso," said the PA. "He's already done things Evel Knievel hasn't done."

On August 4 at Phenix City, he did another. He died.

He was trying to break what is supposed to be a world record, jumping 30 automobiles and a distance of 200 feet on a motorcycle. There wasn't but about $2,000 in it, but he was convinced that immortality and riches would follow.

"Who holds the record now?" I asked.

A man named Bob Gill, he said. From St. Petersburg, Florida, he said.

I said, "Doesn't that tell you something, Bob? There's the guy who holds the record and I never heard of him."

He was going a step further. Everybody else used a ramp to catch their bikes. He'd use nothing. Let the ground catch him. He figured that would be the difference in the fame-obscurity ratio. He ALMOST made it. He cleared 27 cars, but the 28th caught the bike. When they took him to the hospital he was nothing but a mass of broken bones.

He'd laughed at all the perils they were building into Knievel's jump. "As soon as that thing gets in the air," he said, "he's going to let the parachute go and float down. Then they'll say there was some malfunction. He's not taking any chance. He's just taking a lot of people for a ride.

"If he wants to take a chance, let him try what I'm trying at Phenix City."

He did want to thank Evel Knievel, though, for creating the kind of sensation that made it possible for him to be what he was. And to ABC-TV, posthumously, for including his fatal jump in the national special called "One Man, One Canyon." Bob Pleso had always said he was going to make it big.

FOR THE RECORD

CHAMPIONS OF 1974

ARCHERY

National Archery Assn. Champions

Men—Darrell Pace, Reading, Ohio.
Women—Doreen Wilber, Jefferson, Iowa.

National Field Archery Assn. Champions

FREE-STYLE

Open—Tim Moyer, Glendora, Calif.
Women's Open—Barbara Morris, Frankfort, Ky.
Amateur—Terry Ragsdale, White Oak, Tex.
Women's Amateur—Kathy Cramberg, Dallas City, Ill.

BAREBOW

Open—David Hughes, Irving, Tex.
Women's Open—Janis Beverly, Americus, Ga.
Amateur—Mike Flier, Pekin, Ill.
Women's Amateur—Betty Selkirk, Canton, Ill.

AUTO RACING

World—Emerson Fittipaldi, Brazil.
USAC—Bobby Unser, Albuquerque, N.M.
NASCAR—Richard Petty, Randleman, N.C.
Can-Am—Jackie Oliver, England.

Formula 5000—Brian Redman, England.
Trans-America—Peter Gregg, Jacksonville, Fla.; under 2-liters, Richard Weiss, Phillipsburg, N.J.
IMSA Camel GT—Peter Gregg.
IMSA Goodrich—George Alderman, Newark, Del.
U.S. Grand Prix—Carlos Reutemann, Argentina.
Indy 500—Johnny Rutherford, Fort Worth, Tex.
Le Mans 24 Hours—Henri Pescarolo-Gerard Larrousse, France (Matra-Simca).

BADMINTON

United States Championships

Singles—Chris Kinard, Pasadena, Calif.
Women's Singles—Cindy Baker, Salt Lake City.
Doubles—Don Paup, Washington–Jim Poole, Northridge, Calif.
Women's Doubles—Pam Bristol, Flint, Mich.–Diane Hales, Claremont, Calif.
Mixed Doubles—Mike Walker, Alhambra, Calif.–Judiann Kelly, Norwalk, Calif.
Senior Singles—Jim Poole, Northridge, Calif.
Senior Doubles—Jim Poole–Bill Goodman, Wellesley, Mass.
Senior Women's Doubles—Ethel Marshall–Bea Massman, Buffalo, N.Y.

Masters Singles—Ed Phillips, Warwick, R.I.

BASEBALL

World Series—Oakland A's.
National League—East: Pittsburgh; West: Los Angeles; playoffs: Los Angeles.
American League—East: Baltimore; West: Oakland; playoffs: Oakland.
All-Star Game—National League.
Leading Batter (N.L.)—Ralph Garr, Atlanta.
Leading Batter (A.L.)—Rod Carew, Minnesota.
Cy Young Pitching Award (N.L.)—Mike Marshall, Los Angeles.
Cy Young Pitching Award (A.L.)—Jim (Catfish) Hunter, Oakland.
American Association—Tulsa.
International League—Rochester.
Pacific Coast League—Spokane.
Eastern League—Thetford Mines.
Southern League—Knoxville.
Texas League—Victoria.
National Collegiate—University of Southern California.

BASKETBALL

National Association—Boston Celtics.
American Association—New York Nets.
National Collegiate—North Carolina State.
NCAA (Division II)—Morgan State.
NAIA—West Georgia.
National Invitation—Purdue.
Atlantic Coast—North Carolina State.
Big Eight—Kansas.
Big Sky—Idaho State and Montana.
Big Ten—Indiana and Michigan.
Ivy League—Pennsylvania.
Mid-American—Ohio University.
Middle Atlantic—East: St. Joseph's; West: Rider; North: Albright; South: Johns Hopkins.
Missouri Valley—Louisville.

Ohio Valley—Austin Peay.
Pacific-8—UCLA.
Southeastern—Alabama and Vanderbilt.
Southern—Furman.
Southwest—Texas.
Pacific Coast Athletic—Long Beach State.
West Coast Athletic—San Francisco.
Western Athletic—New Mexico
Yankee Conference—Massachusetts.
Knickerbocker Conference—Stony Brook.
AAU—Jacksonville (Fla.) Stars.
Women's AAU—Hutcherson Flying Queens.
Women's Collegiate (AIAW)—Immaculata, Pa.

BIATHLON

World—Juhani Suutarinen, Finland.
U.S.—John Morton, Anchorage, Alaska.

BILLIARDS

World Pocket—Ray Martin, Fair Lawn, N.J.
U.S. Pocket—Joe Balsis, Billings, Mont.
U.S. Women's Pocket—Jean Balukas, Brooklyn, N.Y.
World 3-Cushion—Naboyaki Koyabashi, Japan.

BOBSLEDDING

World Two-Man—West Germany.
World Four-Man—West Germany.

BOWLING

American Bowling Congress Champions

Singles (Regular)—Gene Krause, Cleveland.
Singles (Classic)—Ed Ditolla, Hackensack, N.J.

Doubles (Regular)—Chuck Sunseri-Bob Hart, Detroit.
Doubles (Classic)—Bob Perry, Paterson, N.J.-Tye Critchow, Claremont, Calif.
All-Events (Regular)—Bob Hart, Detroit.
All-Events (Classic)—Jim Godman, Vero Beach, Fla.
Team (Regular)—Olympic Beer, Omaha.
Team (Classic)—Ebonite Corp., Hopkinsville, Ky.
Team (Booster)—Elliott's Jesters, Peoria, Ill.

Women's International Bowling Congress

Singles—Shirley Garms, Island Lake, Ill.
Doubles—Carol Miller, Waukesha, Wis.-Janie Leszczynski, Milwaukee.
All-Events—Judy Cook Soutar, Grandview, Mo.
Team—Kalicak Int. Construction, St. Louis.

B.P.A.A. Open Champions

Men—Larry Laub, San Francisco.
Women—Pat Costello, Carrolltown, Md.

BOXING

World Professional Champions

Flyweight—Susumu Hanagata, Japan, recognized by World Boxing Association; Shoji Guma, Japan, recognized by World Boxing Council.
Bantamweight—Rodolfo Martinez, Mexico; Soo Hwan Hong, South Korea.
Featherweight—Alexis Arguello, Nicaragua, WBA; Bobby Chacon, Sylmar, Calif. WBC.
Junior Lightweight—Ben Villaflor, Phil-

ippines, WBA; Kuniaka Shibata, Japan, WBC.
Lightweight—Roberto Duran, Panama, WBA; Gattu Ishimatsu, Japan, WBC.
Junior Welterweight—Antonio Cervantes, Colombia, WBA; Perico Fernandez, Spain, WBC.
Welterweight—Jose Napoles, Mexico.
Junior Middleweight—Oscar Alvarado, Houston.
Middleweight—Carlos Monzon, Argentina, WBA; Rodrigo Valdez, Colombia, WBC.
Light-heavyweight—Victor Galindez, Argentina, WBA; John Conteh, England, WBC.
Heavyweight—Muhammad Ali, Chicago.

National A.A.U. Champions

106 Pounds—Claudell Atkins, St. Louis.
112 Pounds—Gregory Richardson, Cleveland.
119 Pounds—Mike Ayala, San Antonio, Tex.
125 Pounds—Mike Hess, Albany, Ore.
132 Pounds—James Kenty, Columbus, Ohio.
139 Pounds—Ray Leonard, Washington.
147 Pounds—Clinton Jackson, Las Vegas, Nev.
156 Pounds—Jerome Bennett, U.S. Air Force.
165 Pounds—Vonzell Johnson, Columbus, Ohio.
178 Pounds—Leon Spinks, U.S. Marines.
Heavyweight—Dwain Bonds, Detroit.

World Amateur Champions

Light Flyweight—Jorge Hernandez, Cuba.
Flyweight—Douglas Rodriguez, Cuba.
Bantamweight—Wilfredo Gomez, Puerto Rico.

Featherweight—Howard Davis, Glen
  Cove, L.I.
Lightweight—Vasily Solomin, USSR.
Light Welterweight—Ayub Kalule,
  Uganda.
Welterweight—Emilio Correo, Cuba.
Light Middleweight—Rolando Garbey,
  Cuba.
Middleweight—Rufas Ridkiev, USSR.
Light Heavyweight—Mate Parlov, Yugo-
  slavia.
Heavyweight—Teofilo Stevenson, Cuba.

CANOEING

United States Champions

KAYAK

Singles (500 Meters)—Steve Kelly, In-
  wood C.C., New York.
Women's Singles (500 Meters)—Linda
  Murray, Washington.
Singles (1,000 Meters)—Kelly.
Women's Singles (5,000 Meters)—
  Sperry Rademaker, Floral City, Fla.
Singles (10,000 Meters)—Bill Leach,
  Newport Beach, Calif.
Tandem (500 Meters)—Leach–Mike
  Johnson, Newport Beach, Calif.
Women's Tandem (500 Meters)—
  Sperry Rademaker–Candy Clark,
  Niles, Mich.
Tandem (1,000 Meters)—Bruce Barton,
  Niles, Mich.–Phil Rogosheske, Wash-
  ington.
Women's Tandem (5,000 Meters)—Pa-
  tience Vanderbush Carol Fisher,
  Niles, Mich.
Tandem (10,000 Meters)—Barton–
  Rogosheske.
Fours (1,000 Meters)—Rogosheske–
  Barton–Kelly–Turner, St. Charles, Ill.
Women's Fours (500 Meters)—Clark–
  Fisher–Rademaker–Vanderbush.
Women's Fours (5,000 Meters)—Clark
  –Fisher–Vanderbush–Rademaker.
Kayak Fours (10,000 Meters)—Rogo-
  sheske–Barton–Kelly–Turner.

CANOE

Singles (500 Meters)—Roland Muhlen,
  Cincinnati.
Singles (1,000 Meters)—Muhlen.
Singles (10,000 Meters)—Andy Wei-
  gand, Balboa Island, Calif.
Tandem (500 Meters)—Weigand–
  Muhlen.
Tandem (1,000 Meters)—Weigand–
  Muhlen.
Tandem (10,000 Meters)—Weigand–
  Muhlen.
Fours (1,000 Fours)—Weigand–Muhl-
  en–Eric Evans, Hanover, N.H.–Bill
  Bragg, Los Angeles.

WHITEWATER

Kayak Slalom—Eric Evans, Hanover,
  N.H.
Women's Kayak Slalom—Candy Clark,
  Lafayette, Calif.
Canoe Slalom—Angus Morrison,
  Wayzata, Minn.
Double Canoe Slalom—Al Harris–Dave
  Knight, Philadelphia.

CASTING

United States Champions

Grand All-Round—Steve Rajeff, San
  Francisco.
Angler All-Round—Rajeff.
All Distance—Rajeff.
All Accuracy—Rajeff.
Women's All Accuracy—Ann Strobel,
  New Orleans.

CROSS-COUNTRY

National AAU—John Ngeno, Kenya.
National AAU Team—Colorado Track
  Club.
National AAU Women's—Lynn Bjork-
  lund, Los Alamos, N.M.
National AAU Women's Team—UCLA.
NCAA—Nick Rose, Western Kentucky.

NCAC Team—Oregon.
NCAA Division II—Garry Bentley, South Dakota State.
NCAA Division II Team—Southwest Missouri.
NCCA Division III—David Moller, Rochester.
NCAA Division III—Mount Union.
NAIA—Mike Boit, Eastern New Mexico.
NIAIA Team—Eastern New Mexico.
IC4-A—Dennis Trujillo, Army; College Division: David Moller, Rochester.
IC4-A Team—Massachusetts; College Division: Lehigh.
Heptagonal—Dennis Trujillo, Army.
Heptagonal Team—Navy.

CURLING

World—United States.
U.S.—Superior, Wis.
U.S. Women—Virginia, Minn.
Canada—Alberta.

CYCLING

World

Sprint—Anton Tkac, Czechoslovakia.
Pursuit—Hans Lutz, West Germany.
Road—Janus Kowalski, Poland.
Women's Sprint—Tamara Piltsikova, USSR.
Women's Pursuit—Tamara Garkushina, USSR.
Women's Road—Genevieve Gambillon, France.

National Champions

ROAD RACING

Senior (115 miles)—John Allis, Cambridge, Mass.
Women (34.5 miles)—Jane Robinson, Seattle.
Veterans (46 miles)—Jim Mayers, Costa Mesa, Calif.

Junior (50 miles)—David Mayer–Oakes, Lubbock, Tex.

TRACK RACING

Sprint—Steve Woznick, Ridgewood, N.J.
Women's Sprint—Sue Novarra, Flint, Mich.
10 Miles—Ralph Therrio, Torrance, Calif.
1,000-Meter Time Trial—Woznick.
4,000-Meter Pursuit—Therrio.
Women's 3,000-Meter Pursuit—Mary Jane Reoch, Philadelphia. Junior (Overall)—Gilbert Hatton, El Monte, Calif.

Other

Tour de France—Eddy Merckx, Belgium.

DOGS

Major Best-in-Show Winners

Westminster (New York)—Ch. Gretchenhof Columbia River, German short-haired pointer, owned by Dr. Richard P. Smith, Hayward, Calif.; 3,146 dogs entered.
Trenton—Ch. Sunnybrook Spot On, wire fox terrier, owned by Mrs. Robert V. Clark, Middleburg, Va.; 4,002.
International (Chicago, spring)—Ch. Salilyn's Classic, English springer spaniel, owned by Mrs. Julie Gasow and Barbara Gates, Troy, Mich.; 3,581.
Santa Barbara (Calif.)—Ch. Vin-Melca's Homesteader, Norwegian elkhound, owned by Mrs. Patricia Craige and Mrs. Dian Schiller, Monterey, Calif.; 4,288.
Boardwalk (Atlantic City)—Ch. Cumming's Gold-Rush Charlie, golden re-

triever, owned by Mrs. Robert V. Clark and Dr. Larry Johnson, Princeton, N.J.; 3,809.
Westchester (Tarrytown, N.Y.)—Ch. Sunridges Lil Liza Jane, Great Dane, owned by Marcia and Jay Lawrence, Northridge, Calif.; 2,713.

National Bird Dog Champions

Pointers and Setters—Crossmatch, pointer, owned by Dr. Minor E. Gordon, Claremore, Okla.
Free-for-All—Wrapup, pointer, owned by Jimmy Hinton, Tuscaloosa, Ala.
Continental—Crossmatch.

FENCING

World Champions

Foil—Alex Romankov, USSR.
Epee—Rolf Edling, Sweden.
Saber—Aldo Montano, Italy.
Women's Foil—Ildeko Bobis, Hungary.
Foil Team—USSR.
Epee Team—Sweden.
Saber Team—USSR.
Women's Team Foil—USSR.

United States Champions

Foil—Heik Hambarzumian, San Francisco.
Epee—Dan Cantillon, Detroit.
Saber—Peter Westbrook, New York.
Women's Foil—Gaye Jacobsenu, San Francisco.
Foil Team—U.S. Marine Corps.
Epee Team—Salle Mori, Los Angeles.
Saber Team—New York AC.
Women's Foil Team—Salle Santelli, New York.

National Collegiate Champions

Foil—Greg Benko, Wayne State.
Epee—Risto Hurme, New York U.
Saber—Steve Danosi, Wayne State.
Team—New York U.

FOOTBALL

Intercollegiate Champions

Eastern (Lambert Trophy)—Penn State.
Eastern (Lambert Cup)—Delaware.
Eastern (Lambert Bowl)—Ithaca.
Atlantic Coast—Maryland.
Big Eight—Oklahoma.
Big Sky—Boise State.
Big Ten—Michigan and Ohio State.
Ivy League—Harvard and Yale.
Mid-American—Miami (Ohio).
Missouri Valley—Tulsa.
Ohio Valley—Eastern Kentucky.
Pacific Eight—Southern California.
Pacific Coast AA—San Jose State.
Southeastern—Alabama.
Southern—Virginia Military.
Southwest—Baylor.
Western Athletic—Brigham Young.
Yankee—Maine and Massachusetts.

National League

AMERICAN CONFERENCE

Eastern Division—Miami Dolphins.
Central Division—Pittsburgh Steelers.
Western Division—Oakland Raiders.
Playoff Wild Card—Buffalo Bills.
Conference—Pittsburgh Steelers

NATIONAL CONFERENCE

Eastern Division—St. Louis Cardinals.
Central Division—Minnesota Vikings.
Western Division—Los Angeles Rams.
Playoff Wild Card—Washington Redskins.
Conference—Minnesota Vikings

Super Bowl

Pittsburgh Steelers

World League

Eastern Division—Florida Blazers.
Central Division—So. California Sun.
Champion—Birmingham Americans.
Grey Cup—Montreal Alouettes.

Canadian Professional

Grey Cup—Montreal Alouettes.

GOLF

Men

National Open—Hale Irwin, Kirkwood, Mo.
National Amateur—Jerry Pate, Pensacola, Fla.
Masters—Gary Player, South Africa.
PGA—Lee Trevino, El Paso, Tex.
British Open—Gary Player.
British Amateur—Trevor Homer, England.
Canadian Open—Bobby Nichols, Akron, Ohio.
Canadian Amateur—Doug Roxburgh, Vancouver, B. C.
U.S. Public Links—Charlie Barenaba, Laie, Hawaii.
USGA Senior—Dale Morey, High Point, N. C.
USGA Junior—Dave Nevatt, Merced, Calif.
World Cup (Pro)—South Africa.
World Cup Individual—Bobby Cole, South Africa.
World Amateur (Eisenhower Trophy)—United States.
World Senior (Pro)—Roberto deVicenzo, Argentina.
U.S. Senior GA—James B. Knowles, Londonderry, Vt.
NCAA—Curtis Strange, Wake Forest.
NCAA Team—Wake Forest.
NCAA Division II—Matt Bloom, Riverside.
NCAA Division II Team—California at Fullerton.
NAIA—Dan Frickey, Washburn.
NAIA—U.S. International College.
World Series of Golf—Lee Trevino.
Tournament of Champions—Johnny Miller, Napa, Calif.
PGA Player of Year—Johnny Miller.
Vardon Trophy (Low Average Rounds) —Lee Trevino.
PGA National Team—Hubert Green-Mac McLendon.
PGA Earnings Leader—Johnny Miller.
Westchester Classic—Johnny Miller.
North-South Amateur—George Burns, Port Washington, L. I.

Women

National Open—Sandra Haynie, Dallas.
LPGA—Sandra Haynie.
National Amateur—Cynthia Hill, Colorado Springs.
British Amateur—Carol Semple, Sewickley, Pa.
Canadian Amateur—Debbie Massey, Bethlehem, Pa.
USGA Senior—Mrs. Justine Cushing, New York.
USGA Girls—Nancy Lopez, Roswell, N.M.
Intercollegiate—Mary Budke, Oregon State.
Intercollegiate Team—Rollins College.
Curtis Cup—United States.
World Amateur Team (Espirito Santo Trophy)—United States.
World Junior—Lori Nelson, West Chester, Pa.
North-South—Marlene Streit, Stoufville, Ontario.
Eastern—Lancy Smith, Williamsville, N. Y.
Vare Trophy—JoAnne Carner.

Leader LPGA Earnings—JoAnne Carner.
LPGA Player of Year—JoAnne Carner.

GYMNASTICS

National AA.U. Champions

All-Round—Yoshi Hayasaki, Chicago.
Floor Exercise—John Crosby, New York AC.
Pommel Horse—Joe Percival, Eugene, Ore.
Still Rings—Robert Rice, Philadelphia.
Vaulting—John Crosby.
Parallel Bars—Yoshi Hayasaki.
Horizontal Bar—Yoshi Hayasaki.
Team—New York AC.

Women

All-Round—Joan Moore Rice, Philadelphia.
Balance Beam—Ann Carr, Philadelphia.
Vaulting—Barbie Myslak, So. Conn. GC., New Haven.
Uneven Parallel Bars—Joan M. Rice.
Team—Philadelphia Manettes.

National Collegiate Champions

All-Round—Steve Hug, Stanford.
Pommel Horse—Ted Marcy, Stanford.
Parallel Bars—Steve Hug.
Floor Exercise—Doug Fitzjarrell, Iowa State.
Rings—Keith Heaver, Iowa State.
Vaulting—Greg Goodhue, Oklahoma.
Horizontal Bar—Rick Danley, Indiana State.
Team—Iowa State.

HANDBALL

United States Handball Assn. Champions

FOUR-WALL

Singles—Fred Lewis, Cleveland.
Doubles—Ray Neveau, Oshkosh, Wis.; Simie Fein, Milwaukee.
Masters Singles—Joey Maher, Ireland.
Masters Doubles—Arnold Aguilar–Gabe Enriquez, Los Angeles.
Collegiate Singles—Vern Roberts, Lake Forest A; Peter Appenzeller, Colorado B.
Collegiate Team—Lake Forest.

ONE-WALL

Singles—Al Torres, N. Y.

National A.A.U. Champions

Singles—Steve Sandler, New York.
Doubles—Wally Ulbrich–Jel Wisotsky, New York.
Doubles—Mike Dikman–Artie Reyer, New York.
Masters Doubles—Reyer–Joe Rispoli, New York.

HARNESS RACING

Horse of the Year—Delmonica Hanover.
Pacer of the Year—Armbro Nesbit.
2-Year-Old Trotter—Bonefish.
2-Year-Old Pacer—Alert Bret.
3-Year-Old Trotter—Dream of Glory.
3-Year-Old Pacer—Armbro Omaha.
4-Year-Old Trotter—Colonial Charm.
4-Year-Old Pacer—Armbro Nesbit.
Aged Trotter—Delmonica Hanover.
Aged Pacer—Invincible Shadow.
Leading Driver (Heats)—Herve Filion.
Leading Driver (Earnings)—Herve Filion.
Hambletonian—Christopher T.
Yonkers Trot—Spitfire Hanover.
Kentucky Futurity—Waymaker.

Dexter Cup—Surge Hanover.
Colonial—Keystone Gabriel.
Little Brown Jug—Armbro Omaha.
Cane—Boyden Hanover.
Adios—Armbro Omaha.
Messenger—Armbro Omaha.

HOCKEY

Stanley Cup—Philadelphia Flyers.
National League—East, Boston; West,
Philadelphia.
Most Valuable Player—Phil Esposito,
Boston.
Leading Scorer—Phil Esposito.
World Association—East, New England,
West, Houston, Champion, Houston.
Most Valuable Player—Gordie Howe,
Houston.
Leading Scorer—Mike Walton, Min-
nesota.
American League—Hershey.
Western League—Phoenix.
Central League—Oklahoma City;
Playoffs: Dallas.
North American League—Syracuse.
Southern League—Roanoke.
International League—Des Moines.
World Amateur—USSR; Class B, United
States.
NCAA—Minnesota.
NAIA—Lake Superior State.
ECAC—Division I, Boston U.; II; Ver-
mont; III, Worcester State.
WCHA—Michigan Tech and Minnesota.
Allan Cup—Orillia Terriers.
Memorial Cup—Regina Pats.

HORSESHOE PITCHING

World Champions

Men—Curt Day, Frankfort, Ind.
Women—Lorraine Thomas, Lockport,
N.Y.
Senior—Stan Manker, Lynchburg, Ohio.
Junior—Doug Kienia, Kittery, Maine.
Girls—Lynn Harrison, Hampton, Ohio.

HORSE RACING

T.R.A. Eclipse Awards

Horse of the Year—Forego.
2-Year-Old Colt—Foolish Pleasure.
2-Year-Old Filly—Ruffian.
3-Year-Old Colt—Little Current.
3-Year-Old Filly—Chris Evert.
Older Colt or Gelding—Forego.
Older Filly or Mare—Desert Vixen.
Sprint Champion—Forego.
Turf Champion—Dahlia.
Steeplechase Champion—Gran Kan.

Stakes Winners

Kentucky Derby—Cannonade.
Preakness Stakes—Little Current.
Belmont Stakes—Little Current.
American Derby—Determined King.
Arlington Handicap—Buffalo Lark.
Flamingo—Bushongo.
Gulfstream Handicap—Forego.
Hollywood Gold Cup—Tree of Knowl-
edge.
Jersey Derby—Better Arbitor.
Jockey Club Gold Cup—Forego.
Santa Anita Derby—Destroyer.
Santa Anita Handicap—Prince Dantan.
Washington D.C. International—Ad-
metus (France).
Widener—Forego.
Woodward—Forego.

Foreign

Ascot Gold Cup—Ragstone.
Canadian International—Dahlia.
Epsom Derby—Snow Knight.
Epsom Oaks—Polygamy.
Grand National Steeplechase—Red
Rum.
King George VI and Queen Elizabeth—
Dahlia.
Melbourne Cup—Think Big.
Prix de l'Arc de Triomphe—Allez
France.
Queen's Plate—Amber Herod.

HORSE SHOWS

World Champions

Three-Day—Bruce Davidson, Westport, Mass.
Three-Day Team—United States.
Jumping—Hartwig Steeken, West Germany.
Dressage—Gainer Klimke, West Germany.

American Horse Shows Assn. Champion

Hunter-Seat Medal—Robin Rost, Branchville, N.J.
Dressage Medal—Cyndy Miller, Bloomfield Hills, Mich.
Saddle-Seat Medal—Mary DeNure, Albany, N.Y.
Stock-Seat Medal—Kim Andersen, Napa, Calif.
Combined Training Trophy—Andrew J. Mouw, Leesburg, Va.
Senior Dressage—Kitty Ireland, Los Angeles.

National Horse Show Equitation Champions

Saddle Seat (Good Hands)—Linda Lowary, Tulsa, Okla.
ASPCA Trophy (Maclay)—Alexandra Dunaif, Ossining, N.Y.

ICE SKATING

FIGURE

World Champions

Men—Jan Hoffman, East Germany.
Women—Christine Errath, East Germany.
Pairs—Irina Rodnina-Aleksandr Zeitsev, USSR.
Dance—Ludmilla Pachomova–Aleksandr Gorshkov, USSR.

United States Champions

Men—Gordon McKellen, Lake Placid, N.Y.
Women—Dorothy Hamill, Riverside, Conn.
Pairs—Melissa Militano, Dix Hills, L.I.–Johnny Johns, Bloomfield Hill, Mich.
Dance—Coleen O'Connor, Chicago–Jim Milnes, Addison, Ill.

SPEED

World Champions

Men—Sten Stenson, Norway.
Women—Atje Keulen-Deelstra, Netherlands.
Sprint—Per Bjorang, Norway.
Women's Sprint—Leah Poulos, Northbrook, Ill.

United States Champions

Outdoor—Leigh Barczewski, West Allis, Wis., and Mike Pasarella, Chicago.
Women's Outdoor—Kris Garbe, West Allis, Wis.
Indoor—Allan Rattray, Los Angeles.
Women's Indoor—Peggy Hartrich, St. Louis.

JUDO

National A.A.U. Champions

139 Pounds—James Martin, Sacramento, Calif.
154 Pounds—Pat Burris, Los Angeles.
176 Pounds—Irwin Cohen, Chicago.
205 Pounds—Steve Cohen, Chicago.
Heavyweight—Jack Anderson, Minneapolis.
Open—James Wooley, Houston.
Grand Champion—Irwin Cohen.

WOMEN'S SHIA

105 Pounds—Kay Hummer, Cranford, N.J.
120 Pounds—Diane Pierce, Minneapolis.
135 Pounds—Margaret Thornton, Indianapolis.
150 Pounds—Bonnie Korte, Hazlewood, Mo.
165 Pounds—Christina Penisk, Los Angeles.
Open—Marie Braziel, New York.
Grand Championship—Marie Braziel.

JUNIOR COLLEGES

National Junior College Champions

Baseball—Meramec CC, St. Louis.
Basketball—Mercer County CC, Trenton, N.J.
Bowling—Erie CC North, Buffalo.
Cross-Country—Southwestern Michigan CC, Dowagiac, Mich.
Decathlon—Mike Anderson, Brevard (N.C.) College.
Football—Ferrum (Va.) College.
Golf—Mike Donald, Broward.
Golf Team—Broward CC, Fort Lauderdale, Fla.
Gymnastics—Odessa (Tex.) College.
Hockey—Canton (N.Y.) Agriculture and Technical College.
Judo—Forest Park CC, St. Louis.
Lacrosse—Nassau Community College, Garden City. L.I.
Marathon—Terry Baker, Hagerstown (Md.) CC.
Skiing—SUNY, Morrisville.
Swimming—SUNY, Alfred.
Tennis—Fernando Maynetto, Wingate; Doubles; Martin Vasquez-Paul Fineman, Odessa College.
Tennis Team—Central Texas, Killeen, Tex.
Track (Indoor)—Mesa (Ariz.) CC.
Track (Outdoor)—Mesa (Ariz.) CC.
Wrestling—Northern Idaho CC Coeur d'Alene, Idaho.

LACROSSE

NCAA—Johns Hopkins.
NCAA Division II—Towson State.
ECAC—New England, Bowdoin; Upstate New York; Geneseo; Metropolitan New York; Fairleigh-Dickinson.
Club—Long Island AC.
World—United States.
North—South—South.

MOTORBOATING

Unlimited Hydroplane Races

President's Cup—Pride of Pay 'N Pak, George Henley, Eatonville, Wash., driver.
Gar Wood Trophy—Miss Budweiser; Howie Benns, Grand Island, N.Y.
World Championship—Pride of Pay 'N Pak, Henley.
Gold Cup—Pride of Pay 'N Pak, Henley.
Season Champion—Pride of Pay 'N Pak.
Champion Driver—George Henley.

Distance Races

Griffith Memorial—Sammy James, Miami.
Bahamas 500—Carlo Bonomi, Italy.
Hennessy Grand Prix—Art (Snapper) Norris, Detroit.
San Francisco Tognoli Memorial—Paul Cook, Atherton, Calif.
Hennessy California Cup—Billy Martin, Clark, N.J.
Miami-Nassau—Billy Martin.
National Inboard Champion—Art Norris.
World Offshore Champion—Carlo Bonomi.

MOTORCYCLING

National Champion—Ken Roberts, Modesto, Calif.
Moto-cross Open Champion—Jim Weinert, Laguna Beach, Calif.

PADDLEBALL

United States Champions

Singles—Steve Keeley, San Diego, Calif.
Women's Singles—Kathy Williams, Hazel Park, Mich.
Doubles—Keeley–Len Baldori, East Lansing, Mich.
Women's Doubles—Kathy Williams–Teri Davis, Lansing, Mich.

PARACHUTING

United States Champions

Overall—Sgt. Jack Brake, U.S. Army.
Women's Overall—Debby Schmidt, Joliet, Ill.
Accuracy—Tie among Sgt. Chuck Collingwood, U.S. Army; Jim Lowe, Chicago, and Tom Schapanski, Kissimmee, Fla.
Women's Accuracy—Vikki Herst, Lakewood, Calif.
Style—Sgt. Jack Brake.
Women's Style—Debby Schmidt.

POLO

National Open—Milwaukee
National 16-Goal—Boca Raton, Fla.
National 8-Goal—Oak Brook, Ill.
Intercollegiate—University of Connecticut.
Interscholastic—Midland Lee H.S.
Cowboy—San Jacinto, Tex.

PLATFORM TENNIS

United States Champions

Doubles—John Beck, Bedford, N.Y.–Herb FitzGibbon, New York.
Women's Doubles—Shirley Babington–Marti Cavanaugh, Tenafly, N.J.

RACQUETBALL

Men—Bill Schmidtke, Minneapolis.
Women—Peggy Steding, Odessa, Tex.

RACQUETS

U.S. Open—William Surtees, Chicago.
U.S. Amateur—William Surtees.

ROLLER SKATING

World Champions

Singles—Michael Obrecht, West Germany.
Women's Singles—Sigrid Mullenbach, West Germany.
Dance—Christina Henke–Udo Donsdorf, West Germany.
Mixed Pairs—Sue McDonald, Steubenville, Ohio–Ron Sabo, Painesville, Ohio.

United States Champions

Singles—Darryl Bayles, Delanco, N.J.
Women's Singles—Natalie Dunn, Bakersfield, Calif.
Figures—Keith King, East Meadow, L.I.
Women's Figures—Debbie Palm, East Meadow, L.I.
Mixed Pairs—Mark Rever–Darlene Waters, Pontiac, Mich.
Dance—Debra Coyne–John LaBriola, Whittier, Calif.
Speed—Chris Snyder, Springfield, Mo.
Women's Speed—Robin Wilcock, Thousand Oaks, Calif.
Dance, International—Jane Purrachio–James Stephens, Vineland, N.J.

ROWING

United States Champions

Singles—Sean Drea, Undine, Philadelphia.

Singles Dash—Jim Dietz, New York AC.
Doubles—Dietz–Larry Klecatsky, New York AC.
Pairs—John Campbell–Kurt Kaufman, Vesper, Phila.
Pairs With Coxswain—Bill Miller–Bill Jurgens–Ken Dreyfus, coxswain, Vesper.
Fours—Vesper–New York AC Crew.
Fours With Coxswain—NAAO National Crew.
Quadruples—New York AC.
Eights—NAAO National Crew.
155-Pound Singles—Larry Klecatsky.
155-Pound Singles Dash—Bill Belden, Undine.
155-Pound Doubles—Belden–Fred Duling, Undine.
155-Pound Pairs—John Sonberg–Joe Caminiti, NYAC.
155-Pound Fours—Vesper.
155-Pound Fours With Coxswain—Potomac B.C., Washington.
155-Pound Eights—New York AC.

Intercollegiate Champions

IRA—Wisconsin; Second Varsity, Wisconsin; Freshmen; Cornell.
Eastern Sprints—Harvard.
Mid-America Regatta—Marietta.
Western Sprints—Washington.
Dad Vail—Massachusetts.
Metropolitan, Sulger Cup—Ithaca.
Harvard-Yale—Harvard.
Oxford-Cambridge—Oxford.

World

Singles—Wolfgang Honig, East Germany.
Eights—U.S. National Crew.
Lightweight Singles—Bill Belden, King of Prussia, Pa.
Lightweight Eights—U.S. National Crew.

U.S. Women

Singles—Joan Lind, Long Beach, Calif.
Pairs—Carol Brown–Janet Youngholm, Princeton U.
Eights—Vesper BC, Philadelphia.

RUGBY

English League Cup—Warrington.

SHOOTING

United States Pistol Champions

Men—Sgt. Hershel Anderson, Army, Tracy City, Tenn.
Women—Sfc. Barbara Hile, Army, Lapeer, Mich.
National Trophy—Sgt. Bonnie Harness, Columbus, Ga.

United States Rifle Champions

Smallbore 4-Position—Maj. Lones W. Wigger, Army, Carter, Mont.
Smallbore 4-Position, Women—Gloria K. Parmentier, Alexandria, Va.
Smallbore 4-Position, Civilian—William P. Schweitzer, Lancaster, Pa.
High Power—Jack Sicola, Santa Cruz, Calif.

Grand American Trapshooting Champions

Men—John Steffen, Minnetonka, Minn.
Women—Mrs. Georgie McCown, Newman, Ill.
Junior—Randy Voss, Le Sueur, Minn.
Veteran—A.J. Meyer, Elbe, N.Y.

Skeet Champions

Men—Noel Winters, Baltimore.
Women—Karla Roberts, Bridgeton, Mo.

Senior—Paul Dublin, Jacksonville, Tex.
Veteran—George Vicknair, Baton Rouge, La.
Junior—Mike Schmidt, Prio Lake, Minn.

Men—Piero Gros, Italy.
Women—Annemarie Proell, Austria.

SKIING

World Alpine

Downhill—David Zwilling, Austria.
Slalom—Gustavo Thoeni, Italy.
Giant Slalom—Gustavo Thoeni.
Combined—Franz Klammer, Austria.

Women

Downhill—Annemarie Proell, Austria.
Slalom—Hanny Wenzel, Liechtenstein.
Giant Slalom—Fabienne Serrat, France.
Combined—Fabienne Serrat.

World Nordic

JUMPING

70 Meters—Hans-Georg Aschenbach, East Germany.
90 Meters—Hans-Georg Aschenbach.

COMBINED

Jumping—Stefan Hula, Poland.
Cross-Country—Jan Legiersky, Poland.
Overall—Ulrich Wehling, East Germany.

CROSS-COUNTRY

15 Kilometers—Magne Myrmo, Norway.
30 Kilometers—Thomas Magnusson, Sweden.
50 Kilometers—Gerhard Grimmer, East Germany.

WOMEN'S CROSS-COUNTRY

5 Kilometers—Galina Kulakova, USSR.
10 Kilometers—Galina Kulakova.

National Alpine Champions

MEN

Slalom—Cary Adgate, Boyne City, Mich.
Giant Slalom—Bob Cochran, Richmond, Vt.

WOMEN

Slalom—Susie Patterson, Sun Valley, Idaho.
Giant Slalom—Marilyn Cochran, Richmond, Vt.

National Nordic Champions

JUMPING

Class A—Ron Steele, Levenworth, Wash.
Veteran—Olay Ullan, Seattle.
Class C, Junior—Jim Denney, Duluth, Minn.
Combined—Bruce Cunningham, Mexico, Me.

CROSS-COUNTRY

15 Kilometers—Larry Martin, Durango, Colo.
30 Kilometers—Mike Devecka, Bend, Ore.
50 Kilometers—Ron Yeager, Durango, Colo.
Junior—Bill Koch, Guilford, Vt.

WOMEN'S CROSS-COUNTRY

5 Kilometers—Martha Rockwell, Putney, Vt.
10 Kilometers—Martha Rockwell.
15 Kilometers—Martha Rockwell.

National Collegiate Champions

Downhill—Larry Kennison, Wyoming.
Slalom—Bill Shaw, Boise State.
Alpine Combined—Peil Christensen, Denver.
Cross-Country—Steinar Hybertsen, Wyoming.
Jumping—Didrik Ellefsen, Colorado.
Nordic Combined—Stig Hallingbye, Wyoming.
Team—University of Colorado.

SOCCER

World Cup

Champion—West Germany.

United States Champions

Challenge Cup—New York Greek-Americans.
Amateur Cup—Philadelphia Inter.
Junior—Florrissant Celtics, St. Louis.
North American Soccer League—Los Angeles Aztecs.

Collegiate Champions

NCAA—Howard University.
NCAA—Division II—Adelphi.
NCAA Division III—Brockport State.
NAIA—Quincy College.

Other Champions

English Association Cup—Liverpool.
English League Cup—Wolverhampton Wanderers.
Scottish Association Cup—Glasgow Celtic.
Scottish League Cup—Dundee.
European Cup—Bayern Munich, West Germany.
European Cup Winners Cup—Magdeburg, East Germany.

SOFTBALL

World

Amateur Softball Assn. Champions

Fast Pitch—Santa Rosa, Calif.
Women's Fast Pitch—Raybestos Brakettes, Stratford, Conn.
Slow Pitch—Howard Furniture, Denver, N.C.
Women's Slow Pitch—North Miami Dots.
Industrial Slow Pitch—Aetna L & C, Charlotte, N.C.

SQUASH RACQUETS

United States Champions

Singles—Victor Niederhoffer, New York.
Women's Singles—Mrs. Gretchen Spruance, Greenville, Del.
Doubles—Niederhoffer–Colin Adair, Montreal.
Women's Doubles—Gretchen Spruance–Frances Vosters, Wilmington, Del.
Veterans Singles—Charles Ufford, New York.
Veterans Doubles—Don Leggett, Hamilton, Ont.–Chuck Wright, Toronto.
Senior Singles—Floyd Svensson, San Francisco.
Senior Doubles—William Ketchum, New York–Newton Meade, Philadelphia.

SQUASH TENNIS

Singles—Dr. Pedro Bacallao, New York.
Doubles—Joe Holmes–Frank Satterthwaite, New York.

SURFING

World

Men—Reno Abellira, Haleiwa, Hawaii.

United States Champions

Men—Rick Rasmussen, Westhampton Beach, L.I.
Women—Isabel McLaughlin, New Smyrna Beach, Fla.

SWIMMING

Men's National Long-Course Champions

100-Meter Free-Style—Tom Hickcox, Bloomington, Ind.
200-Meter Free-Style—Tim Shaw, Long Beach, Calif.
400-Meter Free-Style—Tim Shaw.
1,500-Meter Free-Style—Tim Shaw.
100-Meter Backstroke—John Naber, Ladera Oaks, Calif.
200-Meter Backstroke—John Naber.
100-Meter Breast-Stroke—John Hencken, Santa Clara, Calif.
200-Meter Breast-Stroke—John Hencken.
100-Meter Butterfly—Mike Bottom, Santa Clara, Calif.
200-Meter Butterfly—Mike Bruner, Cupertino, Calif.
200-Meter Individual Medley—Steve Furniss, Long Beach, Calif.
400-Meter Individual Medley—Steve Furniss.
400-Meter Free-Style Relay—Gatorade SC, Bloomington, Ind.
400-Meter Medley Relay—Santa Clara (Calif.) SC.
800-Meter Free-Style Relay—Long Beach (Calif.) SC.
1-Meter Dive—Tim Moore, Columbus, Ohio.
3-Meter Dive—Keith Russell, Mesa, Ariz.

Platform Dive—Keith Russell.
Team—Santa Clara SC.

Women's National Long-Course Champions

100-Meter Free-Style—Kim Peyton, Portland, Ore.
200-Meter Free-Style—Shirley Babashoff, Mission Viejo, Calif.
400-Meter Free-Style—Shirley Babashoff.
1,500-Meter Free-Style—Jenny Turrall, Australia.
100-Meter Backstroke—Margie Moffitt, Silver Spring, Md.
200-Meter Backstroke—Wendy Cook, Vancouver, British Columbia.
100-Meter Breast-Stroke—Marcia Morey, Decatur, Ill.
200-Meter Breast-Stroke—Marcia Morey.
100-Meter Butterfly—Deena Deardurff, Cincinnati.
200-Meter Butterfly—Valerie Lee, Mission Viejo, Calif.
200-Meter Individual Medley—Kathy Heddy, Milltown, N.J.
400-Meter Individual Medley—Jenni Franks, New Castle, Del.
400-Meter Free-Style Relay—Mission Viejo (Calif.) Nadadores.
400-Meter Medley Relay—Lakewood (Calif.) Aquatic Club.
800-Meter Free-Style Relay—Mission Viejo (Calif.) Nadadores.
1-Meter Dive—Cynthia Potter, Houston.
3-Meter Dive—Christine Loock, Fort Worth, Tex.
Platform Dive—Teri York, Vancouver, British Columbia.
Team—Missio Viejo (Calif.) Nadadores.

National Collegiate Champions

50-Yard Free-Style—John Trembley, Tennessee.
100-Yard Free-Style—Joe Bottom, Southern California.
200-Yard Free-Style—Jim Montgomery, Indiana.
500-Yard Free-Style—John Naber, Southern California.
1,650-Yard Free-Style—Jack Tingley, Southern California.
100-Yard Backstroke—John Naber.
200-Yard Backstroke—John Naber.
100-Yard Butterfly—John Trembley.
200-Yard Butterfly—Robin Backhaus, Washington.
100-Yard Breast-Stroke—David Wilkie, Miami (Fla.)
200-Yard Breast-Stroke—John Hencken, Stanford.
200-Yard Individual Medley—Steve Furniss, Southern California.
400-Yard Individual Medley—Steve Furniss.
400-Yard Medley Relay—Tennessee.
400-Yard Free-Style Relay—Indiana.
800-Yard Free-Style Relay—Indiana.
1-Meter Dive—Tim Moore, Ohio State.
3-Meter Dive—Rick McAllister, Air Force Academy.
Team—Southern California.

TABLE TENNIS

United States Champions

Singles—Kjell Johansson, Sweden.
Women's Singles—Yukie Ohzeki, Japan.
Doubles—Stellan Bengtsson, Sweden–Johansson.
Women's Doubles—Ann-Christine Hellman–Birgitta Olsson, Sweden.
Mixed Doubles—Nobuhike Hasegawa–Tazuko Abe, Japan.
Senior Singles—Tim Boggan, Merrick, L.I.
Senior Doubles—Bill Sharpe–George Rocker, Philadelphia.

Juniors—Roger Sverdlik, Rockville Centre, L.I.

TENNIS

International Team Champions

Davis Cup—South Africa.
Wightman Cup (Women)—Britain.
Federation Cup (Women)—Australia.
Bonne Belle Cup (Women)—United States.

Wimbledon Champions

Men—Jimmy Connors, Belleville, Ill.
Women—Chris Evert, Fort Lauderdale, Fla.
Men's Doubles—John Newcombe–Tony Roche, Australia.
Women's Doubles—Evonne Goolagong, Australia–Peggy Michel, Pacific Palisades, Calif.
Mixed Doubles—Billy Jean King, Hilton Head Island, S.C.–Owen Davidson, Australia.

U.S. Open Champions

Men—Jimmy Connors.
Women—Billy Jean King.
Men's Doubles—Bob Lutz, San Clemente, Calif.–Stan Smith, Sea Pines, S.C.
Women's Doubles—Billy Jean King–Rosemary Casals, San Francisco.
Mixed Doubles—Pam Teeguarden, Los Angeles–Geoff Masters, Australia.
Junior—Billy Martin, Palos Verdes, Calif.
Junior Women—Ilana Kloss, South Africa.

Other United States Champions

Indoor—Jimmy Connors.
Women's Indoor—Billy Jean King.
Clay Court—Jimmy Connors.

Women's Clay Court—Chris Evert.
Men's 35 Clay Court—Gene Scott, New York.
Amateur Grass Court—Chico Hagey, La Jolla, Calif.
Senior Clay Court—Bob Barker, Port Washington, L.I.
Junior—Ferdie Taygon, Framingham, Mass.
Girls—Rayni Fox, North Miami Beach, Fla.
NCCA—John Whitlinger, Stanford; Division II; Andy RAE, University of San Diego.
NALA—Stan Franker, Texas Southern.
Women's Collegiate—Carrie Meyer, Marymount.

Other Foreign Opens

Australian Men—Jimmy Connors.
Australian Women—Evonne Goolagong.
French Men—Bjorn Borg, Sweden.
French Women—Chris Evert.
Canadian Men—Guilfermo Vilas, Argentina.
Canadian Women—Chris Evert.

TRACK AND FIELD

Men's National Indoor Champions

60-Yard Dash—Herb Washington, Ann Arbor, Mich.
60-Yard High Hurdles—Tom Hill, U.S. Army.
600-Yard Run—Wes Williams, San Diego TC.
1,000-Yard Run—Rick Wohlhuter, U. of Chicago TC.
One-Mile Run—John Walker, New Zealand.
Three-Mile Run—Dick Tayler, New Zealand.
Two-Mile Walk—Larry Walker, Beverly Hills Striders.
Sprint Medley Relay—Adelphi University.

One-Mile Relay—Philadelphia Pioneers.
Two-Mile Relay—U. of Chicago TC.
High Jump—Tom Woods, Oregon State.
Pole Vault—Vic Diaz, Beverly Hills Striders.
Long Jump—Jerry Proctor, Beverly Hills Striders.
Triple Jump—Milan Tiff, Beverly Hills Striders.
35-Pound Weight Throw—Jacques Accambray, Kent State.
Shot-Put—Terry Albritton, Palo Alto, Calif.

Men's National Outdoor Champions

100-Meter Dash—Steve Williams, San Diego.
200-Meter Dash—Don Quarrie, Beverly Hill Striders.
400-Meter Dash—Maurice Peoples, D. C. Striders.
800-Meter Run—Rick Wohlhuter, U. of Chicago TC.
1,500-Meter Run—Rod Dixon, New Zealand.
5,000-Meter Run—Dick Buerkle, New York AC.
10,000-Meter Run—Frank Shorter, Florida TC.
3,000-Meter Steeplechase—Jim Johnson, Club Northwest.
5,000-Meter Walk—John Knifton, New York AC.
110-Meter Hurdles—Charles Foster, North Carolina Central.
400 Meter Hurdles Jim Bolding, Pacific Coast Club, Long Beach, Calif.
High Jump—Dwight Stones, Pacific Coast Club.
Long Jump—Bouncy Moore, San Diego.
Triple Jump—John Craft, U. of Chicago TC.
Pole Vault—Dave Roberts, Gulf Coast TC.
Shot-Put—Al Feuerbach, Pacific Coast Club.
Javelin—Sam Colson, Lawrence, Kan.
Discus—John Powell, Pacific Coast Club.

Hammer—Steve DeAutremont, Beverly Hills Striders.

Other Champions

AAU Decathlon—Bruce Jenner, San Jose, Calif.

AAU—Marathon—Ron Wayne, Oregon TC.

Boston Marthon—Neil Cusack, Ireland.

USTFF Decathlon—Rick Wanamaker, Des Moines.

USTFF Marathon—John Lesch, Chicago UTC.

Women's National Outdoor Champions

100-Yard Dash—Renay Bowen, Lakewood (Calif.) International.

220-Yard Dash—Alice Annum, Sports International, Washington.

440-Yard Dash—Debra Sapenter, Prairie View A&M.

880-Yard Run—Mary Decker, Garden Grove, Calif.

One-Mile Run—Julie Brown, Los Angeles, TC.

One-Mile Walk—Sue Brodock, Rialto (Calif.) Road Runners.

2-Mile Run—Lynn Bjorklund, Albuquerque, N. M.

110-Meter Hurdles—Patty Johnson, La Jolla (Calif.) TC.

400-Meter Hurdles—Andrea Bruce, Prairie View A&M.

High Jump—Joni Huntley, Springfield, Ore.

Long Jump—Martha Watson, Lakewood (Calif.) International.

Javelin—Kathy Schmidt, Los Angeles TC.

Shot-Put—Maren Seidler, Chicago.

Discus—Joan Pavelich, La Jolla TC.

Team—Sports International, Washington.

Other Champions

AAU Pentathlon—Mitzi McMillan, Seattle.

Marathon—Judy Ikenberry, Rialto (Calif.) Road Runners.

Collegiate Pentathlon—Debbie Wilson, Illinois State.

Collegiate Team—Prairie View A&M.

Boston Marathon (First Woman Finisher)—Mrs. Michiko Gorman, Los Angeles.

National Collegiate Outdoor Champions

100-Yard Dash—Reggie Jones, Tennessee.

220-Yard Dash—James Gilkes, Fisk.

440-Yard Dash—Larance Jones, Northeast Missouri.

880-Yard Run—Willie Thomas, Tennessee.

One-Mile Run—Paul Cummings, Brigham Young.

3-Mile Run—Paul Geis, Oregon.

6-Mile Run—John Ngeno, Washington State.

3,000-Meter Steeplechase—Doug Brown, Tennessee.

120-Yard Hurdles—Charles Foster, North Carolina Central.

440-Yard Hurdles—Bruce Collins, Pennsylvania.

High Jump—Randy Smith, Kansas.

Long Jump—Jerry Herndon, UCLA.

Triple Jump—Charlton Ehizuelen, Illinois.

Pole Vault—Ed Lipscomb, Oregon State.

Shot-Put—Jesse Stuart, Western Kentucky.

Discus—Zdravko Pecar, Brigham Young.

Hammer—Peter Farmer, Texas-El Paso.

Javelin—Jim Judd, Oregon State.

440-Yard Relay—Kansas.

One-Mile Relay—UCLA.

Team—Tennessee.

Other Champions

NCAA Decathlon—Runald Backman, Brigham Young.
NAIA Decathlon—James Herron, Cameron State.
NAIA Marathon—Lucian Rosa, Wisconsin-Parkside.

VOLLEYBALL

World Champions

Men—Poland.
Women—Japan.

U.S. Volleyball Assn. Champions

Open—University of California, Santa Barbara.
Women—Los Angeles Renegades.
Senior—Balboa Bay (Calif.) Club Masters.
Collegiate—University of California, Santa Barbara.

Other National Champions

AAU—Men Michiana AC, Chicago.
AAU Women—Dallas AC.
YMCA—Hollywood (Calif.) YMCA
NCAA—University of California, Los Angeles.
NAIA—George Williams College.
JYB—Educational Alliance, New York.

WATER POLO

AAU Outdoor—Fullerton, Calif.
North American Cup-Berlin, West Germany.
College—University of California.

WATER SKIING

United States Champions

Overall—Ricky McCormick, Hialeah, Fla.
Women's Overall—Liz Allan Shetter, Groveland, Fla.
Slalom—Kris LaPoint, Castro Valley, Calif.
Women's Slalom—Liz Allan Shetter.
Tricks—Russ Stiffler, Upland, Calif.
Women's Tricks—Liz Allan Shetter.
Jumping—Mike Suyderhoud, Petaluma, Calif.
Women's Jumping—Liz Allan Shetter.

WEIGHT LIFTING

United States Champions

114 Pounds—Joel Widdel, Dewar, Iowa.
123 Pounds—Sal Dominguez, York, Pa.
132 Pounds—Roman Mielec, York, Pa.
148 Pounds—Dan Cantore, San Francisco.
165 Pounds—Fred Lowe, York, Pa.
181 Pounds—Tom Hirtz, York, Pa.
198 Pounds—Phil Grippaldi, York, Pa.
242 Pounds—Al Feuerbach, San Jose, Calif.
Superheavyweight—James Gargano, Los Angeles.

WRESTLING

National Collegiate Championships

118 Pounds—Gary Breece, Oklahoma.
126 Pounds—Pat Milkovich, Michigan State.
134 Pounds—Tom Sculley, Lehigh.
142 Pounds—Rick Lawinger, Wisconsin.
150 Pounds—Jerrett Hubbard, Michigan.
158 Pounds—Rod Kilgore, Oklahoma.
167 Pounds—Doug Wyn, Western Michigan.

177 Pounds—Floyd Hitchcock, Blooms-
burg State.
190 Pounds—Greg Strobel, Oregon
State.
Heavyweight—Jim Woods, Western Illinois.
Team—University of Oklahoma.

National A.A.U. Free-Style Champions

105.5 Pounds—Dave Range, Garfield
Heights, Ohio.
125.5 Pounds—Rich Sofman, New York
AC.
136.5 Pounds—Don Beam, East Lansing, Mich.
114.5 Pounds—Sergio Gonzales, Ven-
ice.
149.5 Pounds—Gene Davis, Lakewood,
Calif.
168 Pounds—Stan Deziedzic, New York
AC.
180.5 Pounds—Greg Hicks, Lancaster,
Pa.
220 Pounds—Greg Wojciechowski,
Toledo, Ohio.
Team—New York AC.

U. S. Wrestling Federation

105.5 Pounds—Don Cliffe, Chicago.
114.5 Pounds—Jim Haines, Wisconsin,
WC.
125.5 Pounds—Dan Sherman, Athletes
in Action.
136.5 Pounds—Dwayne Keller, Oklahoma.
149.5 Pounds—Joe Tice, U. S. International WC.
163 Pounds—Mike Jones, Oregon State.
180.5 Pounds—Bob Anderson, Athletes
in Action.
198 Pounds—Bill Harlow, Chicago.
200 Pounds—Russ Hellickson, Wisconsin WC.
Unlimited—Mike McCready, Athletes in
Action.
Team—Mayor Daley Youth Foundation,
Chicago.

YACHTING

America's Cup

Winner—Courageous, United States;
Ted Hood, skipper.

North American Yacht Racing Union

Men (Mallory Cup—Vann Wilson, San
Anselmo, Calif.
Women (Adams Cup)—Deborah Free-
man, Beachwood, N.J.
Junior (Sears Cup)—Tom Burton, Deep
Haven, Minn.
Single-handed (O'Day Trophy)—Carl
Buchan, Seattle.
Single-handed Women (Mertz Trophy)
—Jane Pegel, Lake Geneva, Wis.
Single-handed Junior (Smythe Trophy)
—Richard C. Lyons, Huron, Mich.
Club (Prince of Wales Trophy)—Noro-
ton (Conn.) YC.

Ocean and Distance Racing

Block Island—Dynamite, Llwyd Eccle-
stone, Palm Beach, Fla.
Newport-Bermuda—Scaramouche,
Charles E. Kirsch, Sturgeon Bay,
Mich.
St. Petersburg-Fort Lauderdale—Robin
Too II, Ted Hood, Marblehead, Mass.
Los Angeles-Tahiti—Sorcery, Jacob D.
Wood, Salem, Ore.
Victoria B.C.-Hawaii—Tinsley Light,
Henry Grandin, San Francisco.
Vineyard Race—La Forza del Destino,
Norman Raben.
San Diego-Acapulco—Standfast, John
MacAllister, San Diego.
World (27,120 miles)—Sayula II, Ra-
mon Carlin, Mexico.

WHO'S WHO IN
BEST SPORTS STORIES—1975

WRITERS IN BEST SPORTS STORIES—1975

THE PRIZE WINNERS

DWAIN ESPER (Davis Triggers the Explosion), winner of the 1975 news-coverage award, has been a member of the *Pasadena Star-News* sports staff since 1965. He has won the Associated Press and California Newspapers Association awards for best sports stories. He formerly was with the *Hayward Daily Review, Imperial Post Press, San Francisco News,* and other California papers. He is well known for track and field public announcing and for his colorful commentaries on football, basketball, and track. He has appeared in *Best Sports Stories* on numerous occasions, but this is his first award winner.

DR. ROSS THOMAS RUNFOLA (A Model of Legalized Violence), winner of the news-feature award, is an associate professor of social science at Medaille College in Buffalo, New York, who specializes in teaching the Sociology of Sport. As a free-lance sports writer and lecturer he has analyzed the contemporary sports scene as a reflection of American society. This is his first appearance in *Best Sports Stories.*

JOHN S. RADOSTA (Stock-Car Streaking), winner of the magazine award, graduated from New York University in 1935 and became a reporter for the *New York Herald Tribune* in 1941. In World War II he was a correspondent-editor of *Stars and Stripes.* Since joining *The New York Times* in 1945, he has done every kind of writing and editing. This is his first appearance in *Best Sports Stories.*

OTHER CONTRIBUTORS (In Alphabetical Order)

MAURY ALLEN (The Spoiled Brats Take It All) is a sports reporter for the *New York Post.* He began his career with the *Seymour* (Ind.) *Times* after army service, joined the *Levittown* (Pa.) *Times* and then worked for *Sports Illustrated.* In 1962 he joined his present paper. His new book, *Where Have You Gone, Joe DeMaggio?,* was published early this year. In addition he is the author of nine other sports books and is a veteran writer in *Best Sports Stories.*

PETE AXTHELM (Ali—You Gotta Believe!) joined *Newsweek* in 1968 as an associate editor in the sports department and was promoted to general editor in 1970. Previously, he wrote for *Sports Illustrated* for two years and before that was a writer and racing columnist for the now defunct *New York Herald Tribune.* He has written more than 20 *Newsweek* cover stories and his writings have received many citations. He also has contributed many stories to numerous national magazines. He is the author of four books, all of which have been warmly acclaimed, but his *The City Game* (Harper's Magazine Press, 1970) is regarded as the definitive work on Harlem basketball.

CATHERINE BELL (Rosie Casals: Why Hasn't She Lived Up to Her Potential?) was born in England 30 years ago and grew up in Tasmania, Australia. She is a graduate in psychology of the University of Tasmania and now lives in London, where she is an associate editor of *Lawn Tennis* magazine and a free-lance writer. This is her first appearance in *Best Sports Stories,* and she is the first woman writer to appear in these annuals in more than 20 years and the third altogether in the entire series.

IRA BERKOW (The Courage of a Long Distance Runner) is sports editor and senior editor of Newspaper Enterprise Association and writes a three-times-a-week column for the Scripps-Howard feature service. He holds a bachelor's degree in English from Miami (Ohio) University and an MSJ from Northwestern University's Medill School of Journalism, where he graduated in 1963. He is the co-author with Walt Frazier of *Rockin' Steady: A Guide to Basketball and Cool,* and is currently working on a nonsports book entitled *Maxwell Street, Chicago,* to be published by Doubleday next year. He has appeared many times in *Best Sports Stories.*

FURMAN BISHER (The Shot Was a Fizzle) is sports editor of *The Atlanta Journal,* although his current article was done for *The Sporting News.* He has been honored by *Time* magazine as one of the outstanding sports columnists and has merited many inclusions in this anthology. Besides writing for *The Sporting News,* he has free-lanced for many major periodicals and has authored a number of sports books, his latest being *Arnold Palmer—The Golden Year.*

Sam Blair (A Long Chance Loses) is sports editor and daily columnist for the *Dallas Morning News* and has won a variety of national and state awards for his writing on golf, baseball, and football. He is a contributor to such periodicals as *The Sporting News, Golf Digest,* and *Pro Quarterback* and has authored three books—*Dallas Cowboys: Pro or Con?; Staubach: First Down, Lifetime to Go* (with Bob St. John); and *Grant Teaff: I Believe.* He is married to former *Dallas News* White House correspondent Karen Klinefelter.

Peter Bonventre (Ali—You Gotta Believe!) is part of a tandem team in this volume along with Pete Axthelm of *Newsweek.* Bonventre covered the Ali–Foreman fight in Zaire and phoned reports to Axthelm, who put the story together in New York. He is a graduate of the University of Pennsylvania as a journalism major and started his career with *The New York Times* as a news clerk. He was then assigned to the sports department and later went to *Newsweek* as assistant sports editor. He is associate editor of *Newsweek* and president of the Magazine Sports Writers Association. He has been published in many magazines and this is his third appearance in *Best Sports Stories.*

David Casstevens (The Dolphins Win a Game of Inches) has been a full-time newspaper sports writer for the past five years. A Ft. Worth, Texas, native, he received a Bachelor of Journalism degree from the University of Texas at Austin. Before joining *The Houston Post* in July, 1972, he worked at the *Abilene* (Tex.) *Reporter-News,* the *Waco Tribune Herald* and the *Dallas Times Herald.* For the past three seasons he has covered auto racing and the Houston Oilers of the NFL. This is his first appearance in *Best Sports Stories.*

Bud Collins (Connors Buries Rosewall at Wimbledon) has been a columnist for *The Boston Globe* since 1964, covering all subjects from sports to the war in Vietnam. He is also a free-lance television commentator on tennis for NBC, CBS, and PBS. A native Ohioan, he graduated from Baldwin-Wallace College and now lives in Boston. This marks his third appearance in *Best Sports Stories.*

Glenn Dickey (Madden Sends in a Play) was graduated from the University of California, Berkeley, in 1958 and went to work shortly afterward as editor of the *Watsville* (Calif.) *Register-Pajaronian.* In 1964 he joined the *San Francisco Chronicle* as a sports writer and is there at the present time. He has had a book, *The Jock Empire,* published this fall by Chilton and another one, *The Great No-Hitters,* is due for April, 1976, publication. He has done over 40 articles for many national magazines. This is his fourth appearance in *Best Sports Stories.*

Ed Donnally (Where Winning Is God) is a jockey, a native of western Virginia who served his apprenticeship with the Whitney Stables. Since that time he has ridden close to a thousand winners in more than 6,000 races and has even found enough time to complete about 30 semester hours of English and journalism at the University of Maryland night school. He is one of those rarities who can write and ride, and be good at both. He free-lances and writes mostly for *Turf and Sport Digest*. This is his first appearance in *Best Sports Stories*.

DAVE DORR (North Carolina State Ends the Reign of Terror), born in Colorado and raised in Iowa, is a 1962 graduate of the University of Missouri School of Journalism. His writing career began at the *Des Moines Register*. In 1966, he joined the sports staff of the *St. Louis Post-Dispatch*. His specialities are basketball, golf, and track and field. He is also a basketball columnist for *The Sporting News*. This is his first appearance in *Best Sports Stories*.

GERALD ESKENAZI (Tribulations of the Father) has been with *The New York Times* since 1959 and a reporter since 1963. His main interest is hockey and he is generally recognized as one of the experts in this field; he has written about the game from 1965 to 1973 and is the author of seven books on hockey. At present he is doing more feature and investigative writing for the sports department. He has appeared in *Best Sports Stories* on many occasions.

KIM FOLTZ (The Business of Winning) has been associate editor at *Gentlemen's Quarterly* magazine since July, 1973. In his capacity as an editor at the magazine he also coordinated the special sports sections in which his articles appeared. He attended the school of journalism at the University of Utah, where his writing won him two William Randolph Hearst national awards for excellence in feature and investigative reporting and the Rocky Mountain Collegiate Press Award for excellence in intrepretive reporting. This is his first appearance in *Best Sports Stories*.

TED GREEN (Pro Basketball Referee: Job for a Masochist) is finishing his second year as a feature writer with the *Los Angeles Times*. He is a graduate of UCLA with a master's degree in journalism and is winner of a number of scholarships and academic awards from UCLA graduate school. This past year he has done extensive pieces on Bill Walton, Wilt Chamberlin, Joe Namath, and Frank Kush's crazy football camp in the mountains of Arizona. This is his second appearance in *Best Sports Stories*.

WILL GRIMSLEY (Muhammad Ali: Athlete, Folk Hero, World Social Force) has covered the globe in pursuit of stories for the Associated Press. He has reported on five Olympic games, made 12 trips to Australia for Davis Cup tournaments, and has had numerous reportorial chores in every major world capital. He has authored three books—*Golf: Its History, People and*

Events; Tennis: Its History, People and Events; and *Football: Greatest Moments of the Southwest Conference.* He also was supervising editor of *Century of Sports,* a popular book that sold close to 100,000 copies in 1971. This marks his fifth appearance in *Best Sports Stories.*

JIM HAWKINS (The Dodgers Even It Up) has covered the Detroit Tigers for the *Detroit Free Press* for the past six seasons. A 1966 graduate of the University of Wisconsin, he began writing sports for the *Milwaukee Sentinel* while still in school. Later he wrote for the *Wilmington* (Del.) *News-Journal* and the *Baltimore Evening Sun,* concentrating there on golf as well as football and basketball. In 1969 he was selected Sportswriter of the Year in the state of Maryland. He was the winner of the magazine award in *Best Sports Stories* of 1974. This is his sixth appearance in this anthology.

DAVE HIRSHEY (Connors Buries Rosewall at Forest Hills) was graduated from Dickinson College in 1971 with a major in English. He went to work at the *New York Daily News* and at the age of 21 became the youngest sports reporter in New York. He started out by covering soccer, roller derby, and racing. He now covers all sports, specializing in college football, college basketball, and tennis as well as general features. He is an occasional contributor to *Sporting News* and other publications. This is his second appearance in *Best Sports Stories.*

BOB HUNTER (Henry Aaron Was Able) is considered one of the top baseball writers in the country although he operates exclusively out of the West Coast. He began working with the *Los Angeles Examiner* in 1933 and when that paper merged with the *Los Angeles Herald,* he continued as a sports writer and columnist there. His excellent and perceptive reportage of baseball is best attested to by his repeated appearances in *Best Sports Stories.*

HANK INMAN (Was the Ticket Worth the Money?) is a native of Joplin, Missouri. He is a graduate of Central State University, Edmond, Oklahoma, with a B.A. in journalism. Following service with the U.S. Navy Seabees and in Vietnam, he joined the staff of the Waukegan, Illinois, *News-Sun,* whose sports staff was voted best in Illinois for non-Chicago papers. He then went to *The Daily Oklahoman* in Oklahoma City, for which he is now working. This is his first appearance in *Best Sports Stories.*

PHIL JACKMAN (Gentlemen, Start Your Excuses) is making his fifth appearance in *Best Sports Stories.* He is an alumnus of Providence College and after his graduation in 1958 he worked for the *Worcester* (Mass.) *Telegram* until he joined his present paper, *The Baltimore Evening Sun.* He was the Maryland Sports Writer of the Year in '68, '70, and '72. He covers the Colts and Orioles and suffers a great deal over their misfortunes but thrives by making himself a host of readers.

STEVE JACOBSON (The Longest Entry in "Who's Who") has covered all sports from rodeo to the Mexico City Olympics as a member of the sports staff of *Newsday* since 1960, but his specialty is baseball. He is a journalism graduate of Indiana University and served a stretch as copy boy on the *New York Daily Mirror,* whose editors' luncheon tastes are etched in his memory. Once a softball and touch football addict, his athletic efforts are confined to struggles with a tennis racket and skis and chasing a small black and white dog. This marks his second appearance in *Best Sports Stories.*

ROGER KAHN (Where Have All Our Heroes Gone?) has garnered three magazine awards in *Best Sports Stories:* the first one in 1960, the second in 1969, and the last in 1970 with his fine analysis of Willie Mays as both player and person (Willie Mays, Yesterday and Today). He started as a copy boy, then sports reporter with the late *New York Herald Tribune,* went to *Newsweek* as sports editor and finally to *The Saturday Evening Post* as senior editor. He then became a free lancer. He is a graduate of NYU and has authored many fine books, one of which on the old Brooklyn Dodgers and the old HTers, *The Boys of Summer,* was published in March, 1972, by Harper & Row. He has appeared on numerous occasions in this anthology.

DAVE KLEIN (Dear Mr. Garvey) is a columnist for the *Star-Ledger* of Newark, New Jersey, and associated Newhouse Newspapers. In addition, he is the author of 14 books, including *The New York Giants: Yesterday, Today and Tomorrow.* He has also contributed to most of the national periodicals. He attended the University of Oklahoma and Fairleigh Dickinson University. He was the winner of the news-coverage award in 1974 in *Best Sports Stories* and has appeared in the anthology on numerous occasions.

FREDERICK C. KLEIN (The Most Expensive Daily) is a native of Chicago and has been a reporter for *The Wall Street Journal,* where his current story appeared, since 1963. His sports writing experience consists mostly of six months as sports editor of the *Elgin* (Ill.) *Daily Courier-News* in 1960. He has written two books: *The Education of a Horse Player* (Hawthorne Books, 1969) and *News and the Market* (Regnery, 1974). This is his first appearance in *Best Sports Stories.*

TONY KORNHEISER (The Perpetual Motion of Billie Jean King) has been at *Newsday* for five years during which time he has covered sports, culture, and the contemporary scene. He has been published in such magazines as *Sport, New York,* and *Rolling Stone.* A 1970 graduate of Harpur College in Binghamton, New York, he taught school in Newark before joining the *Newsday* staff on his 22nd birthday. This is his third appearance in *Best Sports Stories.*

AARON LATHAM (Tom Seaver in the Locker Room) was born in Spur, Texas, where his father was the high school football coach. He graduated from

Amherst College in 1966 and went on to take a Ph.D. in English at Princeton University in 1970. He was a reporter for *The Washington Post,* where he won the Heywood Broun Award. He also worked as an editor at *Esquire* before coming to *New York Magazine* in 1972. He has published one book entitled *Crazy Sundays: F. Scott Fitzgerald in Hollywood.* This is his first appearance in *Best Sports Stories.*

HAL LEBOVITZ (Don't Jinx the No-Hitter) is a graduate of Western Reserve University who started his career as a high school chemistry teacher but then became a sports writer because of his avid interest in athletics. He started writing for the *Cleveland News* and then went to the *Cleveland Plain Dealer,* where he is now the sports editor. His column "Hal Thinks" is supplemented by his "Ask Hal" column and both have earned him numerous writing honors. He is a past president of the Baseball Writers Association of America and has been included in *Best Sports Stories* many times.

RON MARTZ (The First Year) has been in the newspaper business only four years. He attended the University of Houston following his honorable discharge from the U.S. Marine Corps. He started in newspaper work as general assignment reporter for the *Fort Pierce* (Fla.) *News Tribune,* was named telegraph editor one year later, and the following year moved to the *Cocoa Today.* He took over as assistant sports editor one year later and in August, 1974, moved to present position as staff writer for the *St. Petersburg Times.* This is his first appearance in *Best Sports Stories.*

NEIL MILBERT (Cannonade Charges Through) has covered thoroughbred racing, professional and college football, and boxing for the *Chicago Tribune.* A graduate of Marquette University, he served in the Marine Corps and worked for the *Jersey City* (N.J.) *Journal,* the *Ottumwa* (Iowa) *Courier,* and WEMP radio (Milwaukee) prior to joining the *Tribune.* This is his third appearance in *Best Sports Stories.*

DOUG MINTLINE (What Goes Through a Field Goal Kicker's Mind?) has been with the sports staff of the *Flint Journal* since 1948 and has been its sports editor since 1959. He was named Michigan Sports Writer of the Year twice, and also won the Golf Writers Association (American Columnist Division) award. He has garnered many other writing awards and was appointed to a number of committees including the vice-chairmanship of the Michigan Hall of Fame. This makes his second appearance in this series of sports stories.

JACK MURPHY (The Drama of Hawking) won the 1963 news-coverage prize in *Best Sports Stories* with his World Series piece, "When the World Stood Still." Since 1951 he has been sports editor and columnist for *The San Diego Union.* His fine writing has gained him many honors, including the Corum

Award for 1962 and the presidency of the Football Writers Association in 1965. His work has appeared many times in this continuing anthology.

JIM MURRAY (Not Just Another Pretty Face) writes a daily syndicated column which is distributed by the *Los Angeles Times*. His perceptive, satiric, and humorous thrusts have caused him to be named America's Best Sportswriter of the year for eight consecutive years by the National Association of Sportscasters and Writers. He was born in Hartford, Connecticut, graduated from Trinity College, and started his news career with the *New Haven* (Conn.) *Register*. In 1944 he went to work for the *Los Angeles Examiner* and in 1953 was one of the founders of *Sports Illustrated* magazine. In 1961 he was induced to return to the *Los Angeles Times* as its premier sports columnist. He won a National Headliners Award in 1965 and is the author of two books, anthologies of his own writing. This is his second appearance in *Best Sports Stories*.

MURRAY OLDERMAN (Reggie Jackson: Blood & Guts of the Fighting A's) is a sports editor of Newspaper Enterprise Association and also the sports cartoonist for that syndicate. He is a former president of the Football Writers Association of America. His writing appears in some 500 newspapers throughout the country. Prior to joining NEA, he worked for the McClatchy Newspapers of California and the *Minneapolis Star-Tribune*. He is a native of New York State and received his education at Missouri, Stanford, and Northwestern. His work has appeared several times in *Best Sports Stories*.

DON OLESEN (The Race to Mackinac) is a staff writer on *Insight,* Sunday magazine of *The Milwaukee Journal.* He is a former editorial writer for *The Milwaukee Journal,* former cityside reporter for *The Washington Post,* and before that the old *Washington Daily News.* He received an A.B. degree from Swarthmore (Pa.) College and saw two years of service in World War II as an enlisted cryptographer in the China-Burma-India theater.

JOHN OWEN (The Athletics Levitate into the Lead) is sports editor of the *Seattle Post-Intelligencer.* He previously worked on newspapers in Bismarck, North Dakota, and Yakima, Washington. He is also the author of a sports-oriented cookbook, *The Intermediate Eater.* In recent years he won top honors for best sports story and for sports columns in the state of Washington. He is a graduate of Montana State University. He has appeared in *Best Sports Stories* on numerous occasions.

PHIL PEPE (A Rare Display of Camaraderie) is a graduate of St. John's University in Queens who in 1957 became a member of the *New York World-Telegram* staff, covering the Yankees and college sports. In 1967 he moved to the New York *World Journal Tribune* as a three-day-a-week columnist; then he free-lanced until 1968, when he joined the staff of the *New York*

Daily News, where he now is. He is the author of five sports books, including *From Ghetto to Glory,* on Bob Gibson, Cardinal pitcher. He has appeared in *Best Sports Stories* on many occasions.

JEFF PRUGH (Ebbets Field Revisited) reported for the *Los Angeles Times* for 13 years and is co-author of *The Wizard of Westwood,* the definitive biography of UCLA basketball coach John Wooden. A graduate of the University of Missouri, where he was president of his class in the School of Journalism, Prugh has received awards for profiles of Kareem Abdul-Jabbar and Pete Maravich and for a series on college recruiting. In 1971 he was one of the first American sports writers to visit Castro's Cuba, where he covered the Olympic volleyball trials. This is his third appearance in *Best Sports Stories.*

JOHN SCHULIAN (On the Block: Way of All Flesh) writes regularly about rock and roll and local characters for *The Baltimore Evening Sun.* He covers sports only when the paper's sports department isn't looking or when he can wangle a magazine assignment. He came to *The Evening Sun* four years ago by way of the University of Utah (B.A., 1967), Northwestern (M.S., 1968), and the Army (Spec. 5, 1970). This is his first appearance in *Best Sports Stories.*

NICK SEITZ (The Greatest Golfer in the World) is making his ninth appearance in *Best Sports Stories.* Now editor of *Golf Digest,* he is a graduate of the University of Oklahoma, where he majored in philosophy. Then, at the age of 22, he became editor of the *Norman* (Okla.) *Transcript.* He has won numerous prizes in golf and basketball writing contests.

LEONARD SHAPIRO (The Celtics Sag to the NBA Title) was born in Brooklyn, New York, and raised in Syosset, Long Island. He attended the University of Wisconsin, where he earned a B.A. in 1968, and the University of Missouri, where he received an M.A. in 1970. He joined the staff of *The Washington Post* the same year and has covered all sports, from high schools to the professionals. In 1973 he was named Sports Writer of the Year in the District of Columbia. With Kenneth Denlinger, he is co-author of *Athletes for Sale,* an investigation of college recruiting abuses. This is his first appearance in *Best Sports Stories.*

LAURENCE SHEEHAN (How to Play Second Base) is a contributing editor of *Golf Digest* and *Tennis* magazine. A graduate of Amherst, his writing experience includes one year as a newspaper reporter, three years in Army Intelligence in France, six years with *Golf Digest* and two as editor of *Ski Week* and *Snow Country* magazines. He also edited *Skier's Digest* and *Best Golf Humor.* In addition he has co-authored *Come Swing With Me* with Doug Sanders, *Stan Smith's Tennis Basics,* and *Sam Snead's Key Approach to Golf.* This makes his third appearance in *Best Sport Stories.*

BLACKIE SHERROD (His Final Bow), the executive sports editor of *The Dallas Times Herald*, has garnered just about every important sports writing prize in the country. To name a few: the National Headliners Award; seven citations as the outstanding sports writer by newspaper, radio, and TV colleagues; and over a dozen inclusions in *Best Sports Stories*. As a master of ceremonies and banquet speaker, he has made a reputation almost equal to his writing. He also has his own radio and TV programs.

JOE SOUCHERAY (He's a Throwback—Way Back), who joined the *Minneapolis Tribune* staff in 1973 at the age of 24, is one of the youngest *Tribune* sports reporters. He is a 1971 graduate of St. Thomas College, St. Paul, with a major in journalism and a minor in English. Before joining the *Tribune* staff, he was a magazine editor at Webb Publishing Company, St. Paul, from 1971 to 1973. He has covered many sports events, written many feature articles for *Tribune* sports fans, and also writes a weekly column for "Thursday," a new section which appears every Thursday in the *Tribune*. This is his first appearance in *Best Sports Stories*.

ART SPANDER (A Magnificent 9-Iron Shot Wins the Masters) is a graduate of UCLA and has been writing sports, and occasionally news, for, first, UPI in Los Angeles, then the *Santa Monica Evening Outlook*, and since May, 1965, the *San Francisco Chronicle*. He specializes in golf and pro basketball but is at home writing about any other sport. He has appeared in *Best Sports Stories* several times previously and was the first prize winner for news-coverage in the 1971 volume with a piece on the 1970 U.S. Open. He also won first place in competitions sponsored by the Golf Writers Association and the San Francisco Press Club.

WELLS TWOMBLY (Globetrotters: A Racist Anachronism) is a sports columnist for the *San Francisco Examiner*, turning in six columns a week. His sports reporting has appeared in newspapers in all parts of the country, in this order: East—*Willimanic* (Conn.) *Daily Chronicle;* West—*North Hollywood Valley Times Today;* South—the *Houston Chronicle;* North—the *Detroit Free Press;* and then back to the West to the *Examiner*. In 1970 he won the news-coverage prize in *Best Sports Stories* and in the October, 1974, issue of *Esquire* he was called one of six "super star sports writers." His book about George Blanda won warm acclaim. He has just finished his third book, *Shake Down the Thunder!* He has also just become a syndicated writer for National Newspaper Syndicate.

WALT WALBERT (Death Stalked the River), born in Austria, has lived in Saginaw, Michigan, and Lansing, Michigan, since he was two years old. A graduate of Michigan State University, he has worked full time as a carpenter, building apartments, and part time as a sausage maker, a salesman of electronic parts, a busboy, and a bean loader. He developed his interest in woods lore and wildlife when he was quite young, when he spent most of his spare time in nearby forests and fields observing nature. This is his first appearance in *Best Sports Stories.*

DICK YOUNG (Now Comes the Big Test) joined the *New York Daily News* in 1941 and appeared in the first edition of *Best Sports Stories* in 1944. He was at that time one of the youngest sports reporters in New York City. Since then he has become one of the two most consistent winners in this series with five *Best Sports Stories* awards—two prizes in news-coverage (in 1959 and 1960), two for news-features (1957 and 1966), and one in the magazine category (in 1955). He writes a daily column for the *News* entitled "Young Ideas," and baseball is his major sport.

PHOTOGRAPHERS IN BEST
SPORTS STORIES—1975

THE PHOTO WINNERS

JIM VINCENT (Sit Down Strike), winner of the *Best Sports Stories—1975* action-photo award, has been a staff photographer for the *Portland Oregonian* for eight years. Prior to that he was with the *Oregon Journal* for 11 years. This marks his seventh appearance in *Best Sports Stories*.

JAMES ROARK (Undesignated Pinch Runner Continues Streak), winner of the *Best Sports Stories—1975* feature-photo award in his first try, was born in Chicago and, after graduating from high school and taking one year of college, he joined the Air Force. He completed the Famous Photographers School course and then joined the *Los Angeles Herald-Examiner* as a copy boy. After seven months he became a staff photographer. He spent the first three years on general assignments and for the past two years has been the staff sports photographer.

OTHER PHOTOGRAPHERS (In Alphabetical Order)

AL ALEXANDER (The Evel Knievel Syndrome) has been a staff photographer for *The Columbus* (Ga.) *Enquirer* for seven years. He retired from the U.S. Army, where he pursued photography as an off-duty pastime, in 1966. This is his first appearance in *Best Sports Stories*.

TIM CHAPMAN (Aftermath for Namath) was born in Ohio, raised in Hialeah, Florida, and attended the University of Miami, where he received a B.A. in journalism. *The Miami Herald* has been his resting spot for the past two years. He likes to shoot sports and wildlife pictures and float down rivers in a canoe. This is his first appearance in *Best Sports Stories*.

LEO COHEN (Body Language) attended the University of California and took classes at California College of Arts and Crafts. He has worked in Europe, China, and the Philippines and has been with the *Oakland Tribune* as a staff photographer for 29 years. This is his first appearance in *Best Sports Stories*.

RAY COVEY (Get Back, You Guys) has been with *The Houston Post* since 1956. He was originally from Hartford, Connecticut, and moved to Houston that year, going to work for *The Post* immediately. He attended schools in Connecticut and also did police photography for the Connecticut State Police. He is now assistant chief photographer for *The Houston Post.* This is his third appearance in *Best Sports Stories.*

LOUIE FAVORITE (A Big Extra Point) has been a photographer for the *Titusville* (Fla.) *Star-Advocate* for almost a year. Prior to that he was the film director for a TV station in Pensacola, Florida, where he also free-lanced for the *Pensacola News-Journal.* He attended high school and college in Pensacola. He is 24 years old and this is his first appearance in *Best Sports Stories.*

BARRY FITZSIMMONS (Death Takes a Ride) has been with *The San Diego Union and Evening Tribune* as a photographer for two years. He started with *The San Diego Union* six years ago as a copy kid and worked his way into the photo lab with the help of all of the photo staff there. He has had pictures published in papers throughout the country as well as in several national magazines. This is his first appearance in *Best Sports Stories.*

JOHN P. FOSTER (Round-Up Rough-and-Tumble) is a stringer for *The Seattle Times* who has been teaching photo-journalism at Central Washington State College, Ellensburg, Washington, for the past ten years. He has business-journalism and masters degrees from Indiana University and was editor of the weekly *Hancock Journal* in Greenfield, Indiana. He was chief photographer for the *Roswell* (N. M.) *Daily Record* and later a photographer for the *Indianapolis News.* This is his first appearance in *Best Sports Stories.*

JACK GAKING (Above and Beyond the Call of Duty) has been a staff photographer for the *Roanoke* (Va.) *Times-World* for the past 19 years. He has won numerous awards in photo competitions in the state of Virginia and was named state photographer of the year twice. This is his first appearance in *Best Sports Stories.*

PETE HOHN (Another Cover-Up) is a 1953 graduate in photo-journalism from the University of Minnesota. Since then he has worked for the *Rochester* (Minn.) *Post-Bulletin* and for the last 20 years for the *Minneapolis Tribune.* This is his first appearance in *Best Sports Stories.*

ROBERT JOHNSON (Stripping for Action) is a staff photographer for the *Nashville Tennessean* and attended the University of Tennessee. He broke in by making photographs to accompany sports articles written by his father. This is his second appearance in *Best Sports Stories.*

CHARLES G. KIRMAN (Time Out for Kitty) received a bachelor of science degree with honors in the field of professional photography from Rochester Institute of Technology in March, 1972, and since then has been employed as a staff photographer for the *Chicago Sun-Times.* He has received over 20 local, state, and regional photography awards since joining the *Sun-Times.* This is his second appearance in *Best Sports Stories.*

POWELL KRUEGER (Most Accidents Happen at Home) has been shooting news pictures for Minneapolis papers for over 32 years. He is now on general assignment, with occasional sports coverage, for the *Minneapolis Tribune.* This is his first appearance in *Best Sports Stories.*

FRED MATTHES (A Falsie!) has been a staff photographer for the *San Jose Mercury-News* for 13 years. He has won many awards, including the California Newspaper Publishers Association first prize; Pro Football Hall of Fame first place and honorable mention in the Forest Lawn Press Photographers Annual Exhibit. He has just been elected Region Ten Director for the National Press Photographers Association. This is his third appearance in *Best Sports Stories.*

TOM MERRYMAN (Spectators Goal was the Post) worked in a news agency and portrait studio until he went into service with a Photo Recon Squadron in the Second World War. He has been with the *Cedar Rapids Gazette* for 21 years and is the chief photographer for that paper. His sport shots have merited several inclusions in *Best Sports Stories.*

WILLIAM MEYER (Men with Dash) is a 25-year-old staff photographer for the *Milwaukee Sentinel.* He has been with that newspaper for two years since graduating from the University of Wisconsin (Milwaukee). He competed in track and field sports and won college division All-America honors for the discus in 1970. This is his second appearance in *Best Sports Stories.*

JOE ODEN (Look Ma! One Foot!) has worked for the *St. Paul Dispatch-Pioneer Press* since 1970 after serving a three-year tour in the U.S. Army, the last of which was spent in Vietnam. This is his first appearance in *Best Sports Stories.*

CHARLES R. PUGH, JR. (Help Wanted) won the action-photo award in the 1969 *Best Sports Stories* anthology with a football shot that marked his debut in this sports series. He began his career with the *Johnson City* (Tenn.) *Press-Chronicle* and since 1956 has been with the *Atlanta Journal-Constitution.* He has appeared in *Best Sports Stories* on numerous occasions.

BILL SERNE (Win, Place, and Show-Off) is a graduate of Kent State University and went to work for *The Tampa Tribune* photo department immediately after graduation in 1972. In college he was photo editor for the *Kent Stater* and prior to that was a sports writer for a year. He won first prize in the action category of *Best Sports Stories—1974*. This is his second appearance in the anthology.

EARL SEUBERT (Smeared, Stacked, and Stopped) is an old hand at winning awards for outstanding photography. His photos have been placing in competition since 1948 and he has accumulated more than 100 national, regional, state, and local awards, including the *Best Sports Stories* feature award in 1953. He started on the *Minneapolis Times* in 1947 and went to the *Minneapolis Tribune* in 1948. He became chief photographer in 1962. He has appeared in in *Best Sports Stories* on numerous occasions.

SEYMOUR SNAER (Candidate for a Double Hernia) is a veteran photographer with the *San Francisco Examiner* and the recipient of many distinguished awards as photographer of the year. He is a pioneer in newspaper color photography and his exciting shots have appeared many times in *Best Sports Stories.*

BARRY STAVER (The Coach Was Pleased) has been with *The Denver Post* for the past four years. He graduated in 1970 from Colorado State University with a B.S. in business administration. He prefers to shoot sports assignments. This is his first appearance in *Best Sports Stories.*

BARNEY STEIN (Lunge Time) was a staff photographer for the *New York Post* for 15 years and before that with the now defunct *Brooklyn Times-Union* for eight years. In 1952 he won the *Best Sports Story* photo award with his shot of Ralph Branca and Cookie Lavagetto, both in despair after Branca had thrown a home-run ball to Giant player Bobby Thomson and lost the pennant on the last day. Stein is now retired and living in Sarasota, Florida, and doing free-lance work for the *Sarasota Herald-Tribune.*

THE YEAR'S
BEST SPORTS PHOTOS

SIT DOWN STRIKE

by Jim Vincent, *Portland Oregonian*. This is the winner in the action-photo division. This calf-roping horse sits down and dumps the rider after the loop missed the calf during the 1974 Pendleton Round-Up at Pendleton, Oregon. Rider being dumped is Pax Irvine of Story, Wyoming. Copyright, ©, 1974, The Oregonian.

UNDESIGNATED PINCH RUNNER CONTINUES STREAK

by James Roark, *Los Angeles Herald-Examiner,* is the feature-photo winner in *Best Sports Stories—1975.* It shows San Francisco catcher Ken Rudolph standing in awed silence as the Los Angeles Dodger game is enlivened by a streaker who rounded and touched all bases. Manager Walter Alston made no statement as to whether or not he would appeal the run, but his case was weak because the streaker disappeared after touching home instead of returning to dugout to get his glove. Copyright, ©, 1974, Los Angeles Herald-Examiner.

ABOVE AND BEYOND THE CALL OF DUTY

by Jack Gaking, *Roanoke* (Va.) *Times-World.* Buried under football players, the referee manages to raise his hands and signal a touchdown. The game was played at Lexington, Virginia, between Virginia Military Institute and East Carolina. VMI won the game and the Southern Conference title. Copyright, ©, 1974, Times-World Corp.

LUNGE TIME

by Barney Stein, *Sarasota Herald-Tribune.* When the team from the North ran over the southern football team, Steve Craig made this lunge and grabbed a TD pass from Gary Marangi. The final score was 28 to 7, favor of the North. Copyright, ©, 1974, Barney Stein.

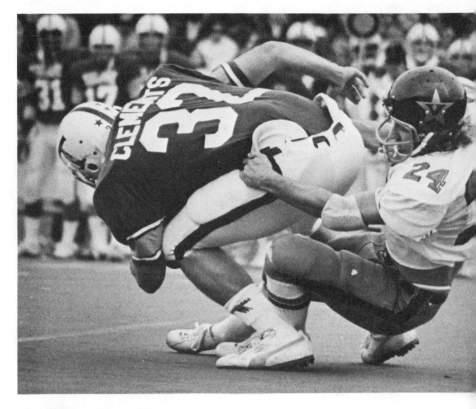

STRIPPING FOR ACTION

by Robert Johnson, *Nashville Tennessean*. Vanderbilt defensive back Ed Oaks holds on for dear life as Tulane running back wonders why he can't get free. Maybe he wouldn't have tried so hard if he'd known what the results would be. However he was soon slammed to the turf and the stands were spared an unseemly spectacle. Copyright, ©, 1974, The Tennessean.

TIME OUT FOR KITTY

by Charles G. Kirman, *Chicago Sun-Times*. A ball boy removes a kitten from the field during a practice at Soldiers Field. The teams were composed of various divisions of the Chicago fire squad. Reproduced with permission from the Chicago Sun-Times. Copyright, ©, 1974, Chicago Sun-Times.

THE COACH WAS PLEASED

by Barry Staver, *The Denver Post*. Denver Bronco coach John Ralston rushes up to linebacker Bill Laskey (45) after Laskey knocked down a pass intended for tight end Bob Moore of the Oakland Raiders. Denver upset the Raiders, 20 to 17, and assured Coach Ralston's job for a few more games at least. Copyright, ©, 1974, The Denver Post.

SMEARED, STACKED, AND STOPPED

by Earl Seubert, *Minneapolis Tribune*. This violent piece of action was deftly
caught by the photographer and exemplifies the tough kind of football
played by the Minnesota Vikings. John Hart is the hapless victim of the
vicious attack, also known as a tackle, by Doug Sutherland during the
play-off game between the St. Louis Cards and the Minnesota Vikings, who
won, 30 to 14. Copyright, ©, 1974, Minneapolis Tribune.

AFTERMATH FOR NAMATH

by Tim Chapman, *The Miami Herald.* Neither Brut, popcorn poppers, or his girl friends can assuage the grief of Jet passer Joe Namath, who has just been intercepted to lose a close game to the Miami Dolphins. Copyright, ©, 1974, The Miami Herald Publishing Co.

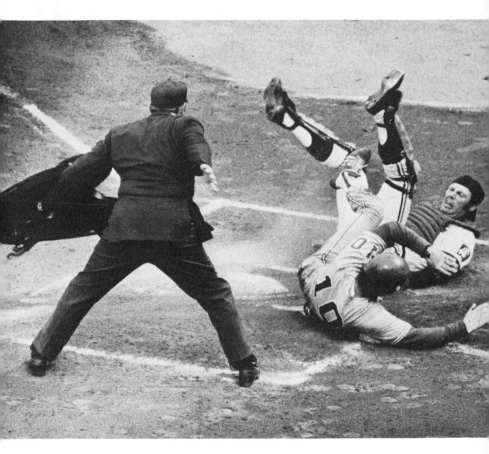

MOST ACCIDENTS HAPPEN AT HOME

by Powell Krueger, *Minneapolis Tribune*. Former Chicago teammates meet again in a collision at home plate as Ron Santo of the Chicago White Sox bowls over Randy Hundley of the Twins to score the Sox first run. The game ended in a 4-to-4 tie when it was called in the sixth because of rain. Copyright, ©, 1974, Minneapolis Tribune.

ANOTHER "COVER-UP"

by Pete Hohn, *Minneapolis Tribune.* In this full court press, where each man is covered personally by his opponent, Minnesota's Rich McCutcheon is boxed in by the press of Michigan State's covering team. Phil Saunders is coming to the aid of his harassed teammate, but press helped State nip Minnesota, 67–66. Copyright, ©, 1974, Minneapolis Tribune.

DEATH TAKES A RIDE

by Barry Fitzsimmons, *The San Diego Union*. A jockey was injured, a horse was destroyed, and another somehow survived a complete somersault after a head-of-the-stretch collision at Del Mar racetrack. Most Precious, ridden by Bill Shoemaker, broke down and veered into Snappy Orbit, sending jockey Francisco Mena flying up and over the head of his mount. Mena fell and Snappy Orbit fell on top of him, the horse's feet straight in the air. Mena suffered a bruised arm, his horse was unhurt even after the complete flip, and Bill Shoemaker's mount, Most Precious, had to be destroyed. Copyright, ©, 1974, The San Diego Union.

ROUND-UP ROUGH-AND-TUMBLE

by John P. Foster, *The Seattle Times.* The official program called this event a "squaw-race," a free-for-all race for Indian women at the Pendleton, Oregon, Round-Up. The woman who had fallen from her mount in the background crawled under the railing to safety. The woman downed at the left was removed on a stretcher, but not seriously injured. Copyright, ©, 1974, The Seattle Times.

WIN, PLACE, AND SHOW-OFF

by William Serne, *The Tampa Tribune*. With illusions of grandeur in the mind of this little mutt, we have a charming depiction of a dog who might work up his way to the Hambletonian and garner the bouquet of roses. Copyright, ©, 1974, The Tribune Co., Tampa, Fla.

BODY LANGUAGE

by Leo Cohen, *The Oakland Tribune.* Julia Greenhalgh, English golfer, furnishes a good example of the way one's body can relate to the situation in hand. Everything about her is involved in this putt . . . legs, face, and stance. However, it was to no avail. She missed the putt and lost the match to Beth Barry of the United States at the San Francisco Golf Club. Copyright, ©, 1974, The Oakland Tribune.

A FALSIE!

by Fred Matthes, *San Jose Mercury-News*. Marv Hubbard, of the Oakland Raiders, watches Dave Elmendorf's (of the L.A. Rams) false start during a heat race in the 50-meter swim event of the decathalon for the March of Dimes charity. When the race was started again Hubbard went on to be the victor. Copyright, ©, 1974, San Jose Mercury and News.

LOOK MA! ONE FOOT!

by Joe Oden, *St. Paul Dispatch-Pioneer Press.* Mariner center-forward Mike
Roe kicks the ball while lying on his back during a St. Paul suburban soccer
game with Sibley. Mariner, with seven wins, clinched the conference championship with a double overtime in this game. Copyright, ©, 1974, St. Paul
Dispatch-Pioneer Press.

CANDIDATE FOR A DOUBLE HERNIA

by Seymour Snaer, *San Francisco Examiner.* This is a YMCA instructor giving a demonstration of weight lifting at the Embarcadero Plaza in San Francisco during a Health Fitness Day sponsored by the YMCA. Copyright, ©, 1974, San Francisco Examiner.

THE EVEL KNIEVEL SYNDROME

by Al Alexander, *The Columbus* (Ga.) *Enquirer*. When Bob Pleso attempted to jump over 30 cars it measured 180 feet, all done without a ramp. The record was 22 cars over 161 feet. His motorcycle hit the windshield of the 28th car and he cartwheeled through the air before he crashed to the pavement and skidded into an embankment. He died two hours later as a result of massive internal injuries. Copyright, ©, 1974, The Columbus, Ga., Enquirer.

GET BACK, YOU GUYS

by Ray Covey, *The Houston Post.* A brief interlude in a Houston Rugby
League game between the Houston alumni and Texas A&M. Copyright,
©, 1974, The Houston Post.

MEN WITH DASH

by William Meyer, *Milwaukee Sentinel*. All the runners wore determined
looks as they came out of the blocks in a trial heat of the high hurdles at
the Wisconsin State high school track meet in Madison in June, 1974.
Copyright, ©, 1974, Milwaukee Sentinel.